S0-BDG-896

FLORIDA STATE
UNIVERSITY LIBRARIES

AUG 12 1997

TALLAHASSEE, FLORIDA

Nuclear Energy and Security in the Former Soviet Union

Nuclear Energy and Security in the Former Soviet Union

EDITED BY

David R. Marples and Marilyn J. Young

WestviewPress

A Division of HarperCollins*Publishers*

HD
9698
F62
N78
1997

All rights reserved. Printed in the United States of America. No part of this publication may be reproduced or transmitted in any form or by any means, electronic or mechanical, including photocopy, recording, or any information storage and retrieval system, without permission in writing from the publisher.

Copyright © 1997 by Westview Press, A Division of HarperCollins Publishers, Inc.

Published in 1997 in the United States of America by Westview Press, 5500 Central Avenue, Boulder, Colorado 80301-2877, and in the United Kingdom by Westview Press, 12 Hid's Copse Road, Cumnor Hill, Oxford OX2 9JJ

A CIP catalog record for this book is available from the Library of Congress.
ISBN 0-8133-9013-3

The paper used in this publication meets the requirements of the American National Standard for Permanence of Paper for Printed Library Materials Z39.48-1984.

10   9   8   7   6   5   4   3   2   1

Contents

Acknowledgements   vii

1 Introduction: Non-Rational Assessment of Risk and the
   Development of Civilian Nuclear Power, *Marilyn J. Young*   1

2 Nuclear Power in the Former USSR: Historical and
   Contemporary Perspectives, *David R. Marples*   19

3 Ukraine, Russia, and the Question of Nuclear Safety,
   Michael K. Launer and Marilyn J. Young   45

4 The U.S.-Russia Joint Electric Power Alternatives Study:
   Nuclear Safety Implications, *Michael B. Congdon*   83

5 Nuclear Power and Civil Society in Post-Soviet Russia,
   Gert-Rüdiger Wegmarshaus   99

6 Ukraine as a Nuclear Weapons Power, *Roman P. Zyla*   121

7 Nuclear Smuggling from the Former Soviet Union,
   William C. Potter   139

Index   167
About the Book   179
About the Editors and Contributors   181

Acknowledgements

This book was published with the support of the Stasiuk Endowment Fund and under the auspices of the Stasiuk Program for the Study of Contemporary Ukraine, Canadian Institute of Ukrainian Studies, University of Alberta. The editors would like to thank Larry Sherfey for providing the cover photograph, Rebecca Ritke for her encouragement of this project in its early stages, Peter Matilainen for supervising the typesetting process, David F. Duke for preparing the index, and Lan Chan-Marples for proofreading the final product.

David Marples

1

Introduction: Non-Rational Assessment of Risk and the Development of Civilian Nuclear Power

Marilyn J. Young

On April 26, 1996, the world observed the tenth anniversary of the accident in reactor unit 4 at the V. I. Lenin Nuclear Power Plant near the village of Chornobyl in what is now Ukraine, an occasion most remarkable in the United States for the lack of fanfare; as human tragedies go, the Chornobyl anniversary was overshadowed by the first anniversary of the bombing of the federal building in Oklahoma City.[1] Quite naturally, most media attention in the U.S. focused on events commemorating that tragedy. This is not to suggest that the Chornobyl anniversary was totally ignored, but the coverage was significantly less than might have been expected for such a momentous event, particularly since the reverberations of that explosion in Ukraine are still being felt around the world today. Thus, it seems appropriate at this juncture to reflect on the state of nuclear power in the post-Chornobyl world.

To this end, we have collected a series of essays addressing diverse aspects of the aftermath of the Chornobyl accident. This volume grew out of a program at the Fifth World Congress of Central and East European Studies, held in Warsaw, Poland in August 1995: "Chornobyl and Nuclear Issues in the Post-Soviet States." Those five papers are here supplemented by pieces solicited from others with an interest in this topic. Some of the contributors to this volume are supporters of nuclear power, some derive their income from the existence of nuclear power, and some are opponents of nuclear technology. It is our hope that we present a balanced view of this controversial issue. In this introduction, I seek to provide a framework for the essays by raising questions for future consideration about the relationship between society and nuclear technology.

It is sometimes difficult to realize that the history of nuclear power is a short one. Uranium fission was achieved in 1939, although its theoretical foundations had been the focus of scientific inquiry since the beginning of the century. The first chain reaction was attained in 1942, and the first experimental production of electricity occurred only nine years later.

Even so, by the 1950s, nuclear power was seen as the future of energy production in the United States and throughout the world. According to proponents, it would provide limitless power at minimal cost ["electricity too cheap to meter"], replacing conventional sources of electricity generation in homes and businesses and, ultimately, in various types of transportation, as well. Commercial nuclear power was the focus of an intense United States government policy initiative, which was grounded in President Dwight Eisenhower's 1953 "Atoms for Peace" speech before the United Nations.[2] Just forty years later, the commercial viability of nuclear energy is in serious doubt. While it provides a substantial percentage of energy production in the U.S. and worldwide, no new plants are foreseen in North America and there are no plans to expand the uses of nuclear energy into the transportation arena beyond the military uses already in existence. Even utility executives are pessimistic about the future of nuclear power. A recent poll conducted by the Washington International Energy Group documents a sharp drop in executives' level of confidence regarding the future of nuclear energy. In this new poll, 39% of the executives surveyed indicated that nuclear power cannot be competitive; only 2% indicated that they would consider ordering a new nuclear plant (down from 10% as recently as 1995); and only 8% believe there will be a resurgence of nuclear power (down from 31% in 1995).[3] In other words, as things stand now, there will never be a nuclear-powered automobile, train, or commercial airplane. After such an auspicious beginning, it is fair to inquire, "What happened?"

First, what has become of nuclear power world-wide? Most of the rest of the world seems to view nuclear power differently than does the United States. While nuclear plants provide about 22% of all electricity in the U.S., in France that figure is closer to 80%. China is undertaking a concerted program to develop nuclear power capability; India and Iran are purchasing nuclear plants from Russia; Kazakhstan is building a plant; and Romania recently brought its first nuclear unit on line.[4] The Metzamor station in Armenia was restarted in 1995 in an effort to combat the dramatic energy deficit in that country. Even Ukraine continues to operate the undamaged reactors at Chornobyl.[5] In contrast, the Watts Bar facility in Tennessee, which came on line early in 1996, is the first U.S. plant to open in many years—and it was ordered in 1970.

The development of nuclear power slowed to a trickle after the accident at Three Mile Island in 1979.[6] According to an official at the Institute of Nuclear Power Operators in Atlanta, Georgia, because of TMI some 8-10 reactor units that had been ordered by U.S. utilities were never built—the orders were canceled. Construction of the Shoreham plant on Long Island (NY) was completed and the facility was granted a Low Power Operating License (start-up) in 1985, but after many years of legal delays it became clear that the plant would never be operated. Due to liability concerns, the facility was sold to the State of New York for $1, and local utility customers had to absorb the total cost of the project without receiving a single kilowatt of electricity; the plant was shut down in 1991.[7]

If TMI severely affected the development of civilian nuclear power in the United States, that development came to a virtual standstill after the 1986 Chornobyl accident. In the ten years that have passed since then, not a single order has been placed in the U.S. for a new reactor unit and seven reactor units have been shut down by their owners. Most of the closings occurred because the plants were not competitive with other sources of electricity; other plants, such as Rancho Seco, were closed for political rather than economic reasons.

The Tennessee Valley Authority (TVA), the non-profit government-owned corporation that operates Watts Bar, has been beset by problems for many years. Once one of the major operators of nuclear plants in the United States, TVA has permanently shut down two facilities (Bellefonte and Sequoyah). In addition, a three-unit plant (Browns Ferry) has been closed for years due to technical reasons.

Virtually all U.S. plant closings have been voluntary, based in large part on financial considerations: given the price tag for bringing old plants up to current safety standards, the refurbishing of aging facilities often makes no economic sense. For example, Trojan nuclear station required new steam generators, but the cost could not be justified given the plant's relatively short remaining service life. Regulatory concerns can also be decisive: Yankee Rowe, the oldest commercial nuclear plant in the United States, was closed because the operator faced the expensive (and, at the time, untested) task of annealing an embrittled reactor vessel, and company officials were not at all certain that the Nuclear Regulatory Commission would authorize restarting the unit after the process had been completed.[8]

It is quite ironic that nuclear power—which was once touted as the low-cost power source of the future—has become exceptionally expensive. Prior to 1982, the cost of commercial plants was approximately $1000 per kilowatt of installed generating capacity; by 1987, that cost had risen to more than $4000. Yet, if costs had continued to increase at the pre-1982 rate, the expected 1987 cost would have been closer to $1500. Needless to say, the increased cost of bringing the plant on-line has been passed on to the consumer.[9] The cost of building a nuclear unit has become prohibitive, some believe, because of changes in the regulatory environment[10] combined with the political situation in most localities—both factors the result of a heightened sense of risk that seems to accompany the use of nuclear power in the United States. This phenomenon has attracted the attention of several analysts, whose work will be discussed below. As background to such a discussion, consider public attitudes toward the construction and operation of nuclear power plants in comparison to perceptions of other risky endeavors.

With respect to exposure of the general public to radiation, nuclear power plants have a remarkable safety record in the United States and Canada. Even the Three Mile Island accident, the worst ever at a commercial facility in this country, resulted in no documented casualties.[11] But the fear of radiation-induced cancer as the result of a potential nuclear accident is rampant among significant elements of the American population, even while they bake themselves in the rays of the warm sun. At the same time, coal-fired plants have produced significantly more effluents than have nuclear plants, and many of these effluents are linked to increases in cancer. Yet there has been no public outcry on this score: rather, the objections to coal-fired energy production have centered on other issues—pollution, environmental degradation, and the health and safety of miners.[12]

Outside the energy field, much greater risk is tolerated in the face of demonstrable harm. The national campaign against smoking, for example, has been slow and has suffered many setbacks. And, even in areas with strict anti-smoking ordinances, the actual incidence of smoking, after dropping for many years, has remained virtually constant and even increased among some populations, most notably teenagers. Europeans generally, Russians in particular, and—especially—Ukrainians who panicked in the aftermath of the Chornobyl accident continue to smoke in great numbers, with virtually no public outcry. Similarly, physicians have been exhorting their patients for decades to avoid excessive exposure to the sun, its radiation a known cause of potentially fatal skin cancer. Yet on any beach, whether Malibu, the Riviera, or the Crimea, one can find on any warm summer day, hundreds, even thousands, soaking up the sun's deadly rays.

While smoking and sunbathing may be considered individual behavior, and the consequences suffered a matter of personal choice, there is no question that automobile casualties cost the lives of tens of thousands of innocent individuals every year. Traffic deaths take a huge toll around the world and are on the rise virtually everywhere. Yet no one has suggested outlawing the automobile. Indeed, it would appear that some technological systems enjoy far greater public tolerance for accidents. In any technology, some margin for error must exist—what Charles Perrow has called the "normal accident."[13] It is not possible for a technology to exist, to interact with human beings, and for there to be no inadvertent failures of the system or its operators. Yet there seems to be a disparity in the way different technological systems are viewed: the automobile is granted greater leeway than is the airplane, for example.

What is it that people fear about nuclear power? If it is increases in background radiation, there are no data to suggest that the operation of power plants has increased radiation in the atmosphere; indeed, the operation of coal-fired plants has been responsible for more radiation release than have nuclear plants.[14] If it is operator error resulting in accidents, the risk is no different from the risk assumed when operating an automobile in the presence of other vehicles. In other words, to put it bluntly, *the fear of nuclear power appears to be non-rational.* U.S. nuclear plants are among the safest in the world; even Three Mile Island—which was technologically more serious than even Chornobyl—resulted in virtually zero radiation release because of the reinforced concrete containment system surrounding all U.S. commercial reactors.[15]

Further, the abandonment of nuclear power makes little economic sense in the present energy environment. In the 1970s, in the aftermath of the oil embargo and the ensuing energy crisis, there was a flurry of activity directed toward the development of alternative sources of energy. Today, that effort has all but disappeared, and in the U.S. the percentage of fossil fuel which is imported is at an all-time high, eclipsing by far the proportion of imported oil prior to the embargo. Yet one hears almost nothing about the dangers of the United States being so dependent on foreign sources of oil to satisfy its energy needs. The one group which is paying attention is the U.S. oil industry: this author recently participated in a random survey designed to test attitudes toward increased off-shore drilling and exploitation of wilderness areas including Alaska's North Slope. The survey was premised on the alarming percentage of oil which is imported, but did not allow for suggestions that alternative sources of energy needed to be developed. The agenda was pretty clear—and it did not include considerations of nuclear, solar, hydro, or other alternatives.[16]

In the remainder of this essay, I will examine some of the explanations which have been offered for the non-rational fear of nuclear power. These explanations break down into five categories: the link between nuclear power and nuclear weapons; the anomalous position of the U.S. government in touting nuclear power while creating fear of weapons of mass destruction; the public relations environment in which nuclear power companies must operate; and, of course, the incidence of nuclear accidents. A major factor in each of these categories is the general lack of credibility afflicting governments in general and the United States government in particular, the perception that the government has been willing to endanger civilians in order to achieve unspecified—and perhaps unjustified—ends. The fifth, and in some ways most interesting, category is the association between nuclear (atomic) power and popular mythology as captured in science fiction and science fantasy.

Almost as soon as scientists began thinking of the benefits of harnessing the atom, their attention was turned to creating weapons of mass destruction. Shortly after the discovery of nuclear fission, the world was rent by war: Science, spurred by fear of the Nazi war machine, marshaled its considerable intellectual resources in support of the Allied war effort.[17] Thus, the public's first real introduction to nuclear science was through atomic explosions, death and destruction in Hiroshima and Nagasaki, mushroom clouds whose images seared the minds of an entire generation, power unlike any the world had known before.[18] For the first time, mankind possessed the ability to destroy itself and to make the earth uninhabitable. The task of dissociating nuclear power from nuclear weapons would prove to be a daunting one.[19]

Much of the difficulty came about because of the anomalous position of the government vis-à-vis nuclear power. On the one hand, the government was in the business of promoting peaceful uses of the atom. In his analysis, Parsons traces the economic effects of a U.S. government policy encouraging civilian nuclear power development. As Parsons describes it, the government took an activist role in stimulating research and development. For example, AEC commissioner T. Keith Glennan openly campaigned for private industry to take the initiative in developing the nuclear generation of electricity, writing articles and making speeches aimed at getting utilities on the commercial nuclear power bandwagon.[20]

Eisenhower's Atoms for Peace plan to the contrary notwithstanding, most government rhetoric during the cold war era was designed to create fear of weapons of mass destruction, i.e., the nuclear threat posed by the Soviet Union.[21] Given the horrific demonstration that introduced the public to nuclear fission at the end of World War II, the subsequent political emphasis on the destructive power of nuclear missiles and bombs could only have reinforced the association between peaceful and aggressive uses of atomic power. This is particularly true if one considers that part of the rhetoric of the Atoms for Peace initiative was based on the realization that the by-products of nuclear fission for energy production could be used in bombs. This fact did not escape the attention of what would later become the anti-nuclear movement.

Finally, the very "conditions of contest" within which nuclear plants operate reinforce the potential for disaster. Consider the amount of time and effort the utilities put into disaster control, informing local residents of what to do in case of an accident—how to evacuate, how to protect themselves.[22] It is, in some ways, reminiscent of the old air raid drills that frightened school children during the height of the cold war. Those children have grown up to be regulators and activists, as well as nuclear engineers and physicists.

It is true that nuclear power plants are not the only enterprises required to give safety warnings and instructions to their customers and constituents. Cigarette and alcohol packages carry warning labels, and airlines are required to instruct passengers regarding evacuation techniques prior to each flight. But these have a documented history of risk: cancer and heart disease in the case of tobacco; the ravages of alcoholism and the effects of small amounts of alcohol on developing fetuses; the large number of lives lost in each airplane crash.

Indeed, the question of airline safety provides a parallel case. Americans, and perhaps other societies as well, are inordinately affected by airline disasters. In part, this may be a function of the increase in world terrorism, and the 1991 destruction of PanAm 103 over Lockerbie, Scotland. But, to a large extent, it is the suddenness and the shockingly large number of instantaneous casualties that affects public perception.[23] As a result, and despite all statistical evidence to the contrary, much of the public believes that air travel is more dangerous than other forms of transportation—most notably, the automobile. The facts, however, are quite different. Out of the thousands of flights each day, and even on the days when an air tragedy does occur, it is almost certainly true that a greater number of people will have died in automobile accidents throughout the world.

This phenomenon is a function of the perception of risk, which does not take into account empirical evidence of risk and which, therefore, fails to conform to Western standards of Cartesian logic. This ability to hold fast to beliefs in the face of contravening evidence is a fascinating topic in itself, but one far beyond the scope of this essay. However, if there is a common thread, it probably lies in the perception of control: generally what people fear about airline travel is the inability to control their own fate in an emergency; most feel that they have greater control in an automobile, despite the unpredictability of drunk and/or reckless drivers, the variables of bad weather, and the growing number of cars on the road, many operated by increasingly aggressive drivers.

Similarly, radiation—characterized as "The Silent Killer" which can be neither seen, felt, smelled, nor heard, and which is under the command of a few powerful utility corporations, government agencies, and university research facilities—represents an inability to control one's own exposure should an accident occur. In this sense, Chornobyl embodied the worst nightmare of both the proponents and opponents of nuclear power: people everywhere tracked the cloud of radiation that, literally, circled the globe, affecting not only the Soviet Union (especially Ukraine and Belarus), but Europe and even North America. The explosion at Chornobyl released far more radiation into the atmosphere than Hiroshima and Nagasaki combined and brought back images of such movie thrillers from the 1950s and 1960s as Neville Shute's *On The Beach*. And the world's population could do nothing except watch, wait, and measure radiation levels. It is, thus, a feeling of helplessness which fuels fear of flying and fear of nuclear power; and, in the case of nuclear power, that helplessness moves in tandem with distrust of government.

Nevertheless, in North America, at least, there exists no incontrovertible documentation for casualties related to civilian nuclear power.[24] Several cases involving people and animals living downwind of the test sites in Nevada and on Pacific Ocean atolls have been documented, but these resulted from weapons testing in the open atmosphere; Western nuclear plants, in contrast, have primary and secondary containment vessels to prevent the release of radiation into the atmosphere. Each time a nuclear accident is reported, however, the image of the silent killer is reinforced, along with the spectre of increased cancer, deformity, and mutation. Perhaps the distinction is one of assumed risk: the smoker, the drinker, and even the airline passenger make an affirmative choice. Those downwind of Chornobyl or the Nevada test site had no choice.

The problem with nuclear accidents, of course, is the public's lack of confidence that its government will be open about the extent and effects of any radiation release. Walter Pasedag, for one, was struck by the open skepticism that greeted his public statements regarding the status of cleanup efforts at TMI.[25] Readers may recall that this distrust was borne out in the Soviet Union's initial handling of information regarding the Chornobyl accident.[26] And while Americans have always had a healthy distrust of their government—any government, for that matter—it may well be that the modern era of suspicion was born in the deserts of Nevada and, nourished at Three Mile Island, reached maturity after Chornobyl. Indeed, the aftermath of atmospheric testing within the continental borders of the U.S. may have been the first time Americans became conscious that their government had lied to them about something which directly affected their health and safety.[27] As a result, few people have confidence in the credibility of the government's information with respect to domestic nuclear incidents.

Fear of nuclear power is based on the incidence of accidents, questions about security, and problems of waste disposal. But each of these comes back to the fundamental concern about radiation, the invisible killer. Historian of science Spencer Weart has traced our concern with radiation to deep-seated, ancient images which, encouraged by early scientists, have been brought to bear on modern nuclear energy.[28] Weart traces the image of nuclear power through four chronological stages. In the first, "Years of Fantasy, 1902-1938," he examines some of the images that have informed our reactions to the development of nuclear science. Among the most striking are the "white cities of the future" and the quest for transmutation. Virtually every culture has its version of the white city—pristine, perfect, without pain or dirt or hunger. In the earliest days of nuclear discovery, many thought that nuclear power might make the white city a reality; science fiction supported this notion with stories set in perfectly functioning atomic powered futures. Similarly, "scientists" almost from the beginning of time have sought the secret of turning metal into gold; because scientists, in creating fission, altered elements, the association to ancient alchemists was easy to make. Other myths that operated alongside these include the notion of the doomsday machine, the death ray, the life-giving ray (one of many two-edged phenomena in the world of scientific development)[29] and the real mutational power of radiation to produce alterations in the genome. In the conclusion to his volume, Weart notes:

> Most of the beliefs and symbols that gathered around nuclear energy were already associated with one another centuries earlier, in a highly structured cluster centered on the tremendous concept I have called transmutation—the passage through destruction to rebirth. By the nineteenth century the themes had become separated from one another, attaching themselves to the new wonders of electricity or to occultism or fantasy tales, surviving only as isolated cultural fragments. But in the early decades of the twentieth century the cluster drew together again around the discovery of nuclear energy. By the 1930s most people vaguely associated radioactivity with uncanny rays that brought hideous death or miraculous new life; with mad scientists and their ambiguous monsters; with cosmic secrets of death and life, with a future Golden Age, perhaps reached only through an apocalypse; and with weapons great enough to destroy the world, except perhaps for a few survivors. In sum, nuclear energy had become a symbolic representation for the magical transmutation of society and the individual.[30]

For every good scientist in a white lab coat, there is, lurking just below the level of consciousness, the mad scientist, ready to blow up the world. In one sense, the love/hate relationship between the public and nuclear power symbolizes public ambivalence toward science itself: for every advance there is a downside, an unintended consequence, an unforeseen side-effect. Value-free science, responsible for so many discoveries that have improved our lives, left the moral and ethical questions to a public ill equipped to understand the science behind personal decisions. Nuclear power might create energy to turn deserts into gardens, but that same power could reduce the most verdant garden to wasteland in a matter of seconds. Indeed, Weart documents the irony: the very images that were supposed to demonstrate how much care is taken to protect the public instead reinforced the deadly nature of radioactive materials.

> Atoms for Peace publicity itself cast inadvertent shadows. For example, countless exhibits, films, and photographs showed concrete shields with thick glass windows, workers hidden in white protective suits, and mechanical "slave" hands for manipulating radioactive substances from a safe distance.... The images were supposed to show how carefully experts protected everyone, but they carried a more archaic message.[31]

As one French author noted, referring to a picture of a face "peering intently through glass at robot hands opening a bottle of isotopes," that very image symbolized "an ever more mechanized Humanity, avid to tear from Nature her eternal secrets, and at the same time fearful of the unknown that can escape from a simple bottle, a modern representation of Pandora's box."[32] For the people of Pripyat and the surrounding villages, Pandora's box was unprotected and now lies entombed in a crumbling sarcophagus.

The tragedy which this volume commemorates was not the first nuclear accident in the former Soviet Union. Information concerning the 1957 disaster at Kyshtym did not surface until many years later, and that involved nuclear waste rather than reactor failure. Nevertheless, as Weart notes, "the minority of nuclear experts who had insisted that radioactive wastes could do serious harm, if badly enough mishandled, were right."[33] The fears epitomized by events such as that at Kyshtym nearly forty years ago found their culmination in the aftermath of the explosion in the No. 4 reactor at Chornobyl in 1986. More than one analyst has commented that the Chornobyl accident may well have been the nail in the coffin of nuclear energy production in the United States.

****

For fifty years, the Union of Soviet Socialist Republics embodied our fears and our notion of evil; psychologists might argue that the United States' morbid absorption with the power of Communism was predicated on a vision of the Soviets as a mirror image of itself: to borrow a phrase, they were our "evil twin"—just like us, only venal. Thus, Ronald Reagan's characterization of the USSR as the "evil empire" struck a resonant chord in the United States and sometimes with the rest of the western world, as well.

More temperate characterizations of the Soviet Union focused on its role as the West's nuclear adversary, possessing, as did the other powers, the ability to destroy us all through the use of nuclear weapons. For a generation that grew up under the mushroom cloud of atomic holocaust, Chornobyl reinforced deep-seated fears about the omnipresent silent killer. And nothing that has been learned about the accident in the intervening ten years has dispelled those fears.

Much of the fear and fascination directed toward the Soviet Union was predicated on its perceived technical competence and ability to compete militarily. The launch of Sputnik I and the flight of Yuri Gagarin shocked the West out of its technological complacency. Furthermore, with its tight control of information and the inability of Soviet citizens to travel to the West unless vetted as trustworthy and circumspect, the USSR was able to maintain a facade of success and efficiency. But when the No. 4 reactor at Chornobyl blew out the roof of the building which housed it, the explosion took with it the Soviet government's aura of technical competence. Chornobyl and its aftermath exposed the incompetence, corruption, and manufacturing inefficiency that have left Russia, Ukraine, and the other former republics in such a sorry economic and political state. Thus, an unforeseen consequence of the tragedy we know simply as "Chornobyl" is a new fear of the former Soviet Union, born of the potential for what we have always dreaded most: the technological accident and the threat of technological blackmail. Each of these ideas is touched on by the essays that comprise this volume.

David Marples begins our discussion with an overview of the history of civilian nuclear power in the USSR. Marples demonstrates that the development of this program represented a shift in Soviet energy policy away from fossil fuel and asks what factors led to this change. His essay traces the progress of energy policy, first in the Soviet Union and then in the independent republics, through the Chornobyl accident and its economic, political, and medical aftermath.

Michael Launer and Marilyn Young describe the general level of safety exhibited in the civilian nuclear power industry of Ukraine and Russia. In their essay, Launer and Young argue that public safety in any potentially dangerous technological industry derives from the organization of management and support services and the presence or absence of a strong safety culture instilled from above.

Michael Congdon also addresses safety concerns raised by the Chornobyl accident; in addition to the absence of a culture of safety, Congdon discusses problems of reactor design and the lack of an independent regulatory body. He describes the safety assistance provided by the West and the conclusions reached by a U.S.-Russia Joint Electric Power Alternatives Study (1995) conducted under the auspices of the Gore-Chernomyrdin Commission.

Gert-Ruediger Wegmarshaus discusses the influence society has on the development of technologies through value structures and the perception of benefits and dangers. He correlates this to theoretical and empirical investigations of risk perception, evaluation, and communication, arguing that if the genesis and maturation of new technologies is largely determined by society, then this thesis should be applicable to the study of technology in Communist and post-Communist societies. In elaborating his argument, Wegmarshaus examines nuclear power in the former Soviet Union in relation to the development of a civil society.

There are many, this author included, who believe that one ultimate result of the Chornobyl accident was the break-up of the Soviet Union.[34] The demise of the USSR as the dominant enemy of the West broached new problems, including the disposition of the Soviet nuclear weapons stockpile and the resultant fears regarding division of weapons-grade fissionable material. The notion of nuclear contraband in the hands of terrorists or outlaw states raises in a different forum the spectre of contamination by exposure to radiation.

Turning to the West's absorption of the USSR as a nuclear adversary, Roman Zyla examines Ukraine's role in the disposition of the Soviet Union's nuclear weapons stockpile. Zyla's argument is that Ukraine was unprepared to become a nuclear power and has been wrongly labeled a "nuclear pariah" by the West because of its negotiating stance regarding the transfer of the weapons to Russian soil.

Finally, William C. Potter explores recent incidences of "nuclear leakage" from the former Soviet Union. It was inevitable that enterprising individuals would take advantage of the lax security of a nation in disarray and attempt to smuggle weapons-usable nuclear contraband out of the country. Potter examines in detail seven cases where nuclear contraband was intercepted; his goal is to isolate behavioral characteristics among the perpetrators.

As promised, each of these essays offers a different perspective on the aftermath of the Chornobyl accident, underscoring the eloquence of Yuri Shcherbak:

Chornobyl has taught the nations of the world a dreadful lesson about the necessity for preparedness if we are to rely on nuclear technology. Humankind lost a sort of innocence on April 26, 1986. We have embarked on a new, post-Chornobyl era, and we have yet to comprehend all the consequences.[35]

Tallahassee, Florida
April 29, 1996

Notes

1.   The explosion at Chornobyl occurred April 26, 1986; the Oklahoma City bombing occurred April 19, 1995.

2.   A terse history of this initiative can be found in R.M. Parsons, "History of Technology Policy—Commercial Nuclear Power," *Journal of Professional Issues in Engineering Education and Practice*, Vol. 121, No. 2 (April 1995): 85-98. Parsons links the fortunes of commercial nuclear power generation to the waxing and waning of governmental technology policy.

3.   This survey can be located on the Internet at: http://www.essential.org/ CMEP/nuclearsafety/020596nukepoll.html.

4.   This is not to suggest that nuclear plants are built without controversy elsewhere in the world. Austrian television, for example, has broadcast numerous commercials opposing the plant at Mohovce, in neighboring Slovakia; the public outcry in Austria, however, has not curtailed construction of the plant. In the old USSR, construction was stopped at many locations, particularly for nuclear powered district heating facilities, and in recent years some projected construction has been postponed because of Russia's economic situation; and Ukraine imposed a moratorium on construction in the aftermath of Chornobyl, although this was lifted in late 1993.

5.   Western governments have been trying for several years to persuade the Ukrainian government to close the Chornobyl plant completely, but Ukraine's chronic energy deficit makes that unlikely. To this end the G-7 nations pledged significant sums in support of the closure. In a recent conversation, Yuri Shcherbak, Ukrainian ambassador to the U.S., indicated that Unit 2, badly damaged in a fire, would be opened in the near future [personal communication, August 1996]. Unit 4, of course, remains entombed in the now infamous sarcophagus. The future of the two remaining units is unclear.

6.   Parsons traces the change in the pace of development to the creation of the Nuclear Regulatory Commission in 1974. Says Parsons, "[The NRC] issued only three operating licenses in addition to five construction permits for nine reactors during their first year of operation. This is compared to 14 operating licenses and construction permits for 23 reactors issued the previous year. The number of

plants planned, under construction, or in operation by the utilities declined drastically after the creation of the NRC—from 218 at the end of 1974 to 120 in 1990." [pp. 91-92]. However, Parsons also believes that there was a marked difference after TMI, characterized by increased cancellations. [personal communication, April 1996].

7. Nuclear Energy Institute, "Historical Profile of U.S. Nuclear Power Development, 1994 Edition," p. 14.

8. The Soviet Union was the first country to anneal aging reactor vessels, conducting such remedial efforts in a number of Warsaw Pact countries.

9. Parsons, 1995, p. 93. According to Parsons, "added measures in the licensing process significantly increased the scope and complexity of engineering, construction, inspection, and documentation. The cost of the measures, when added to the hardware costs of the TMI backfits and the costs of higher inflation during the period, caused total plant costs to escalate much more than previously experienced." Comanche Peak (TX) and Diablo Canyon (CA) each cost approximately US$6 billion for two 1100+MW units. The final Diablo price tag was nearly ten times the original planned cost, in part because of seismic upgrades that the NRC required after construction of the plant had almost been completed. On the other hand, some plants remain cost effective when compared to conventional fuels. In Wisconsin and Minnesota—the Point Beach, Kewanee, and Prairie Island stations are competitive with the cheapest sources of electrical generation.

10. Parsons, 1995, p. 95: "In the writer's experience, the NRC's regulatory attitude caused at least four major impacts on a plant's costs.... Finally, the new way of doing business with the NRC increased the level of documentation and verification to extraordinary levels.... [C]oping with regulatory change was the most significant factor in increasing the cost of nuclear plants."

11. Over the years, the operator of TMI has paid millions in damage claims, none of which was documented as valid. Nevertheless, the operator deemed that settling these claims was more predictable and less expensive than protracted court action.

12. The health and safety of uranium miners was neglected for years, until it came to national attention that this population was suffering adverse consequences on at least the same scale as coal miners.

13. Charles Perrow, *Normal Accidents: Living with High-Risk Technologies* (New York: Basic Books, 1984). See also Charles Perrow, "The President's Commission and the Normal Accident," in David L. Sills, C. P. Wolf, and Vivien B. Shelakski, eds., *Accident at Three Mile Island: The Human Dimension* (Boulder: Westview Press, 1982), pp. 173-184.

14. Keep in mind, however, that the greatest source of increased background radiation throughout the Northern Hemisphere has been the above-ground testing of nuclear weapons conducted by many nations over the past several decades.

15. Ironically, criticisms from the anti-nuclear lobby notwithstanding, TMI proved that well conceived protection systems can shield the public from the potential harm of a severe accident.

16. Walter Pasedag, a physicist with the U.S. Department of Energy, has indicated that, in any event, our ability to exploit hydroelectric power is pretty much exhausted [personal communication, April 1996]. The number of geographic areas with appropriate topography for hydro is limited, and dam construction faces many of the same ecological constraints that nuclear operators do.

17. The conventional wisdom is that their Nazi counterparts were on the verge of creating nuclear weapons.

18. In his essay for this collection, Gert-Ruediger Wegmarshaus uses as the foundation for his analysis the thesis developed by Gar Alperovitz that the atomic bombs were dropped on Hiroshima and Nagasaki for largely geo-political reasons having more to do with a vision of the postwar world than with the reduction in U.S. casualties. For a dissenting analysis of the decision to drop the bombs, see Robert P. Newman, *Truman and the Hiroshima Cult* (East Lansing: Michigan State University Press), 1995.

19. Some observers believe that the Nuclear Regulatory Commission was created in order to separate civilian applications of nuclear power from military ones. For others, the fact that the Atomic Energy Commission functioned both as operator and regulator—an inherently inconsistent situation—was a paramount consideration. In any event, the effect achieved by passage of the 1974 Energy Reorganization Act was to regulate civilian plants without hampering military research and development. However, as far as separating perceptions is concerned, the effort came too late, for the link was already forged in the public mind.

20. The irony here is that, according to Parsons [p. 87], the electric companies were not particularly interested until the government made it financially attractive for them and, in some instances, hinted that failure to comply would result in increased regulation. Another scholar takes a different perspective, arguing that a small number of businessmen and industrialists, "chiefly from the electrical industry, resolved not to be left behind when the atomic revolution arrived.... In the early 1950s, they began to urge Congress toward new legislation that would lower secrecy and other barriers." See Spencer R. Weart, *Nuclear Fear: A History of Images* (Cambridge: Harvard University Press, 1988), p. 161 and the references cited therein.

21. Interestingly enough, one scholar has argued that Eisenhower's proposal was disingenuous: the real motivation was to find a way to control nuclear weapons proliferation; the only way to do this was to have inspection rights, which would be possible only as a condition attached to a grant of nuclear energy technology. See Martin J. Medhurst, "Eisenhower's Atoms for Peace Speech: A Case Study in the Strategic Use of Language," *Communication Monographs*, 54 (June 1987).

22. For an excellent analysis of the inconsistency inherent in letting nuclear utilities create the materials used to transmit risk information to the public, see Louis Gwin, *Speak No Evil: The Promotional Heritage of Nuclear Risk Communication*, Praeger Series in Political Communication (New York: Praeger, 1990).

23. Perception is also affected by media coverage: the constant repetition of the images of disaster and tragedy magnify that news to the exclusion of the thousands of uneventful flights occurring daily. By bringing disaster into high relief, the incidence of such tragedies is distorted against the background of safe travel.

24. In the 1950s and 1960s, after the opening of the Shippingport reactor in Pennsylvania (1957), there were assertions of adverse effects on fetuses and children downwind of the facility. The documentation for these claims, while receiving much public attention, was never scientifically validated.

25. Personal communication, May 1996. As part of his assignment, Pasedag—who then worked for the TMI operator—often spoke in public, providing information to the media and to ordinary citizens in the Harrisburg, PA area.

26. Many observers, including at least one contributor to this volume, feel in retrospect that the subsequent openness of the Soviet government as the tragedy of Chornobyl unfolded consisted more of smoke than substance. At the time, however, the change from the original knee-jerk regression to pre-glasnost' practices was taken at face value by even the International Atomic Energy Agency (IAEA).

27. Most commentators trace the loss of innocence to the Gary Powers incident, when the Soviet Union shot down the U-2 spy plane overflying their territory and then-President Eisenhower initially lied, claiming that the U.S. had no such surveillance program. Eisenhower later admitted the lie, acknowledging both the program and the captive Powers; ultimately, the U.S. exchanged a captive Soviet spy for the American pilot. I would not dispute this chronology, for it was long after the U-2 incident that the American public became aware of the effects of atmospheric weapons testing; however, the direct effects of that realization, I would argue, are more far-reaching and continue to affect perceptions of government credibility today, particularly where nuclear facilities are concerned. Ironically, many believe that the government response to Chornobyl broke the social covenant between that government and the people of the USSR.

28. See Weart, pp. 3-74.

29. Radiation itself reinforces these images in the form of radiation therapy which, properly applied, can eliminate incidences of cancer; but when misapplied. it can itself produce deadly cancer in addition to the unpleasant, sometimes horrific side-effects of the treatment.

30. Weart, p. 421. The image of transmutation—the passage through destruction to rebirth—is reminiscent of the Russian legend of the firebird, immortalized in the ballet by Stravinsky.

31. Weart, p. 177.

32. Martin, Charles-Noël, "Humanité de plus en plus mécanisé," in *Promesses et menaces de l'énergie nucléaire* (Paris: Presses Universitaires de France, 1960), p. 250.

33. Weart, p. 299. For more information about Kyshtym, see Zhores Medvedev, *Nuclear Disaster in the Urals*, (New York: Norton, 1979).

34. See Marilyn J. Young and Michael K. Launer, "Redefining Glasnost in the Soviet Media: The Recontextualization of Chornobyl," in Marsha Siefert, ed., *Mass Culture and Perestroika in the Soviet Union*, (New York: Oxford University Press, 1991), pp. 102-104. See also Yuri Shcherbak, "Ten Years of the Chornobyl Era," *Scientific American* (April 1996): 4.

35. Shcherbak, "Ten Years of the Chornobyl Era," p. 49. Like the practice followed in this volume, Ambassador Shcherbak uses the Ukrainian spelling Chornobyl, rather than the more common Russian rendering: Chernobyl.

2

Nuclear Power in the Former USSR: Historical and Contemporary Perspectives

David R. Marples

Introduction

The Soviet Union lays claim to the development of the first civilian nuclear power station at Obninsk, a nuclear research station near Moscow, in 1954. However, the application of the atomic weapons program to the energy needs of the country did not commence in full for a further 15 years. The foundations of the Soviet nuclear power program were established therefore in the Brezhnev period. The reasons for its development have never been explained satisfactorily. In the early 1970s, the USSR was the world's largest producer of oil—it accounted for approximately half the world's known reserves—and gas; and occupied second place in the output of coal. In terms of energy resources, it could lay legitimate claims to self-sufficiency. Output of oil in the Soviet Union had risen from 31.1 million tons in 1940 to 147.9 in 1960 and 353.0 million tons in 1970. Over the same period, output of gas soared from 3.2 million to 45.3 and 197.9 thus a rise of more than 60 times. Coal production also continued to increase substantially throughout the 1960s and 1970s, from a total of 509.6 mmt in 1960 to 624 mmt a decade later.[1]

All three fuels were critical to energy output in the Soviet Union, but they appeared to meet the needs of the country adequately, in addition to providing (especially in the case of oil and gas) valuable exports that could bring hard currency to the country. What factors led to the change in policy and to the development of an expansive program in nuclear energy?

First, the costs of energy production had begun to rise, commencing in 1970 and increasing throughout that decade. As one energy expert has noted, the USSR failed to address this dilemma through the application of more modern techniques and increased extraction, and an improvement in general management over this period. Rather, to maintain output, the planners were obliged to raise continually the share of energy in industrial investment.[2] One could append to that assessment a failure to raise energy prices above the levels fixed by the state, which were well below the market level. Soviet oil output had peaked by the mid-1970s and the regime recognized the need to conserve valued nonrenewable energy reserves.

As for coal, the valuable coking coal of the Donbas coalfield had been badly depleted after more than a century of exploitation. There were thus two simultaneous developments in the coal industry: a reorientation of priorities and investment from the European coalfield to those of Siberia and the Far East; and the marked decline of the famous Donetsk Basin as a source of energy supplies for Soviet electricity production.[3] The decline of the country's largest coalfield—that is, easily extractable coal supplies were used up—signalled the end of the legendary exploits of a mining community that had produced a Stakhanov, and which in official propaganda epitomized the image the state wished to convey of the Soviet working man, laboring for the glory of the state and for whom no sacrifice was too great.[4] Perhaps as a result of this image, the authorities had belatedly turned attention to the problems of the Donbas region.

Second, factors of geography began to play a major role in Soviet energy policy. Since 90% of the country's known natural resources lay east of the Ural Mountains, the perennial problem henceforth would be to transport these resources to the consumer in the European part of the country. Eastern Europe represented a significant factor in this equation. The countries of Eastern Europe, with the exception of Poland (which had an abundance of brown coal), were critically lacking in energy resources. The USSR had long adopted a role of energy supplier to its political allies within the Council for Mutual Economic Assistance. However, given the rise in costs and the need for hard currency, it was no longer economically expedient to provide these countries with subsidized oil and gas. An alternative had to be found. Both the European USSR and Eastern Europe were energy consumers. Because of the distance to be covered, transportation costs were also high. Moreover, losses of coal in particular during transportation were especially heavy.

Third, output of existing energy resources was subject to huge fluctuations and uncertainty. The Soviet authorities sought a form of energy that could provide a "guaranteed" output each year to meet required needs both internally and for export. Soviet industrial planning was as notable for its anticipated precision as well as for its general inefficiency of operation. When an energy program was formulated in 1983 at the beginning of the administration of CC CPSU General

Secretary Yuri Andropov, the goals were longterm conservation of energy supplies, maintenance of the levels of oil output, and rapid development of both gas and nuclear power.[5] Nuclear power was perceived as the solution to a likely future shortfall of energy output.

Fourth, the centralization of Soviet industry rendered extensive debate on any form of energy production unnecessary. Critics have suggested that energy construction was subject to the whim of bureaucrats in Moscow rather than discussions at the regional level. The Ministry of Power and Electrification of the USSR was the key institution in the development of energy policy. No separate ministry existed for the various branches of energy production. A separate ministry was already in place to supervise atomic weapons development, namely the secretive Ministry of Medium Machine Building, the failings of which have been illustrated by a former Soviet scientist.[6]

The authorities resolved therefore to meet the growing energy costs and the annual rise in the need for electricity with the development of a civilian nuclear power program. The key questions were twofold: where to locate the new installations to best meet existing needs; and what types of reactors to use. There is little evidence that outside the realms of esoteric debate, there was any detailed discussion or cost factoring of such items as nuclear waste disposal or long-term monitoring of reactors that had lived out their natural lifespan. Moreover, though the question of water supply is critical for nuclear power installations, the planners did not take into account the overall impact of reactors on the future water supplies of the various regions. As for location, logic suggested that the stations would be built for the most part in the European regions of the country, particularly in key industrial areas and border regions (those stations that were to produce electricity for export), and close to major cities. The second issue was to pose far more serious problems for the Soviet authorities.

The First Soviet Reactors

The original civilian nuclear reactor developed at the experimental plant at Obninsk (Russia) was of the channel type based on a graphite moderator. It was thus deemed logical to conduct research into this type of reactor, the prototype for military production. The Beloyarsk station near the Caspian Sea at Shevchenko was based on two tiny reactors with a total capacity of 300 megawatts, but it represented the pioneer project for the channel-type reactors. They were brought into service in 1963 and 1967, and the former was the first operative civilian reactor in the country. In 1965, the authorities commissioned the construction of graphite moderated reactors based on channel structure or, to use the Russian acronym, an RBMK, close to the city of Leningrad (St. Petersburg), at Sosnovy Bor. The task was entrusted to the Kurchatov Institute of Atomic Energy and the Scientific Research and Construction Institute of Electro-Technology, which were ordered to synthesize their current experience to develop this new reactor. It came into operation in 1973, and reached its maximum size of 4,000 megawatts (based on four 1,000-megawatt reactors) in 1981. Each reactor had about 1,690 channels.[7]

The RBMK was developed as an exclusively Soviet type of reactor for military purposes. Economically it was regarded as an efficient reactor as it could be refuelled on line and did not require lengthy maintenance periods. Identical RBMK-1000 stations were subsequently constructed at Kursk, Chornobyl, and Smolensk. In 1983 an RBMK-1500 station at Ignalina in Lithuania came into service, which remained the largest capacity reactor in the Soviet Union until the dissolution of the USSR in 1991.[8] A further RBMK station was planned at Kostroma in central Russia. Despite such rapid expansion, the RBMK was a deeply flawed reactor that became unstable if operated at low power. It has been speculated that the prime defect lay in the construction of the control rods, which could not be inserted into the reactor core at an adequate depth.[9] It was also a design that did not provide for a large-scale accident taking place above the reactor. It was not built with the shell or containment dome common to western reactors. Altogether, according to scientists at the Kurchatov Institute of Atomic Energy, the reactor was designed with at least 32 significant defects, rendering the first generation of this reactor group among the most dangerous reactors operating in the world.[10]

The second reactor type, developed concomitantly with the RBMK, was the water-water pressurized reactor, or VVER. Manufactured at the Volgodonsk plant in the Rostov region, the original site for this type of reactor was the Novovoronezh station, which first came into operation with a VVER-210 reactor in 1964, and two VVER-440 reactors in 1971 and 1972. This reactor was developed on a broad scale as further stations were established on the Kola peninsula (1973), Metzamor in Armenia (1976), Rivne and Mykolaiv in Ukraine (the first reactors coming on line in 1980 and 1982 respectively), Kalinin (1984), Zaporizhzhya (Ukraine, 1984) and Balakovo (1985). The Novovoronezh-5 reactor saw the expansion of capacity size to 1,000 megawatts in 1980, and thereafter the VVER-1000 became the most common type of Soviet reactor and the basis for future expansion, though research was conducted on the manufacture of reactors of much larger capacity.[11]

Nuclear power at this same time became a focus of cooperation between the Soviet Union and its East European satellites, which began a power-sharing exercise through the so-called MIR (peace) grid, though there were frequent accusations of "power stealing," particularly between Hungary and Romania. However, the brunt of the production was conducted in the USSR. The VVER-type reactor was manufactured elsewhere only in the former Czechoslovakia though it was installed at various other sites in Eastern Europe: Bulgaria (the Kozloduy plant); Hungary (the Paks station); and East Germany. The reactor type was also the model for the station in Finland, and was exported to Vietnam and Mongolia. Some East European countries opted for western-designed reactors. Yugoslavia's first reactor was designed by Westinghouse; while the Romanian station at Cernavoda was based on the Canadian CANDU (the first reactor came into service only in 1995).[12] Energy-needy countries such as Poland, Hungary and Romania were able to tap into the so-called MIR grid that provided energy from Soviet stations, mainly based in Ukraine. Both South Ukraine (Mykolaiv) and Khmelnytsky plants in Ukraine were manufactured with investment and the use of manpower from the countries concerned: Romania and Bulgaria in the former case; Poland in the latter.[13]

Nuclear Power Development in the Eleventh Five-Year Plan

The key period in the growth of the Soviet nuclear industry was that of the Eleventh Five-Year Plan (1981-1985), which made projections to the year 2000, at which time the industry was to have accounted for 30% of the electric power produced in the Soviet Union, and over 60% of that in border republics such as Ukraine and Lithuania. In 1986, it is estimated that some 36,000 megawatts of capacity were at the planning and construction stage, based predominantly on the VVER model. A new series of this reactor type was under construction with new "energy units" or additional reactors at the following sites: South Ukraine (Mykolaiv), Zaporizhzhya, Rivne, Khmelnytsky (all in Ukraine), Balakovo, Kalinin and Rostov (Russia); with planning work under way for the commencement of construction of the Bashkir and Tatar nuclear power stations. Altogether 45,400 megawatts of capacity were under construction by the spring of 1986.[14]

The entire program came under review as a result of the world's worst nuclear power disaster at Chornobyl station in Kyiv Oblast of northern Ukraine. This accident has given rise to a plethora of literature, both scholarly and otherwise.[15] What follows below is therefore a ten-year review of the major results rather than an attempt to reformulate the series of events. It can be stated with impunity that the psychological impact of the Chornobyl accident on the nuclear power industry in the Soviet Union was enormous and that its psychological ramifications have continued to have an impact on those post-Soviet countries that continue to use or are considering the use of nuclear energy.

The Impasse: 26 April 1986

Perhaps more than any other event in modern history Chornobyl has generated emotions and wildly fluctuating interpretations. There is no consensus on many issues even today. In late April 1986 there were various predictions of the future casualty rate from cancer in the European part of the (former) USSR. The lowest such total, provided by the Soviet authorities, was about 2,500; the highest, that of Dr. John Gofman of the University of California, was 500,000. Such data were based primarily on the amount of radiation entering the atmosphere and eventually landing in the soil and forests; the amount of Chornobyl radiation received by the population, particularly the evacuees from the area and the so-called "liquidators" or cleanup workers.[16]

Scientists also have differed on the amount of low-level radiation that can be tolerated by the human body. During the aftermath of Chornobyl, the Academy of Medical Sciences of the USSR developed the "35 rem concept," signifying that over a normal 70-year lifespan, the average human could safely tolerate—in addition to natural background radiation—35 rems (full body count), or 0.5 rems per year. The concept was greeted with outrage in Ukraine, particularly among environmental groups such as Zelenyi Svit, which argued that for some residents, the 35 rems had been surpassed in the days after the accident. The conception of a 35-rem limit never received official approval from the legislature of Ukraine.[17] Ukraine, together with other affected countries such as Belarus and Russia, eventually replaced the 35 rem concept with a 7-rem limit over a lifetime.[18]

The new Ukrainian radiation tolerance law also led to some difficulties. As in all the affected countries, it is calculated according to ground contamination since aside from within and around the damaged reactor itself, there is little contamination in the air at present. It is measured principally by the radiation fallout of Cesium-137 (though the amount of strontium and plutonium in the soil is also taken into account), but the fallout has not been uniform. Far from it. Areas 300 miles from the nuclear plant have been found to be contaminated whereas some clean spots can be found relatively close to the destroyed reactor unit. What it has meant inevitably is that the Chornobyl fallout area has become much wider, since today all those areas in which the population can acquire only an addition 0.1 rems per year are now included in the fallout zone. For Ukraine, it meant, for example, that areas as distant as the provinces of Volhynia (300 miles west of Kyiv) became contaminated zones. As a result the Chornobyl problem has become an almost insuperable burden for the newly independent government of Ukraine.

The Accident

The Chornobyl nuclear power station is located in the north-central part of Ukraine, about 90 miles north of the capital city Kyiv, with its 2.5 million inhabitants. Built in the 1970s, there were six reactors by April 1986, four in operation and two under construction. It is a graphite-moderated plant (acronym RBMK), one of several of this design in the former Soviet Union, but the only such plant in Ukraine. (The others, as noted above, are Sosnovy Bor, near St. Petersburg, Kursk, Smolensk, and Ignalina in Lithuania.) The technology of the station had been criticized by western nuclear experts. Its fundamental safety problems were to render the Chornobyl disaster a more dangerous accident than might otherwise have been the case.

The experiment on April 25-26 was a test of safety equipment that had been tried previously at both the Chornobyl-3 reactor and the Kursk station in Russia. To prevent a reactor automatic shutdown, operators had dismantled emergency shutdown devices, but an operator error almost brought down the reactor's power to zero before the removal of safety rods from the core caused a power surge. We now know that the design of the safety rods themselves was faulty and the attempt subsequently to shut down the reactor by plunging the rods back into the core may have contributed to the dramatic power surge which blew the roof off the fourth reactor building. Neither the plant manager nor the chief engineer was on hand at the time of the accident, a steam explosion at 1.23am on April 26.

The immediate events in the aftermath of the explosion are well known. The ensuing graphite fire with extremely high levels of radiation took a heavy toll especially on firemen and first-aid workers. The Soviet government response was slow, and Ukrainian officials, operating by precedent (previous accidents had been concealed successfully from the general public), were reluctant to take the initiative in making decisions to evacuate those in the vicinity. Initially, about 40 hours after the accident, a 10-kilometer-radius zone around the reactor was evacuated, commencing with the city built for plant employees—Pripyat—2 miles to the north. After May 2, when the Gorbachev Politburo dispatched two officials to the scene, Egor Ligachev and Nikolay Ryzhkov, the zone was extended to 30 kilometers.

The radiation levels were unprecedented for a civilian nuclear power plant accident and for almost two weeks radiation continued to escape from the gaping hole in the reactor. It was eventually blocked off using both machine and human methods, the crudest being the use of "volunteers" to traverse the reactor roof, fling a shovelful of hot graphite chunks into the gaping hole, and be removed from the area. Such work was highly hazardous. Safety equipment and clothing were inadequate and the toll was heavy. After 30 days, military reservists conducted the bulk of the decontamination work. At the same time the evacuated population had been informed that it would be moved temporarily and that enough belongings must be taken to last for three days. The westward evacuation path, however, emulated that of the radiation cloud, meaning that a reevacuation was soon necessary.

About 116,000 people were removed from the 30-km zone which stretched into the Byelorussian SSR (Belarus). From the Ukrainian side, 76 settlements or towns were evacuated, with 91,000 residents. The amount of land contaminated in Ukraine was not known until the spring of 1989. Revelations from the Narodychi Raion in Zhytomyr Oblast, 200 miles to the west, indicated that radiation levels there after the accident had been as high as 3 rems per hour.[19] Cesium levels in the soil attained 100 curies per square kilometer in places (15 curies had been designated as the tolerance limit warranting immediate evacuation). Such information caused widespread panic among the population and contributed to the notion that the authorities had deliberately misinformed them as to the real impact of Chornobyl. This viewpoint was partially true, though the majority of officials in Zhytomyr and Kyiv were unaware of the actual radiation levels. Such feelings were given weight by the official decision of the Third Department of the USSR Ministry of Health to classify all health information pertaining to Chornobyl as top secret. The consequence was an absurd situation in which even those suffering from acute radiation sickness could not bring official attention to their plight since officially they were diagnosed as having some ailment unrelated to radiation exposure from the Chornobyl accident. Official secrecy has also rendered all health information relating to this event highly suspect.

Since 1989, and the declaration of independence by Ukraine and Belarus in August 1991, the picture has become much clearer. In Ukraine after Chornobyl, 123,000 hectares of agricultural land were taken from cultivation in the republic, in addition to 136,000 hectares of forest. Further evacuations of population from regions such as Narodychi brought the Ukrainian total to around 160,000 people. Using the criterion of 1 curie per square km of cesium in the soil, the area of Ukraine contaminated amounts to more than 40,000 sq kms encompassing around 2,200 towns, villages and hamlets. An estimated 3.2 million people have been affected, of which about one 1 million are children, that is they either live in irradiated regions or have been evacuated from the same. According to official Ukrainian statistics, 2,148,969 people today live in areas suffering from contamination.[20]

In Belarus, it has been estimated that the republic received about 70% of the high-level fallout in the former Soviet Union. Estimates of the affected population vary between 1.9 and 2.2 million, or approximately 20% of the population. They live in 3,668 settlements, including 53 towns.[21] Belarus also received over 60% of the high-intensity fallout of more than 40 curies/square kilometer in the soil, principally in the Homel' and Mahileu regions. One scientist has broke down the population living in highly contaminated zones of the republic as follows:

TABLE 2.1. CESIUM CONTAMINATION OF SOIL IN THE REPUBLIC OF BELARUS[22]

Level (cu/km2)	No. of Inhabitants
over 40	9,821
15-40	120,003
5-15	709,502
1-5	1,485,193
Total	2,324,519

The eastern region of Brest Oblast was adversely affected by the fallout of radioactive iodine, which encompassed about 80% of the republic. Cesium and strontium are the principal problems in the soil today.[23]

Low-level fallout in Russia has encompassed a very wide area of approximately 50,000 square kilometers in total (i.e., over 1 curie per square kilometer), and the Bryansk region has been seriously contaminated though once again official secrecy concealed the situation there for some time.[24] In December 1991, 18 oblasts of Russia registered contamination levels of more than 1 cu/km2 of cesium in the soil. This fallout encompassed 20% of Ryazan Oblast, and large areas of Tambov Oblast, Mordova and Udmurtia. In Russia, in contrast to the affected areas of Ukraine and Belarus, evacuations of those subject to high dose loads was not conducted by the authorities and monitoring of food contamination was negligible. Coal miners from Tula region spent time constructing a concrete seal under the damaged fourth reactor—one of the most hazardous operations in the aftermath of the accident—and then returned

home to a highly contaminated region, all to almost no official attention.[25]

Evacuations

By the spring of 1995, some 130,000 people had been evacuated from
contaminated zones in Belarus. The vertical migration of radionuclides
into the soil here has been minimal—about 1-2 centimeters per year[26]—
and thus because of the longevity of the radionuclides (some three
decades of half-life for both Cesium-137 and Strontium-90), the situation
has not improved over the course of the decade. The population now
receives 70% of its intake of radioactive iodine, cesium or strontium
directly through the food chain.[27]

Evacuation has been dependent in theory upon the precise level of
radiation in the soil, and zones have been divided accordingly, with 15
curies/square kilometer of cesium the minimum limit for immediate
evacuation; 5-15 curies for subsequent evacuation; and 1-5 curies of
cesium the level at which families have a *right* to evacuation if they are
unable to obtain clean supplies of food and water. Often these stipula-
tions remain more on paper than reality. In December 1995 in Ukraine,
for example, 5,500 families, 1,500 of which had children, were still
awaiting removal from the areas of *obligatory evacuation* in the Poliske
Raion of Kyiv Oblast.[28] Like other families, these have consumed
contaminated food products in their native villages for almost a decade.
In January 1996, a further 12,000 families were evacuated from contaminated zones of Ukraine.[29]

The levels of radiation, as noted, vary considerably. Studies have
indicated that the worst affected oblasts in Ukraine are those of Kyiv,
Chernihiv and Zhytomyr, and these have received the bulk of attention.
However, significant radiation fallout has been found well south of the
city of Kyiv, in Kirovohrad and other central regions. Low-level fallout
reached Rivne and Volyn oblasts of the far northwest, and 72 raions in
12 Ukrainian oblasts embracing 4.5 million hectares of agricultural land
have registered contamination of the soil sufficient to warrant concern.[30]
Radiological probes in the Kyiv region have indicated that the content of
radioactive cesium and strontium in rivers and lakes had increased
markedly over the past years and in underground waters exceeds the
permissible level by over 100 times.[31] How can one put these figures
into perspective?

They indicate first of all that Chornobyl contamination affected 6.6%
of all Ukrainian territory; 7.4% of all agricultural land; and 1.6% of all
forests, based on official statistics for the years immediately prior to the

accident. The evacuations entailed the construction of new residences for resettlers in ecologically clean zones, and the erection of a completely new city for Chornobyl plant operatives and their families, called Slavutych, and located in western Chernihiv Oblast, about 42 miles northeast of Chornobyl. In 1995, Slavutych had 28,000 inhabitants (as compared to the 45,000 who lived in the now abandoned Pripyat).[32] How do the above statistics translate into human casualties?

The Human Toll: Health Consequences of Chornobyl

Human casualties from Chornobyl can be divided into several categories: the initial firemen and first-aid workers; the liquidators; the evacuees; and the population living in regions of high radiation fallout. When the USSR established a Government Commission to deal with the consequences of the disaster, the official death toll was given as 31, 28 of whom had reportedly died from radiation-related causes. That figure then remained static and additional deaths were not added. Some high-level figures succumbed to the effects of Chornobyl, including the Ukrainian film director, Volodymyr Shevchenko and possibly even Borys Shcherbyna, the first chairman of the Government Commission. The suicide of Valery Legasov, the head of the Soviet delegation to the International Atomic Energy Agency (IAEA) in Vienna, on the second anniversary of Chornobyl was clearly linked to that accident. Ostensibly Legasov could not live with the knowledge that the nuclear industry had commissioned the station despite information that the Chornobyl plant contained some 32 fundamental design flaws.[33]

In 1990 I interviewed an official of the Pripyat Industrial and Research Association who was visiting Canada, and whom I had first met at the Chornobyl plant the previous year. He noted then that about 5,000 liquidators had died since the accident, some of whom had suffered heart attacks. The liquidators were predominantly young men in their 20s and thus should not normally have died from such a cause. A more recent figure offered by the Ukrainian National Committee for the Radiation Protection of the Population is 5,722 deaths among liquidators.[34] In addition the former decontamination crews suffer from various ailments. Almost 50% of those liquidators resident in Ukraine have some ailments, most notably skin diseases, digestive and breathing problems.[35]

Reliable information on the number of civilian deaths is the most difficult to ascertain, for two reasons. First, the international scientific community has been negligent in providing an accurate picture of the true health situation in the areas affected by Chornobyl. The 1991 study, the International Chornobyl Report (ICR), which was undertaken by a group of experts working under the auspices of the IAEA, attempted to assure the world that the health impact of Chornobyl had been exaggerated; that although the possibility of thyroid gland cancers and leukemia in the future could not be discounted, in 1990-91 there was no evidence of serious health concerns. Rather there was a great deal of psychological tension and stress, some of which had been generated by constant evacuations of people who would have preferred to stay in their homes.

From the perspective of 1996, it is easy to criticize such a report as outdated, but evidence suggests that even by 1991, health problems related to Chornobyl were already becoming apparent. In November 1995, speakers attending a WHO conference in Geneva, Switzerland noted the correlation between a new outbreak of thyroid gland cancer among children and radiation fallout from Chornobyl.[36] The ICR investigation team did not, however, examine liquidators or evacuees. The results ascertained therefore were perhaps not so surprising. Nonetheless, the Report was circulated widely as an attempt to provide a current account of the health problems, or lack thereof, generated by Chornobyl.

Information released by the Ukrainian government has been equally problematic, though from a different perspective. The Ukrainian Health Ministry was initially under the leadership of Anatoly Romanenko who assured the public that no serious health consequences would accrue from Chornobyl. His successor Yury Spizhenko was more open, whereas some six ministers later, today's Ukrainian Health Ministry has produced alarming figures—125,000 Chornobyl-related deaths[37]—without published corroboration. In today's climate, which has seen furious arguments about casualty totals, such a decision was unwise in the extreme. That the death toll is in the thousands is clear—as that for liquidators above demonstrates—but it has to be verified with adequate evidence.

Since Chornobyl, major health problems have arisen in a number of areas. In the heavily contaminated regions, the incidence of morbidity generally has risen in alarming fashion. The portrait of newly independent nations in health crisis is an accurate one, though it must be regarded within the general perspective of health care as a whole: shortage of funds; a general lack of nutritious food in some communities; unhealthy lifestyles, including the smoking of cigarettes and high consumption of alcohol; and the lack of adequate pharmaceutical provisions, especially outside major cities. Neither Belarus nor Ukraine have seen as yet a rise in the number of leukemia cases as a result of Chornobyl. Conversely thyroid gland cancer, especially among children, has seen an unexpected rise in both countries. This disease, which was rare among children prior to the disaster (1-2 cases per year in Ukraine), has risen markedly since 1990 and has developed almost exclusively in the heavily irradiated areas. In the north-central areas of Ukraine, for example, the rise in incidence among children is 8-10 times.[38]

This particular form of cancer is a highly aggressive form which can mestastasize rapidly if not operated upon promptly. Virtually all the new cases have arisen in children born or conceived prior to the accident— hence it is affecting an older age group with the passing years. In about 40% of cases, repeat surgery is necessary. Initially the cause of the disease was believed to be radioactive cesium, but the consensus of the World Health Organization and other bodies at a major conference in Geneva in November 1995 was that it arose through the fallout of radioactive iodine, the major radionuclide released by the explosion, but one that has a half-life of only 8 days.

The situation has been made worse by the fact that northern Ukraine and southern Belarus have iodine-deficient soils, meaning that the thyroid glands of children in particular would take in and be saturated by iodine in the air. Thyroid-related illnesses, but not cancer, were common prior to the accident. Medical specialists maintain that thyroid gland cancer has a 90% cure rate. Hence with totals today approaching 900 children (Ukraine and Belarus) and continuing to rise in 1995, one can anticipate that at least 100 deaths will ultimately result. Among both adults and children in Ukraine, the numbers have also continued to rise: 1,389 in 1991; 1,408 in 1992; and 1,616 in 1993.

Thanks to the research of Dr. Evgeny Demidchik, head of the Thyroid Tumor Clinic in Minsk, basically complete statistics are available for the Republic of Belarus for the period 1986-1995. Prior to 1986, the average incidence of thyroid gland cancer among children (expressed hereafter as TGCC) was about one case per year for the republic. Little increase was seen until 1989-90, when the total rose from 7 to 29 per year. Since 1990, the annual totals have risen sharply. In 1991 the total was 59, in 1992, 66; 1993, 79; 1994, 82; and in 1995, there were 91 cases for an overall total of 424.[39]

Even more revealing than the figures are the locations of those children with thyroid cancer. The highest incidence of TGCC is in Homel' Oblast, which has 226 of the 424 cases to date, or 53.3%, while Brest Oblast has 97 cases. In Vitebsk region, to the far north and beyond the range of the fallout of radioactive iodine, there were no cases of TGCC recorded last year, and there have been only 7 since records were kept.[40] The relationship between iodine and TGCC is today generally accepted by the scientific community, despite initial skepticism. According to Demidchik, the vast majority of the children who have contracted the disease were born or conceived prior to the Chornobyl disaster, meaning that the youngest group is in the 9-10 age range. However, Demidchik stresses that those children who were under the age of 5 at the time of

Chornobyl are the most susceptible to the disease.[41] The TGCC will likely kill about 10% of its victims. To date, thyroid gland cancer is the single most serious and pervasive disease to result directly from Chornobyl, and unfortunately it has not yet peaked.[42]

One can supplement the above figures with a report from Belarus compiled by V.B. Nesterenko, the Director of the Institute of Radiation Safety.[43] Observing the contaminated regions in 1993 as compared to figures for 1992, he noted that from a register of 1.95 million people, including 467,671 children; the number of endocrinological illnesses and of diseases of the nervous system had doubled; diseases of the lungs had increased by 76%; of digestive organs, by 79%; anomalies in growth by 80%; oncological illnesses by 27%; and thyroid gland cancer by 30%. In Nesterenko's view enhanced radiation has served as a catalyst in the general rise in diseases in that republic.

Even more alarming has been the incidence of disease among victims of Chornobyl when compared to that of the general population, particularly when applied to evacuees living in the midst of others in major cities. Oncological diseases in the city of Minsk compared to 1986 were higher overall, but twice as high among evacuees as compared to the general population; diseases of the digestive system were 6 times higher; and cancer of the thyroid gland rates were more than 33 times higher than the average for the city population as a whole.[44] One could repeat this example elsewhere. The point, however, is clear: the disaster at Chornobyl has exacerbated a general health crisis in Ukraine and Belarus; but the incidence of various diseases is much higher among those who were in the vicinity of the reactor or else took part in the decontamination campaign afterward, in the summer and fall of 1986.

Dealing with the sort of problems engendered by Chornobyl would pose problems for any government in the world. For Ukraine and Belarus they are simply impossible to overcome given their current financial situations. In the budgets of these republics as a whole, funds allocated for Chornobyl have been squeezed in recent years. According to the chair of the Ukrainian parliamentary Committee on the questions of the Chornobyl Catastrophe, Volodymyr Yatsenko, writing in March 1995: in 1992, Chornobyl funds constituted 15.7% of the state budget; in 1993, 7.4; in 1994, 5%; and the plan for 1995 [it was not fulfilled] was a mere 3.4%, or 80 trillion *karbovantsi*. Adequate funding, he admitted ruefully, would require the deployment of 20% of state funds, a totally unrealistic proposition. Under such circumstances, and with Chornobyl-related costs growing rather than declining, the young Ukrainian state has been forced to request international aid for Chornobyl problems. These entail not only expenses for evacuation, new housing, and health care, but also for the twin dilemmas of the closure of the Chornobyl plant itself, and the construction of a new covering, or *sarkofag* over the destroyed fourth reactor unit.

The Recovery of the Atomic Energy Industry, 1992-1995

Russia

The recovery of the nuclear industry in the countries of the Commonwealth of Independent States (CIS) has been notable. In late 1992, spokespersons for the Russian atomic power industry (Rosenergoatom) announced an ambitious new program for the expansion of nuclear energy in Russia, with emphasis on plant construction in the remote areas of the federation. The program—though it lacked adequate funding—represented a symbolic resurgence of the nuclear power lobby in Russia, the offshoot of the former Ministry of Nuclear Power and Engineering, almost seven years after the Chornobyl disaster. The scientists anticipated that nuclear power could resolve Russia's current energy problems in the oil and gasfields. They also noted that three reactors had been at an advanced state of construction in 1986 (Balakovo-2; Kalinin-3; and Kursk-5) and could quickly be brought into operation. New reactors for existing units were designated for the Kola peninsula, Sosnovy Bor (St. Petersburg), Khabarovsk and Kostroma, and new units were also anticipated at Novovoronezh, the oldest and original location of the VVER reactor in Russia.[45]

The goal of the new program was declared to be to raise capacity at Russian atomic power stations from 20,000 megawatts to 37,000 megawatts by the year 2010. The program thus appeared to be a modest one, but it nonetheless signified a radical change of view in ruling circles about the viability of nuclear energy as a leading power source for the future. A decline in the production of oil and gas in recent years is likely to continue and will perhaps be compensated by a resurgent nuclear power industry. The program, as outlined, appears to be divorced from reality in more than one respect. The Russian government lacks the resources at present to finance such a program. Rather the press conference illustrated the desire of those involved in atomic energy to restore its place as a future energy alternative.

Ukraine and Belarus

In turn, those neighboring states in the CIS that have long been dependent upon Russian energy supplies—Ukraine and Belarus in particular—have also been obliged to address the question of, in the former case, the further development of nuclear energy and, in the latter case, the creation of a domestic nuclear energy program from the beginning.

Facing economic crises, the newly independent states of Ukraine and Belarus began to address the question of nuclear power development in 1992-93. In both cases, the authorities faced a huge psychological barrier in that the population, having suffered the brunt of the radioactive fallout and the medical repercussions of Chornobyl, was very wary of any nuclear power program. For the planning authorities, however, the immediate concern was the state's inability to cover the costs of imports of oil and gas in hard currency payments.

Ukraine and Belarus appeared to follow the lead of Russia on the nuclear power issue. However, the ultimate decision has lain with the individual state leaders. In Ukraine's case, nuclear energy seemed a logical alternative to traditional energy fuels. Nuclear energy was already responsible for over 30% of total electricity output and hence could hardly be abandoned outright without drastic repercussions on the population. Ukraine in 1992 had five existing stations with a total of 14 reactors. Moreover, like Russia, it possessed several reactor complexes at an advanced stage of construction: Zaporizhzhya-6; Khmelnytsky-2; and Rivne-5. They had been halted by a 1990 moratorium placed on further reactor building and operation by the Ukrainian parliament.[46] This moratorium was lifted in 1993.

Two Ukrainian stations could thus be brought into service within a period of 6-18 months and the synopsis within energy circles was that they could make a significant impact upon the Ukrainian economy. In 1992, for example, the Zaporizhzhyan station alone (with five reactors operational) produced 31.5 billion kilowatt hours of electricity, or 13.3% of total output in Ukraine, and the equivalent of 12 million tons of coal, or 7.6 million tons of oil expended for the same output of electricity at thermal power stations.[47] One Ukrainian scientist declared that a single unit at the Chornobyl station—then under review (see below)—could supply the entire city of Kyiv, population 2.5 million, with electricity.[48]

In Ukraine also, the pro-nuclear lobby was able to marshal some convincing arguments in favor of a renewed program. By 1993, the government was under strong pressure to lift its moratorium on new construction. For example, the Ukrainian Supreme Soviet received a petition early in 1993 from the city of Enerhodar, the city that houses the workers and operatives of the Zaporizhzhya station, to end the moratorium forthwith. One petitioner noted that France, a country of comparable size in area and population to Ukraine, had 56 reactors in service compared to Ukraine's 14. Other relatively small countries were also pursuing the nuclear option: Japan had 43 reactors in an area almost half that of Ukraine; South Korea planned to bring into service 18 new reactors at its atomic power stations by the year 2010.[49]

Turning to the Republic of Belarus, the only reactor under construction at the time of Chornobyl—a nuclear power and heating station some 20 miles east of Minsk—was abandoned in 1988 after widespread public protests. The location of the republic, however, has rendered it very susceptible to the effects of any nuclear accident involving Soviet manufactured RBMK reactors. On the northwest border is located the Ignalina station, an RBMK-1500, on Lithuanian territory. Some 40 miles to the east is the RBMK-1000 near Smolensk; and 15 miles to the south of the southern border is the Chornobyl station itself. Cynics have therefore argued that Belarus might profitably pursue its own program since the dangers of an accident from a domestic station could hardly surpass those from the stations along the borders of the country. As Russian oil supplies to Belarus have varied according to the timeliness of payment, Belarus's nuclear power lobby has become a significant one. Four possible sites have been selected for the country's first nuclear power station, while scientists have argued that the cost of importing nuclear fuel from Russia is considerably less than the price for imported Russian oil and gas.[50]

Nevertheless, opposition to such plans remains significant. In 1994, an argument against nuclear power in the republic was propounded by Professor B.P. Savitsky of the International Ecological Academy in Belarus. He noted that Belarus required annually about 38.5 billion kilowatts per hour (Kw/hr) of electricity and that the chief users of power were industry, utilities, transport and street lighting. Belarusians have been wasteful in their consumption of what was long considered cheap energy supplies. As for nuclear power, the country has no nuclear fuel or waste storage facilities, thus even if Belarus constructs its own power stations it will still be dependent on other countries for both these processes and also for spare parts required to maintain such plants. Moreover, the construction of a domestic nuclear power station would have to start from zero. It probably could not be completed until the period 2005-2010, at which time it might at best provide about 7% of energy needed. It is thus in his view a futile endeavor, but one that has come to light because the pro-nuclear lobby has managed to eliminate research on alternative sources of energy.[51]

The Debate over the Chornobyl Station

Nineteen ninety-three was the pivotal year for the Ukrainian nuclear power industry. In this year, a dramatic reversal of policy occurred as a result of the efforts of a strong pro-nuclear lobby, and Ukraine's continuing energy difficulties. When the decommissioning of the Chornobyl plant began in this year, with the planned removal of the second reactor from the grid (it had been shut down after a fire in 1991),[52] there was a chorus of protests at the highest level, advocating delay and even abandonment of the schedule to take the reactor out of service. A government official pointed out that once fuel had been removed from the reactor core, the process of decommissioning would be almost impossible to reverse. In his view, money spent on making Chornobyl more reliable and safe would be wasted if the plant was closed down. About 270 million rubles (in 1984 prices) had been expended on improvements, almost 25% of which was devoted to work on the reactor itself. In the official's view, these changes had rendered Chornobyl one of the safest of the former Soviet RBMKs.[53]

The above comments found further backing from Bronislav Pschennikov, a candidate of technical sciences from Kyiv. Pschennikov acknowledged that Chornobyl in retrospect should not have been brought back into service in 1986.[54] That decision was basically a political one to display to the world that the consequences of Chornobyl had not been as substantial as first feared. It was a decision that exposed thousands of workers to very high levels of irradiation. Nevertheless, he added, the Chornobyl reactors had been the subject of serious study. Since 1986, several improvements had been introduced: the reactor was provided with a higher enrichment of uranium; its shutdown time was reduced significantly; new laws were issued preventing experiments without the presence of the plant director and chief engineer. Radiation levels had also fallen each year and by 1993 were at only 20% of the permissible norm. According to the principal builder of the station and its chief scientist, the first reactor unit could operate at Chornobyl until 1997, and the third unit until 2001. Pschennikov also noted that developed countries such as Britain continued to operate stations that were much older than Chornobyl, and dated to the 1950s. The then president Leonid Kravchuk was noncommittal in the face of international pressure to close the plant, pointing out that an international research center for the nuclear industry could be established at the station, using the city of Slavutych, 40 miles to the east in Chernihiv Oblast as a base for the workers.[55]

Other observers in Ukraine noted in the spring of 1993 that with enhanced safety and ecological awareness, Chornobyl could continue to operate and benefit the Ukrainian economy.[56] Ukraine has, however, like other non-Russian republics, suffered the loss of several thousand nuclear experts since gaining its independence in August 1991, mainly through the decision of qualified Russian technicians to return to Russia.[57] This deficit of well qualified specialists has been compensated partially by the convocation of a number of high-level international conferences and meetings in the republic that was the location of the world's worst nuclear accident. In the spring of 1993, for example, a high level conference of the International Atomic Energy Agency (IAEA) was held at Enerhodar, in which nuclear experts from Sweden, the United States, Spain and Ukraine participated.[58] There the IAEA specialists had an opportunity to examine the construction of the new, sixth reactor that, once on line, would render Zaporizhzhya the largest nuclear plant in the world. This conference followed a "successful" meeting between Kravchuk and IAEA Director Hans Blix in December 1992, during which the Ukrainian president declared that his country could not survive without nuclear energy, a clear indication that the moratorium was about to be lifted.[59]

Despite the increasing success of the pro-nuclear campaign in the former republics of the Soviet Union, an IAEA delegation visited the Chornobyl site in the spring of 1994 and declared the reactor too dangerous to remain in service.The U.S. Nuclear Regulatory Commission agreed with this verdict and its director suggested that international organizations and financial institutions should assist Ukraine to commission its three almost completed reactors which would then compensate for the loss of the Chornobyl station.[60] In the spring of 1995, after strong international pressure, Ukraine's new president, Leonid Kuchma, informed representatives of the European Union and G-7 countries that he would halt operations at the Chornobyl station by the year 2000.[61] Much hope was placed on a summer 1996 of the G-7 countries in Moscow that encompassed the question of Chornobyl and provided further financial aid to Ukraine to deal with Chornobyl at over $3 billion.

These hopes have yet to be realized. By the fall of 1996, not only was Ukraine complaining that it had yet to receive any of the promised funds, though it did close down the second reactor by 30 November without any guarantee that the closure would be a permanent one, but also the nuclear power authorities announced that plans were afoot to restart the second reactor unit closed since 1991. It is plausible that some statements may have been issued to put pressure on the G7 countries to provide the first installment of funds. Conversely, there is a substantial body of scientific opinion in Ukraine that believes that the Ukrainian nuclear power industry has been unjustly criticized and indeed the focus of international concern whereas ostensibly dangerous RBMK reactor units in Russia and Lithuania are ignored. In addition, as we have observed, many specialists believe Chornobyl to be among the safest of the former Soviet nuclear power stations.

While fallacious, these arguments have been fuelled not only by what can be termed the Soviet nuclear tradition, but also by the international scientific community. There are numerous examples of western special-ists—particularly leaders of the IAEA—visiting the Chornobyl station in the aftermath and even several years after the Chornobyl disaster and offering laudatory comments about the improvements made. When an IAEA team went to Chornobyl in April 1994 and declared the reactors there unsafe by international standards, the remarkable factor was not the statement, but the length of time required to reach such a conclusion: eight years since the major disaster. Sergey Parashyn is not alone in his view that the Chornobyl plant could operate to the end of its natural lifespan. The highly flawed structure of such reactor types is well known and but one factor. It must also be taken into consideration that the Ukrainian economic situation in 1996 had led to a situation in which operators and other personnel were not paid wages for months at a time. However efficient station personnel might be, material hardships lead with certainty to industrial accidents and even more serious events.

What has occurred in Ukraine is the survival of nuclear power as a short-term solution to an energy and general economic crisis. A lobby that appeared powerless after the worst industrial accident in history has recovered from its inertia and is beginning once again to assert its authority in economic decision-making. Further evidence of the revival of nuclear power was the restarting of the Metzamor reactors in Armenia in 1995, in a dangerously seismic zone, and the current dominance of nuclear power in the energy production of several countries in Central and Eastern Europe: Lithuania; Hungary; and Bulgaria. In all the above cases, there is international concern regarding the safety of reactors in operation; the use of obsolete equipment; the lack of training or irregular wages provided to plant operatives; and the general levels of safety consciousness.

Conclusions

Unfortunately, the Chornobyl story is far from over. The covering over the damaged reactor will have to be replaced within the next 10-15 years. Moreover, even the proposed closure of the nuclear station may be dependent on an improvement of Ukraine's energy situation. Elsewhere in the CIS countries, the nuclear power plants are notably lacking in safety procedures and since 1991 accidents have been frequent, including a fatality at the Zaporizhzhya station in 1993.[62] The new Russian program was announced before funds had been assigned. At the time of writing it appeared to be inconceivable that the Russian government would allocate such funding. Hence both Russia and Ukraine remain very much dependent on the charity of international organizations both to fund a future program and to render it safe.

In the meantime, the two Slavic states and other members of the CIS have demonstrated an alarming tendency to "muddle through" and maintain present operations at nuclear power plants with reduced levels of safety. Hence while the RBMK has now been almost universally condemned as a dangerous reactor, and attention has periodically been focused on the need to stop operations at Chornobyl, very little has been said about the remaining five stations still in operation, including the giant Ignalina station, once bitterly opposed by the Lithuanian Sajudis, but now responsible for some 80% of that country's electricity supply. The question of continued operations at such plants must be discussed by the IAEA and other international organizations if the world is to avoid a major nuclear accident in the immediate future. Despite the world's worst nuclear accident, nuclear power in the territories of the former Soviet Union today is less safe than it was in 1986.

The Republic of Belarus, which has suffered the most from the Chornobyl disaster in terms of both medical repercussions and radioactive fallout, faces perhaps the greatest dilemmas of all. It has metamorphosized from Communist rule into a presidential dictatorship with a rubber-stamp parliament reduced to a rump of 110 members and an unstable political structure. Evidence suggests that scientific planners may seek ready answers to complex questions, and that a nuclear power program could be undertaken without an adequate infrastructure or financial backing. Under such circumstances, the political authorities would not find it in their interests to publicize the alarming health statistics, including the impact of the nuclear disaster of more than a decade ago.

It is worth noting finally that the situation in the former Soviet Union owes much to the irresponsible optimism of many in the international nuclear industry, who first collaborated with the Soviet authorities in minimizing the impact of a major catastrophe and then saw fit to promote the industry at every opportunity, even when it must have been apparent that neither Russia nor Ukraine were in an economic position to develop nuclear power further. Nuclear power has thus been placed at a higher priority than energy conservation or viable energy alternatives. It is being promoted, at times cynically, in areas of the world in which the best adjective that can be applied to the workforce is "disillusioned." Safety workers remain unpaid for months at a time, stoppages for "incidents" are frequent, and several of these in the case of Ukraine have been potentially dangerous. Many of the current nuclear power plants in the former Soviet Union are reaching the end of their natural lifespans but few provisions have been made for their removal from the grid and longterm conservation.

The nuclear industry has a history in the former Soviet Union that now spans more than four decades. It is a timespan that has seen several accidents, of which two—Kyshtym and Chornobyl—can be characterized as catastrophes. It is hard to conceive of another industry that has managed to wreak such damage to the environment in such a short space of time. It is worthwhile suggesting therefore that energy planners here and elsewhere in the world consider a number of alternatives before resolving that nuclear power is indeed "the wave of the future."

1. Are there conceivable energy alternatives?
2. How far would the energy shortage be assuaged by rigorous methods of energy conservation?
3. What impact will the establishment of the industry have on the surrounding landscape?
4. In the event of an accident are there major population centers that will be affected, and can these be conceivably evacuated?

In the case of Russia, one could make a strong case that nuclear power is simply unnecessary and that its loss would not adversely affect the power supply. One could also concede that the development of the oil and gas industry has also had extreme consequences for the native communities of western Siberia. We have also noted an argument that for Belarus, nuclear energy will not alleviate the energy deficit. This leaves Ukraine, the location of Chornobyl, and a country that was very much the victim of irresponsible and poorly conceived plans of authorities based in Moscow.

Thus far Ukraine's actions in the sphere of nuclear energy are not appreciably different from those of the Moscow predecessor; namely to develop nuclear power as the only conceivable energy alternative while putting pressure on western industrialized countries to come up quickly with funds to compensate the agreed upon closure of the Chornobyl station itself. As Michael Launer has noted, the closure of Chornobyl by the year 2000 appears increasingly unlikely. The dividing line between authentic financial needs of the state and calculated bargaining techniques is a fine one. One need hardly add that the similarity of Ukraine's behavior as an independent state to its actions as a virtually mute partner of the Soviet Union constitute one of the major paradoxes of the post-Soviet era. The history of nuclear power in the former Soviet Union is not a happy one. Unfortunately the future looks no brighter than the past, not least because of a fundamental failure to explore adequately the alternatives to this form of energy.

Notes

1. Central Statistical Administration of the USSR, *Narodnoe khozyaystvo SSSR v 1984g.* (Moscow, 1985), p. 166.

2. Thane Gustafson, *Crisis amid Plenty: The Politics of Soviet Energy under Brezhnev and Gorbachev* (Princeton, NJ: Princeton University Press, 1989), pp. 35-36.

3. David R. Marples, *Ukraine Under Perestroika: Ecology, Economics and the Workers' Revolt* (New York: St. Martin's Press, 1991), pp. 178-188.

4. Despite official rhetoric, the coalfield rarely had trouble-free periods. The difficulties in the pre-Stakhanov period of the 1930s are described in Hiroaki Kuromiya, "The Commander and the Rank and File: Managing the Soviet Coal-Mining Industry, 1928-33," in William G. Rosenberg and Lewis H. Siegelbaum, eds., *Social Dimensions of Soviet Industrialization* (Bloomington and Indianapolis: Indiana University Press, 1993), pp. 146-165.

5. Gustafson, *Crisis amid Plenty*, p. 242.

6. Grigorii Medvedev, *The Truth About Chernobyl* (New York: Basic Books, 1993).

7. A.M. Petros'yants, ed. *Atomnaya nauka i tekhnika SSSR* (Moscow: Energoatomizdat, 1987), p. 22.

8. The Ignalina station began operations in 1983.

9. Victor Snell, "Introduction," in David R. Marples, *The Social Impact of the Chernobyl Disaster* (London: The Macmillan Press, 1988).

10. For a discussion of the safety problems at Chornobyl, see for example, Alexander R. Sich, "The Shutdown Question," *The Bulletin of the Atomic Scientists*, Vol. 52, No. 3 (May/June 1996): 36-37.

11. Petrosyants, *Atomnaya nauka i tekhnika SSSR*, pp. 21-23.

12. It led to a minor public outcry in Canada as a result of concern about exporting such technology to authoritarian regimes. In November 1996, a Canadian deal with China initiated by the Canadian Liberal government of Jean Chretien sparked similar protests.

13. David R. Marples, *Chernobyl & Nuclear Power in the USSR* (London: The Macmillan Press, 1987), pp. 51-70.

14. *Energetika SSSR*, p. 169. While accidents were not reported at Soviet nuclear power stations, there is ample evidence of construction problems at the various sites, including in one case the collapse of a reactor building on its foundations. I have chronicled such dilemmas in Marples, *Chernobyl & Nuclear Power*, pp. 79-90.

15. Among the Chornobyl literature has been some notable contributions from Russian, Ukrainian, and Belarusian authors. They include in approximate chronological order: Solomea Pavlychko, *Letters from Kiev* (Edmonton: Canadian Institute of Ukrainian Studies, 1992); M.I. Bobneva, ed., *Chernobyl'skiy sled: mediko-psikhologicheskie posledstviya radiatsionnogo vozdeystviya* (Moscow, 1992); Institute of Sociology, National Academy of Sciences of Ukraine and the Democratic

Initiatives Research-Educational Center, *Sotsial'ni naslidki Chornobyl's'koi katastrofy: Rezul'taty sotsiolohichnykh doslidzhen' 1986-1995 rr.* (Kharkiv: Folio, 1996); and especially Ya. V. Malashevich, chief editor, *Charnobyl: pohlyad praz dzesyatsihoddze* (Minsk: Belaruskaya Entsyklopedyya, 1996).

16. Discussed in David R. Marples, *The Social Impact of the Chernobyl Disaster* (New York: St. Martin's Press, 1988), Chapter 1.

17. Alla Yaroshinskaya, *Chernobyl'. Sovershenno sekretno* (Moscow: Drugie Berega, 1992), p. 100.

18. In Belarus, the new law was implemented in December 1991, but it has not been accepted as the most valid means of determining the danger to the population residing in such areas.

19. I have discussed these events at length in Chapter 3 of my book *Ukraine Under Perestroika* (1991).

20. *Holos Ukrainy*, May 5, 1995, p. 2.

21. V.B. Nesterenko, *Mashtaby i posledstviya katastrofy na Chernobyl'skoy AES dlya Belarusi, Ukrainy i Rossii* (Minsk: Pravo i ekonomika, 1996), p. 20.

22. V.B. Nesterenko, "Glavnye problemy minimizatsii i preodoleniya posledstviy Chernobyl's'koy katastrofy: alternativnye nauchnye kontseptsii," in III Mizhnarodny kanhres, *Svet paslya Charnobylya: osnovnye nauchnye doklady* (Minsk: Belarusian Charitable Fund 'For the Children of Chernobyl', 1996), p. 53. It should be noted that the total figure in Nesterenko's calculation is higher than the official total of people affected by Chornobyl in the Republic of Belarus.

23. I have dealt with this subject at length in David R. Marples, *Belarus: From Soviet Rule to Nuclear Catastrophe* (Basingstoke, UK: The Macmillan Press, 1996), Chapter 3.

24. See Michael Launer and Marilyn Young's paper in this volume.

25. Nesterenko, *Mashtaby i posledstviya*, pp. 29-30.

26. "Chernobyl'skaya katastrofa, ee posledstviya i puti preodoleniya na territorii Belarusi: Natsional'nyy doklad," cited in II Mizhnarodny Kanhres, *Svet paslya Charnobylya* (Minsk, 1994), p. 2.

27. *Nabat*, No. 11, 1995, p. 9.

28. *Uryadovyi kur'yer*, December 12, 1995, p. 2.

29. *Holos Ukrainy*, February 7, 1996, p. 2.

30. Ibid., June 7, 1995, p. 4.

31. Ibid., April 26, 1994, p. 1.

32. Ibid., January 6, 1996, p. 4.

33. See, for example, Marples, *Ukraine Under Perestroika*, pp. 20-25.

34. *Holos Ukrainy*, June 7, 1995, p. 4.

35. *Pravda Ukrainy*, June 16, 1995, p. 1.

36. Cited in *Science*, Vol. 270, December 15, 1995.

37. Cited in *Vil'na dumka* (Lidcombe, Australia), January 28, 1996, p. 1.

38. *Holos Ukrainy*, May 5, 1995, p. 2.

39. Correspondence of Dr. E.P. Demidchik with the author, February 2, 1996.

40. Ibid. The author has conducted three interviews with Dr. Demidchik in Minsk in the period 1993-95 and the conclusions presented below derive from those meetings.

41. Evgeny Demidchik, "Interes k Chernobyl'skoy probleme ne dolzhen prekrashchat'sya," *Nabat*, No. 9 (September 1995): 3.

42. According to one source, which in general greatly understimates the medical impact of Chornobyl on the population of the former Soviet Union, there are altogether over 1,000 cases of TGCC today and a further 3,000 are anticipated. "Chernobyl, cancer, and creeping paranoia," *The Economist*, March 9, 1996, p. 81.

43. V.B. Nesterenko, "Gor'kaya pravda o posledstviyakh Chernobyl'skoy katastrofy dlya Belarusi," *Nabat*, No. 11 (November 1995): 8.

44. Ibid., p. 9.

45. Information about the new program was announced at a press conference in Moscow on January 20, 1993.

46. The other stations operating in Ukraine are Chornobyl itself and South Ukraine (Mykolaiv). The latter is part of a vast energy complex which includes two hydroelectric stations. The moratorium stalled not only the fourth reactor at the Mykolaiv site, but also work on the hydroelectric stations. See *Robitnycha hazeta*, December 18, 1992, p. 3.

47. *Pravda Ukrainy*, April 24, 1993, p. 2.

48. *Vechirniy Kyiv*, April 29, 1993, p. 2.

49. *Pravda Ukrainy*, April 29, 1993, p. 1

50. Marples, *Belarus*, Chapter 5.

51. B.P. Savitsky, "Belarus' i atomnaya energiya: Problemy i perspektivy," in *Svet paslya Charnobylya* (1994), pp. 23-24.

52. According to the then director of the former Ukrainian State Committee for Nuclear and Radiation Safety (now part of the Ministry for the Protection of the Environment and Nuclear Safety), Nikolay Shteinberg, though the Ukrainian parliament had resolved to close unit two permanently on October 22, 1991, this decision was also reversed on October 22, 1993, when the moratorium was lifted. Paper presented at a conference on nuclear safety Monterey Institute of International Studies, April 1994.

53. *Pravda Ukrainy*, April 29, 1993, p. 3.

54. Chornobyl's reactor number one was back on line only five months after the major accident, on October 1, 1986. The second reactor followed a month later. Reactor three, which posed more serious problems in the light of its adjoinment to the destroyed fourth reactor, was returned to the grid only in December 1987. See Marples, *Social Impact*, p. 207.

55. *Vechirniy Kyiv*, April 29, 1993, p. 2. Slavutych was constructed as a center for Chornobyl workers to replace the evacuated city of Pripyat, which was

declared uninhabitable after the Chornobyl disaster. For an account of the radiation situation there on the eve of its construction, see the secret protocol of the USSR Council of Ministers, "Concerning the site for the construction of a new settlement for the permanent habitation of the personnel of the Chernobyl nuclear power plant and their family members." Secret Protocol, circa August 13, 1986, cited in Alla Yaroshinskaya, *Chernobyl': sovershenno sekretno* (Moscow: Drugie berega, 1992), pp. 466-467.

56. *Pravda Ukrainy*, April 22, 1993, p. 1.

57. *News From Ukraine*, No. 15, April 1993, p. 2.

58. *Pravda Ukrainy*, April 17, 1993, p. 2.

59. *Demokratychna Ukraina*, December 22, 1992, p. 1.

60. Information of Ivan Salin, then director of the U.S. Nuclear Regulatory Commission at the conference on nuclear safety, Monterey Institute of International Studies, April 1994.

61. Marta Kolomayets, "Ukraine to shut down Chornobyl by 2000." *The Ukrainian Weekly*, April 16, 1995, pp. 1,4.

62. *UPI*, May 22, 1993.

3

Ukraine, Russia, and the Question of Nuclear Safety

Michael K. Launer and Marilyn J. Young

Introduction: Safety and Fear; Economics and Environmental Awareness

The purpose of this paper is to describe the general level of safety exhibited in the civilian nuclear power industry of Russia and Ukraine, to examine the various factors—both technological and institutional—that impinge upon safety improvements, and to provide an assessment of prospects for the future. In contradistinction to the oft-expressed opinion that operational safety in the nuclear industry is primarily dependent upon technical excellence of the equipment itself, together with the level of training achieved by operations and maintenance personnel, this paper shall argue that such factors are derivative. We believe, in fact, that public safety in any potentially dangerous technological industry derives from the organization of management and support services and, further, that the relative level of safety is societally determined: in other words, it is primarily dependent upon economic and political factors. Moreover, the linchpin that unites or impedes safety efforts at all levels—operational, managerial, and governmental—is the presence or absence of a strong safety culture instilled from above. On the most abstract level, indeed, the cardinal consideration may be the social contract existing between any government and the people it governs.

Many argue that nuclear power is inherently unsafe, hence that it cannot be made safe, so the technology should be abandoned and all existing facilities throughout the world closed. Critics point to the accidents at the Three Mile Island nuclear station (near Harrisburg, Pennsylvania in the U.S.) and at the Chornobyl nuclear station (located some 100 kilometers north of Kyiv, the capital of Ukraine) as ample proof of their position. As a form of argument, this is ideological in the extreme, relying more upon emotion and an appeal to fear of the unknown than upon reasoned judgment or the consideration of factual evidence. To demonstrate this point, we would cite the virulent campaign that was waged unsuccessfully in Austria to force termination of construction activities at power plant sites in Slovakia (particularly the Mohovce station) and the Czech Republic. Opponents of nuclear power generation have purchased television air time to run advertisements that juxtaposed still pictures of completely harmless concave cooling towers—which most people seem to think are the reactor units them-selves—to stock footage of nuclear test explosions in the Pacific.

Nevertheless, these arguments need to be taken seriously, if only because they are so persuasive. Two factors are of utmost importance. First of all, there is fear of the atom—that odorless, colorless, invisible destroyer stalking the earth. This, of course, is the legacy of the A-bomb, so much in the news throughout much of 1995 because of the fiftieth anniversary of the devastation wrought in Hiroshima and Nagasaki. For any analysis of "nuclear politics" to be complete, one must take this fear into consideration. In the Introduction to this volume, Marilyn Young discusses some of the factors impinging on the willingness of society to fully accept nuclear power plants in its midst. Secondly, one must consider the very notion of "safety": how is this concept defined and what does it actually mean? We would argue that there exist competing definitions of "safety" and that the issue of nuclear power development worldwide ultimately will be decided as the result of public persuasion: whichever side projects its definition most effectively will win. (At the moment, to be sure, it is the naysayers who are ascendant.) We shall discuss this factor in greater detail to provide a background for the remainder of our analysis.

The TMI accident occurred when personnel in the unit control room incorrectly diagnosed a dangerous situation; the accident was exacerbated because their emergency instructions were ill-suited to the task of restoring normal operating conditions given the actual situation that had developed. What might have been a scary, but manageable scenario got completely out of hand, and the resulting accident nearly proved to be the realization of an engineering nightmare—a molten agglomeration of radioactive fuel and metallic structural elements that threatened to "eat" its way through the thick concrete slab underlying the damaged power unit. Other than an actual nuclear explosion, nothing more terrifying than the release of all that radioactivity into the environment could be imagined. As a matter of fact, however, virtually no radiation escaped the thick, negatively pressurized containment facility made of reinforced concrete.[1] Obviously, the protective measures that had been designed into the power plant were sufficient to cope with a severe accident that went far beyond what anybody would consider acceptable.

So, do the events at TMI demonstrate that nuclear power is safe or unsafe? That all depends. Is safety defined by the absence of accidents or by the capability of handling them when they occur? To a great extent, the answer to the latter question is determined in the political arena; purely technical issues may be, and often are, overshadowed by policy concerns, and policy concerns are driven largely by societal pressures.

Many opponents of nuclear power production argue that no accidents are acceptable, regardless of the consequences that ensue. This ideology of "zero tolerance" requires assurances of absolute safety before a technology is deemed acceptable; TMI must, by definition, prove the technology unsafe. Indeed, many minor accidents that never had the capacity to create damage to people or the environment would prove exactly the same thing. But no technology, not even the most benign, is absolutely safe. Well over a decade ago, Professor Charles Perrow of Yale University propounded the theoretical notion of a "normal accident"—the idea being, simply, that no technology is fail-safe, that not only are malfunctions to be expected, in reality they are unavoidable (a statistician would call them "anticipated events"). For this reason, measures must be taken in the design and operation of technological systems to minimize the consequences of accidents when these (inevitably) occur. Society, in turn, will determine by consensus how many accidents are tolerable, how severe they may become before the public demands that the technology be abandoned. All of this is based on some sort of cost-benefit calculus that factors in both the potential good which is derived from the technology and the potential harm which may ensue from its application.

An obvious example of the application of this theory (long before its actual formulation by Perrow) occurred in the United States in the early days of the consumer movement, when Ralph Nader published a treatise entitled *Unsafe At Any Speed*.[2] This was an indictment of a specific make of automobile. Nader's premise was essentially that of an engineer: equipment breaks down, people make mistakes, and accidents happen— therefore, a vehicle must protect its occupants in the event that a specific range of accidents occurs (in the nuclear industry, these are called "design basis" accidents). Improvements in safety are defined by an engineer as *those activities or mechanisms which (1) increase the probability of an adequate response in the event that a design basis accident occurs or (2) expand the envelope of design basis accidents that can be compensated for by the available equipment.* As indicated by the title, Nader believed that the vehicle in question would not protect its occupants in any accident scenarios whatsoever. Largely as a result of Nader's activities, which were excoriated by industrialists at the time, Americans now drive safer and more efficient vehicles. Such changes result from a combination of technological innovation and quality control; but they cannot be brought into existence without public pressure, legislative action, governmental regulation, and/or enlightened industrial managers endowed with a realistic sense of what it takes to ensure the profitability of their businesses.

It turns out that Americans, by and large, are actually very tolerant of technology's underside, to the extent that this is almost a national characteristic. In some instances, the risk potential is negligible in comparison to the potential benefits. For example, adverse reactions to immunization, while not unheard of, occur so infrequently that most parents routinely vaccinate their children against a broad spectrum of devastating and not so devastating diseases. And, yes, some babies die in the process. By and large, however, unless it happens to your baby, most people understand that the risks inherent in the process of immunization are a small price for society to pay when compared with the death, disease, misery, and financial cost of failing to immunize the general population.

Even when the risks are more palpable, most people take what they consider to be reasonable precautions and go about their business. The most obvious example, again, is the use of automobiles. Between forty and fifty thousand individuals are killed in the United States each year as the direct result of vehicular accidents, with hundreds of thousands more injured. The economic cost is staggering; the cost in pain and suffering among victims and their loved ones is incalculable. Yet, that doesn't keep people from driving. It doesn't even inspire many of them to buckle their seat belts, or to buy new tires when the old ones wear out, or to obey speed limits, or to stay sober.

With respect to power production at civilian nuclear facilities, most developed societies have determined a level of technological safeguards that they consider adequate to protect the population from exposure to even minimal significant doses of radioactivity. With those safeguards in place, nuclear power has been allowed to function. Over time, these requirements have become increasingly stringent. Many plants that were designed and commissioned some two decades ago may be deemed uneconomic by their owners, since the facilities are reaching the end of their design life and the cost of retrofitting the latest safety enhancements is staggering. Some of these safety measures were not required when the old plants were designed and constructed; others simply didn't exist at the time.[3]

Many countries, of course, have no nuclear program; and some, bowing to public pressure after the Chornobyl scare, have terminated existing programs. The United States, where these decisions are often made at the local level, has witnessed the following circumstances: the Seabrook plant on Long Island (New York) was built but never operated after citizens sued over the lack of emergency escape routes; and another in California was closed by public referendum after the utility had spent several years and much money turning a deficient facility into one of the best in America. In Wisconsin, one of the country's lowest-cost producers of electricity, the Point Beach nuclear station is under tremendous financial pressure due to an impending corporate merger, the reluctance of the state Public Utility Commission to grant a rate increase in the face of anti-nuclear sentiment, and certain administrative decisions taken by the Nuclear Regulatory Commission that may directly effect operating efficiency of the station.

Thus the economic decision to build and operate a nuclear facility depends to a great extent upon the political climate in the jurisdiction that will be affected. The political climate, in turn, depends upon public perception. For the U.S. industry to have any chance at survival, there must be no more serious accidents anywhere in the world. But that alone may not be sufficient to ensure economic viability. Assiduous regulatory enforcement and the delays occasioned by citizen law suits are directly translated into increasing costs and decreasing profitability, even when the utility triumphs in court. The practical effect in the United States has been to eliminate all domestic projects for more than a decade, although American corporations are participating in projects overseas. While there are some signs that the U.S. domestic situation is changing, and research into advanced reactor designs has continued unabated with significant government funding, the fact of the matter is that no utilities have chosen to take the financial risks inherent in bringing a new plant on stream. That said, it is still true that generating electricity through the use of nuclear power at existing facilities remains cost effective throughout most of the world even when the cost of decommissioning is taken into account. If full weight is accorded the environmental costs of fossil fuel generation, the economic advantages of the nuclear sector become even more pronounced. Trapped between the Scylla and Charybdis of fossil fuel pollution, on the one hand, and a deep antipathy in the populace for further nuclear development, on the other, the United States has turned its attention to energy conservation. The results have been nothing short of spectacular, but the lessons cannot profitably be transferred to Central and Eastern Europe because only a rich nation with a strong economy can afford the developmental costs that make energy conservation a significant mechanism for fine tuning energy sector developmental needs.

Society, then, ultimately determines whether or not a specific technology will enjoy widespread application. In a market economy, the situation is fairly straightforward. Society defines the required level of perceived benefit, an acceptable level of risk, and the price it is willing to pay (none of these factors is immutable, of course). Industry, if it sees a sufficient market and can meet the requirements within the available pricing structure, applies the technology in its business activity. How the requirements are defined, however, is a political question.

It may strike some people as ironic, but the nuclear power production industry in Russia and Ukraine faces exactly the same pressures as are encountered in the West, although the severity is different for each factor, as are the root causes of the difficulty. Political pressure against continued development of nuclear power in the former Soviet Union literally exploded onto the scene shortly after Chornobyl blew up.[4] It remained a strong factor through the 1990 parliamentary elections, at which time it was almost impossible for even communists to win competitive election without a serious ecological plank in their political platform.[5] Also in 1990, moratorium on the development of nuclear facilities was instituted in Ukraine, and several new units under construction were halted. In many instances, the units were as much as 40% completed; some were even farther along.[6]

Starting in 1991, political and economic woes brought nascent environmental concerns to a standstill. In Lithuania, public appreciation for the existence of the Ignalina RBMK plant sky-rocketed in the frigid month of February 1991 after Soviet President Gorbachev cut off oil shipments as part of the crackdown on nationalist separatism that also resulted in an attack by troops of the OMON on the radio-TV center in the republic's capital. However, the best example of changing attitudes may be the Armenian situation, where the region's only nuclear power plant had been shut down several months after the terrible earthquake hit in December, 1988. Over the years, oil and gas pipelines leading into Armenia were destroyed as the civil war with Azerbaijan for control of Nagorno-Karabakh dragged on, and a blockade continued of the only rail line for delivering coal; Armenians had to make do with less and less electricity, and the supply of heat and lighting was eventually reduced to as little as two hours per day. Under the circumstances, opposition to nuclear power dissipated, and with significant foreign aid from Russia the power plant—which had deteriorated significantly during the shutdown—was brought back on line in 1995 much more quickly than most Western observers felt was advisable.

Nevertheless, in Ukraine and Belarus, the two Soviet republics most devastated by Chornobyl, significant public resistance to nuclear power remains. Indicative of this are repeated complaints by government officials that the population is suffering from "radiophobia"—by which they mean a psychological and psychosomatic malaise bordering on hypochondria in which anything that goes wrong with the health of the individual is immediately ascribed to the consequences of radiation exposure as a result of the accident. Which is not to say that these consequences have been mild;[7] only that not every illness that has occurred over the past decade resulted from the radiation effects.[8]

Even in these countries, however, economic chaos has led to a softening of opposition to nuclear power. Overall generation of electricity has plummeted in the Ukraine due to the collapse of the economy; nevertheless, the country faces an energy shortage, and cheap nuclear power is playing an ever increasing role in its energy balance. Because Ukraine cannot afford the world prices for oil and gas being charged by its No. 1 supplier (Russia), nuclear plants now produce nearly one half of all the electricity generated in the country.[9] As will be described below, energy politics, nationalist sentiments, and public safety issues have become inextricably intertwined.

As far as fear of the atom is concerned, few places outside of Japan can compete with Ukraine. To a large extent, this fear was created throughout the Soviet Union by the government's propaganda machine: for the duration of the Cold War, the word "nuclear" was inextricably associated with the words "weapons," "war," and "destruction." Analogously, in the United States, the generation of the Fifties grew up with bomb shelters, air raid drills in school, and the pervasive fear that "godless commies" were going to try to vaporize "God-fearing Americans" out of existence with "The Bomb." Even after the Chornobyl accident, the Gorbachev government insisted on associating the "heroic" efforts of the Party and the Soviet people to combat this disaster with powerful allusions to defeating the Nazis during World War II. The government defended its helplessness before the devastating radiation release from the explosion by insisting that the accident "proved" the necessity for avoiding nuclear war, the proportions of which would dwarf the consequences of a mere industrial accident.[10]

Economics is all about bottom line analysis. The bottom line in this story is that both Russia and Ukraine are exceedingly poor countries with economic, demographic, environmental, and medical statistics in the lowest decile of the world's nations.[11] They are Third World economies struggling not to tumble into Fourth World status. Can they afford nuclear power, which is an extremely expensive technology to operate and maintain? Absolutely not. Can they afford to do without nuclear power? Again, absolutely not. Given the state of the environmental depredation in the two countries, even greater reliance on fossil fuels (assuming they could afford to purchase them) would doom the land to long term tragedies worse even than the current situation, which is bad enough.[12] And the energy conservation strategy being pushed so insistently in Eastern Europe by the American government is unlikely to succeed in Russia or Ukraine, since consumer consumption is so low compared to Western countries, and there does not exist the technological infrastructure needed to manufacture high-efficiency motors, refrigeration units, and other industrial equipment.[13]

The Mechanisms for Enhancing Safety

What are the available means for enhancing safety, as that term is broadly defined above: those activities or mechanisms which (1) increase the probability of an adequate response in the event that a design basis accident occurs or (2) expand the envelope of design basis accidents that can be compensated for by the available equipment? Generally, these means fall into four categories: hardware; procedures; the organization of management and support services; and safety culture. Each category will be discussed in turn.

None, of course, exists in a vacuum: for example, procedures, whether formal or informal, must of necessity take into account the available equipment.[14] And, often, inadequacies in one area can be compensated for by modifying one's approach to other activities. For example, the Soviet nuclear industry has always had to function in the face of a lack of written instructions for its operators (the reasons for this are complex, but include the following: unavailability of paper, duplicating machines, and computers resulting from a systemic compulsion for information control and secrecy; the fact that all things nuclear, including civilian power generation, were highly classified activities; and the low priority placed on any industrial activities other than actual production, resulting in a lack of resources for training). Thus it became expedient to insist that all plant operators, including equipment operators, hold college degrees in engineering. By contrast, American power plants, which devote a remarkably high percentage of their resources to training, routinely hire people right out of high school, technical school, or the military.

Equipment

The Soviet Union had a history of building simple, durable equipment: machine guns, tanks, airplanes, even space craft were all of the "Volkswagen" variety—easy to build, easy to run, easy to repair. They had to be, because little expense was devoted to stockpiling tools and spare parts or, again, to training people in equipment operation. Soviet diesel engines are the envy of American specialists because they can generate more power at lower rpms than can Western diesels—as long as you can get them to run at all, which is a significant problem at nuclear plants. On the other hand, Soviet industry was—and remains—deficient in designing precision equipment, electronics, and other "high-tech" components. What they lacked mostly was a technological infrastructure. Throughout all branches of learning and all sectors of the Soviet economy, lots of money was spent on "science," but almost none on "technology." As a result, theoretical capabilities have always far outstripped practical applications.[15] When senior engineers first began to visit the United States on technical exchanges, they would just shake their head ruefully as they pondered the simplicity, ingenuity, and *widespread availability* of products such as Post-it Notes, Pampers, and moist towelettes! Even today, budding Russian entrepreneurs complain about how difficult it is to turn a bright idea into a manufactured product. The most obvious result of this situation, ultimately, is the low standard of living available to the population. Everything sort of works, like plumbing and elevators, but just barely and not always.[16] Everything is as primitive and simple as it can be, yet still function. Nothing is pretty, or easy, or convenient.[17]

American specialists generally agree that the design of basic equipment for Soviet pressurized water reactors (known as VVERs, in contradistinction to the Chornobyl-type graphite moderated channel reactor known as the RBMK) is pretty good. This includes the reactor unit itself—in essence a sophisticated way to boil water—as well as the piping, pumps, steam generators, turbines, and various other pieces of equipment. Some facets of the Soviet design are admirable: they have much more water storage capacity, which gives them more time to react to certain kinds of emergencies; the steel used has a lower cobalt content than does American steel, so the overall level of radiation on-site is lower; they seem to have sump screens that work especially effectively and that may play a role in the low ambient radiation levels; and, as noted, they make good diesels. Soviet plants have some equipment that American plants lack, and they lack some things commonly found in American plants, such as power-operated relief valves on pressurizers. Other items have a completely different design (compare vertical U.S. steam generators with horizontal Russian ones), but it is not clear which type is better, since each poses significant problems for operations and maintenance personnel. On the whole, both U.S. and Soviet reactors are good at heating water, creating steam, and producing electricity.

What the Soviet designed units do not have are sophisticated electronic instrumentation and controls, measuring equipment, or fire[18] and emergency protection systems equal to those in the West. As a matter of fact, one of the best power plants in the world, the Finnish plant at Lovisa, combines a Soviet reactor with Western controls. The Czechs are now building an amalgam unit at Temelin, which will feature a Skoda-built Soviet reactor combined with Westinghouse I&C equipment.

One sees a number of conscious trade-offs in the way Soviet units were designed. For example, the spent fuel pool in VVER units is located inside containment: this limits its maximum size, which causes complications in other areas, but provides a certain amount of additional protection. Russian engineers will declare, privately, that they have no faith in the integrity of the domestically manufactured steel pool liner, and, were a leak to occur, at least all of the radioactive cooling water would be localized. Similarly, Soviet plants have three completely independent sets of emergency protection equipment, called "safety trains," compared to two in U.S. plants. The presence of the extra safety train offsets the lower reliability of the equipment, particularly of the safety system pumps and the power supply from the emergency diesel generators.

Chornobyl-style reactors, of course, have no containment structure whatsoever. Rather, they are enclosed in what amounts to a glorified utility building. Like the U.S. reactors at Hanford, Washington, Soviet RBMKs were designed with one purpose in mind—to produce weapons grade plutonium (generating electricity was just secondary, an added bonus). A premium was placed on keeping the plant in operation, and refueling takes place while the reactor is running;[19] PWR/VVER units, whose primary function is electricity generation, have to be shut down for a month or more in order for refueling to take place. There are other design features in the RBMK that make it extremely unstable in certain operating environments. With no containment to serve as the last barrier against disaster, circumstances were perfect for turning a bad accident into a national tragedy. A large number of modifications have been introduced to the original RBMK design since the Chornobyl accident, although not all functioning units in either Russia or Ukraine have instituted all the changes yet. However, even the upgraded units are inherently unstable (technically, they have a "positive reactivity coefficient" in all operating modes), although less so than before.

Despite design changes and the progress that has been made recently, improving equipment reliability to any significant degree is an unresolvable problem for Russia and Ukraine, if to do this they have to rely on their own resources. The lack of market competition, inadequate technological infrastructure, government run manufacturing facilities, and a cumbersome approval process for new equipment makes it nearly impossible that improved controls, measuring devices, or fire suppression systems will appear on the domestic market in this century. Nor is either country likely to develop a computer manufacturing industry anytime soon. Such items are available from foreign suppliers, but the power plants themselves are strapped for funds, and neither economy (particularly in Ukraine) is strong enough to allow large-scale purchases of imported equipment.

Fortunately, a great deal of technical assistance has been provided, and continues to be made available, by G-7 countries. Most of the equipment—valued in the tens of millions of dollars—has been donated in the form of humanitarian aid: as such, it should be exempt from import taxes, duties, and fees. However, the customs and tax administrations in both Russia and Ukraine are run as independent fiefdoms within the government, and even the existence of international accords such as the Gore-Chernomyrdin Agreement has not been sufficient to resolve the financial and bureaucratic "turf" issues. As a result, much of the foreign aid has languished for months in customs warehouses, and only by paying the duty on equipment or invoking political pressure at the ministerial level and above has it been possible to get some shipments delivered to their destinations. Slowly but surely, such administrative problems do get resolved, and the process should work better in the future. But foreign governments have found themselves in the unlikely position of offering both equipment and hard currency—to pay for contract work as a means of providing funds with which additional equipment might be purchased—only to find out that it is extremely difficult to give either away.

Procedures

Prior to the Chornobyl accident, and for approximately three years thereafter, Soviet power plants had no written operating procedures and very few written training materials. Of course, training materials were superfluous, because they also had no formalized training.[20] To this day they have no written maintenance or repair procedures. However, since 1989 a collaborative U.S.-Soviet effort (and successor projects with the Russian Federation, Ukraine, and several Central European countries formerly in the Soviet sphere of influence) has disseminated information regarding American emergency operating procedures. This approach relies on a response to symptoms, regardless of the cause, rather than attempting to diagnose what has happened during a tense emergency situation on the basis of incomplete information.[21] A vigorous exchange program consisting of quarterly discussions in Eastern or Central Europe and semi-annual training sessions in the U.S. has led to the development of draft procedures for selected power units. After six years of development and a painfully slow regulatory approval process, on May 1, 1996, a full set of these procedures was finally implemented at one VVER unit in Novovoronezh, Russia. In order to implement the new procedures, operating crews had to be trained to work with them, which entailed creation of a training program, as well.

The Eastern European operators who have participated in the program have gone through a remarkable psychological transformation. After an initial period during which American industry experts gave lectures on various aspects of operations and training, the operators set about writing their own procedures, with the Americans reviewing the drafts and providing commentary. For the Russians and Ukrainians, this was a new and far from pleasant experience: culturally they were not prepared to have foreigners criticize their efforts in an open forum. Soviet society had not developed the notion of constructive criticism, and the first few meetings included a lot of awkward silent moments.[22] Gradually, however, as the procedure writers became accustomed to the methodology, as trusting relationships developed among the participants, and as the drafts became better over time, the give-and-take produced exactly the results that the Americans had hoped for: honest discussions laced with praise, criticism, and humor. More importantly, gradually and nearly imperceptibly there have occurred significant transformations in the way power plants are operated in that part of the world. In a recent discussion of a hypothetical accident scenario, one of the Americans asked whether or not the Ukrainians would shut down a damaged reactor coolant pump and continue operating the unit using the undamaged pumps. The surprising answer he received was, "We're not allowed to do that anymore."[23]

Management and Support Services

Soviet managers generally were not advocates of the Dale Carnegie approach, nor did they subscribe to the tenets of Total Quality Management. Take into account the top secret, quasi-military status of civilian nuclear power, and it is easy to understand why a less than enlightened management style prevailed. To a very great extent, it still does. By and large, major enterprises are still run by the same people who ran them in the days before democratization and the temporary banishment of the communist party. And a remote Soviet village dominated by one industry or one manufacturing facility resembles nothing so much as an American coal-mining company town. The plant manager was mayor, king, and deity. Literally he could make you or break you. Plus there was the KGB or Savak or whoever. Not a pretty picture.

Managers were under tremendous pressure to meet production targets ("fulfilling the plan")—little else mattered. Failure to do so meant that everyone in the enterprise lost bonuses, which amounted to as much as 75% of one's base pay. One could be removed for cause, or for no reason at all. Under the circumstances, it is not surprising that the management paradigm was authoritarian and top-down. When nothing matters except production, it is not surprising that few funds are expended on irrelevant luxuries such as training or environmental protection. Nor is safety a high priority when a run-the-plant-at-all-costs mentality prevails.

Running a power plant meant keeping the plant running whenever possible. Particularly in the winter, when energy consumption throughout Europe increases sharply (it is easy to forget how far north Europe is situated). The ramifications can be seen everywhere in the system. One of the reasons the undamaged Chornobyl units were brought back on-line so quickly (Units One and Two returned to service prior to the end of 1986 and *before construction of the Unit Four sarcophagus was completed*; Unit Three returned to service in 1987) can be seen in the need to cover an expected energy shortage—fossil fuel plants that should have been shut down during the summer months had been forced to keep running, since the accident had put 4,000 megawatts of generating capacity out of commission. Soviet engineers knew that without their annual inspection and preventive maintenance, those fossil plants were unlikely to remain functional throughout the winter.[24]

As the Ukrainian economic crisis intensified during 1992-1994, the disparity in effective salary between Russia and Ukraine grew exponentially. The Ukrainian currency, which had been at parity with the Russian ruble when the Soviet Union was officially dissolved, dropped in value sharply, with the exchange rate quickly reaching the 20-to-1 range.[25] The break-up of the union also meant there were no longer any government constraints on residence or employment, and many of the most qualified plant personnel, largely Russian by birth and nationality, returned home to better paying jobs. Still, one cannot run a power plant without operators, and the Ukrainians found themselves hard pressed to put qualified people in the control rooms around the clock. A variety of incentives, including pay raises and tax concessions from the federal government, were instituted to stem the tide, but only the continued decline of the Russian economy coupled with a dearth of further vacancies at Russian power plants slowed down the loss of experienced personnel. The problem was especially critical at Zaporizhzhya nuclear station, since plans were underway to start up Unit Six toward the end of 1995—in typical "old Soviet Union" fashion, the reactor went critical (achieved a self-sustaining chain reaction) just prior to the new year. The extra people required to staff this unit, in the face of a dwindling supply of experienced operators, has necessitated a decrease in the overall experience of control room personnel, and even less time is available to provide continuing training.[26]

A nuclear power plant, like any other complex organization, has many constituent elements not directly engaged in power production, but necessary nonetheless for work to continue. Among the most important ·support activities are maintenance, training, procurement, and planning. Each area is beset by a number of difficulties, the most critical of which are not susceptible to easy solution: these are lack of money to support their activities, and specifically a lack of modern equipment, including office automation, to increase the efficiency and work capacity of the unit. It is difficult to say which division is worst off. In a country where apartment dwellers routinely steal light bulbs out of hallways and car owners lock their windshield wipers in the glove compartment whenever they leave their cars, it should not be surprising that repair shops lack the necessary equipment, supplies, or spare parts. Still, it *is* surprising to see a fully operational blacksmith shop in a modern power plant, or to watch electricians rewinding cores for electric motors because replacements are not available.

The planning department at an American nuclear facility has a staff numbering in the dozens. It coordinates all activities that require participation from more than one department or unit in the plant administration. For example, if routine servicing of a pump motor is to be performed, Operations, Maintenance, Supply, and perhaps Quality Assurance people are called into play: Operations isolates the pump and certifies that other equipment is in the proper configuration—e.g., that valves are closed to keep water or steam from reaching the spot where the servicing is to occur—so that work may proceed safely; Supply needs to get the proper materials ready for use and possible delivery to the work location; and the Maintenance people will actually do the work. QA may have to inspect everything and run post-maintenance tests; then operators need to reconfigure the lines for normal plant conditions. Meticulous records are kept on everything; regulators and lawyers are everywhere. All of this is planned in advance, work is scheduled and logged, unit supervisors are informed so that they can schedule crews or plan their own activities. The maintenance supervisor must be certain that personnel sent to do the job have passed qualifying training on the activity. Everyone involved has a written procedure to follow, all of which are developed, maintained, and distributed electronically. Without massive logistical support (LANs, high-volume duplicating machines, computerized inventory records, etc.), even the simplest task can become chaotic. When a unit outage is planned, and the activities of hundreds of people over a span of 35-80 days need to be coordinated, the planning process begins months in advance. When major modifications are planned, engineering personnel need to perform a wide range of time-consuming activities.

Without putting too fine a point on things, suffice it to say that this process is not duplicated at a Russian or Ukrainian plant. A specific example should highlight the differences. Both American and Soviet reactor units have chronic difficulties with steam generators. Replacing them is a major headache requiring that the affected unit be shut down (in the United States, this entails the loss of perhaps $500,000 per day in revenue from the electricity not being generated), and having direct costs in the tens of millions of dollars. At an American station, the planning for this activity can take upward of three years. Coordination is essential, since the unit cannot operate while the modification is taking place, and every extra day the unit must be shut down costs so much money. Ideally, the actual process of replacing a unit's old steam generators should take less than two months.

By contrast, a leading Ukrainian specialist described the process at his plant, presumably with a great deal of hyperbole, as follows: the chief engineer calls a meeting on Tuesday and explains that next week we have to begin replacing the steam generators on a unit. Zaporizhzhya has replaced steam generators on at least three of the five units that have been in operation for a while. Never has the process taken less than a year to complete. This is not particularly a safety issue, but it helps explain a number of factors—economic, organizational, and cultural—that do have a direct bearing on the safe operation of a nuclear power plant.

One specific factor needs to be mentioned here. When major equipment is replaced at a Western plant, the utility generally has a choice of suppliers, and it attempts to purchase the best replacement part at the best competitive price. In Eastern Europe, there is at most one supplier for a given piece of equipment (let us recall that blacksmith shop!), the item may or may not be in stock, the price will be whatever the manufacturer chooses to charge—Russia and Ukraine were, and to a great extent remain, state run industrial monopolies—and in all likelihood, even if it is possible to obtain the part, it is of exactly the same design as the one that went bad, so if the problem is generic to the item as designed you can be certain that you will have to replace this one, too.

Safety Culture

The notion of a safety culture is difficult to define, but the results of its absence in a nuclear plant (or anywhere else, for that matter) are immediately obvious. Safety culture is an existential philosophy—establishing safe operation as the highest value to which all others are subordinated, including the generation of electricity and profits. If one tries to function so as to eliminate accidents, no matter how unlikely they are, then some accidents will not happen.[27] The operative question is, "What if...?," and the difficulty is that one can never prove which accidents did not happen, only that the general frequency is up or down.

Safety culture is a habit—doing things in the same way every time so that, if something is done when your brain is in neutral, it is likely that it was done correctly. Good examples from everyday life include always putting on your seat belt as soon as you get into a car, always turning off the iron before walking away from the ironing board, always locking the front door behind you when you enter your home.[28]

Safety culture is an attitude of respect—caring about yourself, your co-workers, the environment, even the equipment you work with, and doing everything possible to safeguard them all. Marine drill sergeants instill the attitude that your rifle is your best friend and should be treated as such. Any supervisor can tell a lot about the people he/she works with just by observing how they handle their tools and their personal belongings.

Ultimately, safety culture is also good business, since a safe, well operated enterprise is more likely to be a profitable one. Just ask any civil lawyer. At the extreme end of the spectrum, the nuclear industry in the West fully realizes the public temperament is such that the next serious accident at a commercial facility will be the last—the political pressure to shut down the whole industry will be insurmountable. That fact, indeed, explains to a great extent the amount of attention, money, and effort being devoted by Western governments and by private industry to improving nuclear safety in Eastern and Central Europe.

Safety is manifested in the way a facility is operated, but it stems from management. Management must devote the resources necessary to make safety a reality, either on its own merits (safe is better than dangerous) or for purely business reasons (safe is more profitable than dangerous). Unfortunately, safety is not necessarily more profitable. The best analogy may be environmental protection. Pollution safeguards are extremely expensive, and in many circumstances it is considerably cheaper for a manufacturer to pollute than not to. This is where government must step in. A strong set of laws, diligently enforced by a regulatory agency, and a system of punitive measures, imposed by the courts, to extract a sufficiently large penalty from polluters—large enough to make them pay attention and change their ways—has proven to be the only mechanism capable of enforcing socially acceptable behavior on enterprises without a social conscience.

In theory, it is society at large that dictates what behaviors are acceptable, how the public interest is defined, and to what extent governmental action is the proper mechanism (as opposed, for instance, to market forces) for adjusting private behavior. These are the classic issues of representative democracy, but they are equally valid regardless of the form of government. One may go so far as to claim that they are the defining issues of any society. In the current American political situation, it is probably true that most citizens believe these issues are inadequately addressed: about as many believe there is too much government interference in the lives of individuals or the activities of business as believe exactly the opposite. All of these people, on both sides of these issues, should visit Russia!

Levity aside, this discussion naturally leads to consideration of governmental politics on national and international levels, the regulatory environment in any jurisdiction, and the ways in which policy impinges on plant management, plant operation, and the availability of technology. In our opinion, national policy, industrial regulation, and plant management are inextricably entwined. It is only after a thorough analysis of the global factors involved that one can reach sound conclusions regarding the safety of nuclear power in Russia and Ukraine, prospects for improving safety, and the changes that must be instituted in society and at the plants themselves for meaningful improvement to occur.

Government, Politics, and the Economy; Regulation and Performance; Society and Safety

The areas of national policy that most affect the conduct of business in the nuclear industry today are economics and international relations. After the breakup of the Soviet Union, international relations expanded to include complex interactions among the successor states, particularly Russia, Ukraine, and Kazakhstan. Keep in mind, however, that perhaps the greatest change came several years earlier, when the veil of secrecy over all things nuclear was lowered. Indeed, were it not for the removal of security restrictions and the general relaxation of control over the flow of information within Soviet society in the late 1980s, prospects for increasing civilian nuclear power safety would be nil.[29]

In the realm of economics, the most significant policy decisions relate to the problem of government subsidies. Even before the breakup of the USSR and the implementation of economic reforms (the largely abortive shift to a "market economy"), authorities instituted a policy of "self-financing"—in effect, a requirement that all enterprises and most governmental agencies except the military and security establishments generate sufficient revenues to cover their own expenses. The practical effect on agencies has been to slash their appropriations from the federal budget, resulting in a scramble to exact fees from industrial sources for the services that had previously been provided at no identifiable cost.[30] Industrial enterprises have been compelled to function on the revenues generated by the products they manufacture and sell, despite the fact that most remain government owned and operated.

In olden days (i.e., pre-perestroika) the Soviet economic system operated within a framework of strict price controls on all domestically produced goods and services, particularly on raw materials and labor, and an elaborate system of internal fund transfers that allowed the government to maintain the fiction of economic viability. It was a deficit ridden system which diverted nearly two-fifths of the country's GNP to support its military establishment and which was propped up by the international sale of natural resources for hard currency. In fact, the whole arrangement resembled nothing so much as a fragile house of cards based on interlocking subsidies. When the subsidies were curtailed, the structure collapsed.

Had the new system been instituted consistently (read: in a draconian manner) the effect would have been devastating, but perhaps relatively short-lived—if one judges by events in Poland.[31] The problem is that for political reasons the government could not really live with its own decision, since to do so would potentially engender greater unrest in an already shaky political situation. Further, the inability of Gorbachev and, after him, Yeltsin to control Central Bank policy crippled all attempts at economic reform. Rather than force the closing or restructuring of major industrial enterprises (with the attendant immediate increase in unemployment and decline in domestic production, but offering the hope of a steady medium-term rebound in capacity utilization and infrastructure development) the Central Bank continued to increase the money supply at will and to provide hopelessly inefficient major enterprises with massive unsecured loans intended to cover their current operating expenses. This simply exacerbated all stresses within the system without remedying any of the underlying causes. Too much money (in the form of wages for unproductive labor) chased too few goods, and consumer competition for relatively scarce supplies of imports allowed domestic producers to raise prices with no regard for quality improvement, but with artificially created impunity from the economic consequences of their actions.

What has resulted is a nearly insurmountable problem of non-payment outside the realm of the cash economy on the street. Enterprises everywhere—particularly large, government-operated manufacturers and raw materials producers—owe staggering amounts to their suppliers and employees.[32] Thus a new system of inadvertent subsidies has been created, but the effects are not spread evenly throughout the economy, and the deficit is no longer being covered by raw material exports.[33]

As far as the energy industry is concerned, the situation has become fairly desperate. In Ukraine, which does not fabricate nuclear fuel and which also lacks easily accessible oil and gas reserves of its own, all of these products must be purchased from Russia at prices close to world levels. Passing along these costs to the consumer would bankrupt the economy immediately. Rather, the price the Ukrainian government (acting as the national cartel that purchases and distributes electricity) pays to itself (as the producer of that electricity) does not cover the cost of production.[34] Even in Russia, where the established price theoretically does cover production costs, the industry is mired in the non-payment morass. Moreover, both governments have mandated that supplies of heat and electricity not be curtailed in the winter, despite the fact that neither individuals nor enterprises can pay their bills.[35] Of course, to do otherwise in such a northern climate would doom millions to death: a policy no government that purports to care about its citizens could adopt. In effect, the energy industry generally and the nuclear sector most specifically,[36] has shouldered the brunt of the problem.

These economic woes reverberate throughout the nuclear industry: plant personnel work without pay, as do non-plant workers who live in the company towns, so individuals with marketable skills such as programming tend to leave the industry; moreover, management does not have the resources required to pay for necessary goods and services, much less to finance safety enhancements that must be purchased abroad and paid for in hard currency.

Policy decisions obviously play an important role. Frequently, however, there is little coordination between national policy and its implementation on the ministry level, so it may seem as though there is no policy whatsoever. For example, the current policy of the Russian government with regard to civilian nuclear power is that everything should be done to further the sector's development in the future. New plants are to be built, and construction that was stopped during the 1989-1993 moratorium is to be resumed. On the other hand, existing power plants are often forced to shut down operating units in good condition because of insufficient industrial demand for the generating capacity. Not only does this practice put additional economic pressure on the nuclear plants, it also increases the number of unanticipated plant evolutions, which increases the possibility that problems may arise.[37]

Even where national policy is well defined, the policy itself may contribute to the persistence of safety problems. For example, the Soviet government did not feel comfortable having to ask for or rely on foreign assistance after the Chornobyl accident, despite its obvious and, to some limited extent, admitted inability to cope with the clean-up or with construction of the protective sarcophagus. In addition to any security issues that may have been involved, Soviet national pride interfered with initial attempts by foreign governments to provide aid. It was only through the intercession of Armand Hammer, the late private industrialist who had long-standing ties to the Soviet Union, that the government accepted the offer of any technical and medical assistance whatsoever.[38] Even so, the official position of the government was that the Chornobyl clean-up effort represented a triumph of Soviet science and technology over the forces of nature and, moreover, that it demonstrated the organizational strength of the Communist Party in focusing the heroism and generosity of the people to resolve such a terrible problem. For all intents and purposes, it was claimed, the Soviet Union was left to struggle with Chornobyl on its own.[39] In addition, the help that *was* accepted was later ridiculed: since 1989 a number of commentators in the USSR and its successor states have reacted negatively to the unsuccessful efforts of Dr. Robert Gale to help the most critically ill patients.[40]

On the other hand, only a pronounced change in governmental policy, fostered by continued improvement of relations with the West, made it possible for the USSR to propose in 1988 that an international organization be created to assist in the distribution of information regarding operational experience and unforeseen events among civilian nuclear facilities worldwide.[41] Only a genuine thaw of cold war hostility made it possible for the superpowers to embark upon the first bi-lateral efforts to increase safety at Soviet designed nuclear facilities in 1989.[42] Those efforts, which focused initially on regulatory issues and the development of emergency operating procedures, continue even today.

Naturally, a certain amount of suspicion, resentment, and wounded pride accompanied the acceptance of Western aid. Soviet bureaucrats and technical experts were put off by a variety of foreign attitudes and policies. These included: the belief that local staff were not capable of deciding what needed to be done; the insistence that most of the available funds be directed at foreign companies (working as contractors in conjunction with ministries or national laboratories) rather than at Soviet or successor state institutes; and—in the case of U.S. Nunn-Lugar appropriations for disarmament, dismantlement, and nuclear materials accountancy—the legislative requirement that the Soviet and successor state governments make "good faith contributions" far exceeding their ability to pay or their institutional capacity to pry appropriations out of legislatures that were inimical to international cooperation and, during some periods, simply not functioning in any normal manner. Representatives of the United States Department of State and Department of Defense, ignoring the realities of politics and the lessons one might have learned from American appropriations disputes, took the position that Russian and other governmental officials need merely "snap their fingers" and the required appropriations would miraculously appear.

Equal, if not greater, significance must be ascribed to attitudes and policies that dominated relations among the Soviet successor states themselves. We shall focus here on two specific issues, spent fuel storage and the fate of the Chornobyl plant.

The Communist dominated Russian Duma elected in 1990, and ethnic Russians generally regardless of where they lived in the Soviet Union, were furious at political maneuvering by Ukraine and the Baltic republics that would ultimately result in the dissolution of the country. In January 1991, when Gorbachev was persuaded by hard liners to cut off oil supplies to Lithuania—and to allow violent intervention by special units of the police (OMON) and military (Spetsnaz) in order to disrupt government broadcasting there—local residents were spared from freezing only because the Chornobyl-type RBMK power plant at Ignalina continued to function. Deep seated anti-nuclear sentiment that had existed at least since the tragic accident nearly five years earlier evaporated instantaneously: it was replaced by an even more intense reaction against Russia and Russians.[43] Shortly after the political reorganization of the Soviet Union, Moscow, for its part, passed highly restrictive and essentially vindictive legislation. Among the steps taken was a ban on the transportation of spent nuclear fuel across the new borders of the Russia Federation from countries of the "near abroad," as the former Soviet republics were called.

This action was directed specifically against Lithuania and Ukraine, although it also affected Kazakhstan to some extent. It hit particularly hard at Ukraine, which has five operating nuclear power plants. Aside from Chornobyl, most of the remaining units incorporate the 1000 MW VVER reactor design: this system has particularly limited capacity for storing spent fuel, since the fuel pool is situated inside containment.[44] The practical effect of this design decision is that spent fuel can be stored at the plant for only a relatively short period, as opposed to American units, which can retain on-site all of the fuel that will be expended during the full 40-year service life of the station. With no domestic capability for storing or reprocessing nuclear fuel off-site,[45] and with regulations limiting the amount of on-site storage more severely than even the design constraints would dictate, Ukraine found itself in an untenable position: there was no way the country could become energy independent in the foreseeable future.

Politically, of course, it was unacceptable to let Russia have such a stranglehold on the well-being of the nation. Accordingly, in early 1993, officials at the largest Ukrainian station[46]—Zaporizhzhya NPP—on their own initiative entered into negotiations with French and American consortia for the design and construction of a storage facility to be located adjacent to the plant. Ultimately, a contract was signed with the Americans, and operation was supposed to begin at the end of 1995. However, Ukraine's financial woes have plagued this expensive project from its inception, so that it has moved along in fits and starts, although a substantial contribution from the United States government—provided as humanitarian aid—allowed work to proceed more smoothly. In addition, licensing delays have been numerous at every stage in the development process. In late summer 1996 approval was obtained for site preparation and pad construction, but as of New Year's Day 1997, the nuclear regulatory agency of Ukraine had yet to authorize fabrication of the storage casks or loading of any spent fuel. This despite the fact that Zaporizhzhya, with its sixth unit started up, has been producing more than half of the nation's electricity, and despite the fact that several of the units there are in violation of the requirement that enough free space be left in each spent fuel pool to allow for a complete unloading of the reactor core in the case of an emergency. As will be discussed below, the interplay here of Ukrainian economic policy, safety regulation, and national energy requirements is extremely complex.

The continued operation of Chornobyl—and particularly Western diplomatic efforts to force closure of the facility—remains a delicate issue. Negotiations have been conducted virtually since the first days of Ukrainian independence. In the spring of 1994, a combined State Department/Department of Energy delegation from the United States visited Kyiv to determine how much it would actually cost to shut down the station and to support long term maintenance and surveillance activities. As was widely reported subsequently in the press, Ukrainian officials set up three significant roadblocks. Two of the impediments were financial, the third touched more on national pride than on any other consideration.

First of all, Ukraine insisted that closing Chornobyl would not be possible unless construction was completed on new units at Rivne, Khmelnytsky, and Zaporizhzhya—work that had been stalled by the moratorium declared back in Soviet days—because the country could not do without the 3,000 MW of installed capacity at Chornobyl there that was still being utilized. Immediately the cost went from under one billion USD to almost three billion. Secondly, Ukraine insisted that the West finance relocation of the 28,000 people whose lives would be disrupted if the station were shut down. Since Ukraine had no independent capability of providing jobs, housing, schools, or hospitals for these people, it included these costs in estimates of the total assistance package that would be required. Although difficult to assess in advance, these expenses surely pushed the total bill beyond the four billion dollar level.

Nonetheless, representatives of the G-7 countries have seemed willing to pay this price. On at least three occasions since early 1994 announcements have been made to the effect that an agreement had been reached between the president of Ukraine (there have been two in this time period) and foreign diplomats concerning the plant closing. Despite much ballyhooing in the West, however, none of these agreements has ever been ratified by the Ukrainian parliament, and it is not at all clear that Ukrainian government officials have ever bargained in good faith on this issue.

Perhaps the greatest stumbling block to closing Chornobyl has nothing at all to do with finances. Rather, paramount here is national pride, both internally and with direct respect to Russia. Nationalist elements in the Ukrainian parliament, as well as many high ranking government officials individually, resent the tremendous pressure being applied to Ukraine in this regard. They believe that the West is unfairly treating the nation like a child who has misbehaved and who is being singled out for punishment as a means of delivering a lesson to its siblings. Of even greater saliency is the belief that Ukraine is being treated in a discriminatory manner because, of all the Soviet-designed RBMK units built in Eastern Europe,[47] it was their misfortune that the one which blew up is located on Ukrainian soil. Anytime this issue is broached, whether formally at negotiating sessions or informally in private conversations, Ukrainians put forth the following argument: either RBMKs are dangerous or they are not; if they *are* dangerous, then all of them are dangerous, not just the ones at Chornobyl; if the remaining operational units at Chornobyl[48] should be closed because the West judges them to be dangerous, then all such units, and particularly the ones located in the Russian Federation, should also be closed; if the West is not willing to put equal pressure on Russia to close down its many RBMK units, then why should Ukraine submit to such pressure?[49]

Ukrainian political considerations relate not only to diplomatic affairs. They also have important ramifications for domestic economic policy generally and for the energy sector specifically. Currently being played out is a titanic turf struggle between Goskomatom, the ministerial level agency that oversees operations at the nation's civilian nuclear power stations, and the directors of the specific stations. Plant managers want control of their own operations. In particular, they want the freedom to threaten major electricity consumers in their service area with termination of service if bills are not paid. Currently, of course, both Russian and Ukrainian plants have to make do with no payment whatsoever for the electricity they produce, late and/or partial payment, and even payment in kind. For example, most of the staff at Balakovo nuclear station in eastern Russia drive shiny new cars because a near-by assembly plant has been paying its electricity bill in vehicles for the last couple of years. Last year at Zaporizhzhya, the plant manager had to find an American company that was willing to take delivery of a large amount of refined aluminum (which the station had received in lieu of cash payment) and arrange for the delivery of needed equipment and supplies from the U.S., just to realize some tangible benefit from the station's electricity production.

National policy, of course, is that no electricity consumer, and particularly no major industrial enterprise, face the threat that power might be cut off. This controversy lies at the heart of a different sort of power struggle currently at issue in Ukrainian courts. Late in 1995 Goskomatom tried to remove the director at Zaporizhzhya, Vladimir Bronnikov, who had the foresight to go on sick leave (making it illegal under Ukrainian law to remove him from his post). In turn, Bronnikov has sued to overturn the pending order that would effectively fire him. In a related maneuver, Goskomatom forced a rewrite of the Zaporizhzhya spent fuel storage facility contract, so that the actual customer was the governmental body, and not the power plant itself.[50]

This is not to say, however, that the power plants and Goskomatom cannot work together when it suits their common purpose. This is exactly what happened when Zaporizhzhya attempted to get regulatory approval for the start-up of Unit Six. Actually, this story goes back to 1989, when Zaporizhzhya sought to obtain regulatory approval from Moscow to start up Unit Five. Things had already changed considerably at Gosatomnadzor, the Soviet nuclear regulatory commission, since the dark days of Chornobyl. Armed with new powers and a national mandate, GAN had started to flex its regulatory muscle despite sorely inadequate staffing and funding. The deputy minister for nuclear operations, Nikolay Shteinberg, sent a commission headed by Aleksandr Gutsalov that was empowered to determine whether or not to grant permission for the new unit to begin commercial operation. Gutsalov determined that there were over 75 deficiencies, some major and some minor, that needed to be eliminated prior to start-up. Political pressure on Shteinberg to cave in was tremendous, because the Soviet government wanted the unit operational, but he stood his ground until a compromise of sorts was reached. Shteinberg forced the plant manager, the same Vladimir Bronnikov, to agree in writing that he would assume personal responsibility for ensuring that all the deficiencies would be addressed. In effect, Bronnikov had to plead guilty, in advance, to all criminal charges arising from any possible accident that might occur in the future, thus absolving the national government of responsibility.[51]

When Ukraine gained independence, Shteinberg was named head of its regulatory body, which following the Soviet model had ministerial status. Shteinberg brought with him many scientists, technical experts, and senior officials, including Georgy Kopchinsky, who became deputy minister [Gutsalov remained in Moscow and ultimately assumed Shteinberg's old post]. Shteinberg, an advocate of U.S.-style regulatory activity, was disturbed by the fact that Zaporizhzhya Unit Six was being completed without regard for new, stricter design standards that had come into force a few years after the start of construction. He gave the station until 31 December 1994 to bring the unit on line or be faced with meeting the revised standards. When the plant failed to meet that deadline, an unresolvable conflict was created.

The Ukrainian government in 1995 proved to be just as anxious to start up the new power unit as the Soviet government had been six years earlier. The country was facing a serious energy shortfall, despite the economic downturn of recent years, and Kharkiv, the nation's second largest city, experienced power outages and planned cutoffs of heat and electricity during the 1994-1995 winter period. It is difficult to impute causality without insider knowledge of the situation, but shortly after the new year had begun a decision was made to downgrade the regulatory agency from an independent ministry to a division of the environmental protection ministry, which had the effect of undercutting Shteinberg's ability to apply pressure to Goskomatom, the Ministry of Health, or other entities that now outranked his regulatory body in the administrative organization of the country's executive branch. Subsequently, Goskom-atom, acting this time on behalf of and with the full support of the power plant, convinced advisors of President Kuchma that the regulatory body had to change its policy with regard to Unit Six. This led to a confrontation, and Shteinberg was forced to choose between resigning or accepting a set of conditions that countermanded his previous authority. Shteinberg, internationally famous as the chief engineer who had restarted the undamaged Chornobyl units back in the fall of 1986, elected to step down from his government post and enter the private sector. Once again, Kopchinsky and others loyal to Shteinberg also resigned, leaving the regulatory agency even less able to exercise its authority and fulfill its responsibilities. In a recent conversation, Shteinberg was asked if Zaporizhzhya Six would have been allowed to go critical in August 1995 had he remained at the helm of the regulatory agency. "That's a hard question," he answered, "Probably, but under different conditions."[52]

It is clear, despite vigorous enforcement activity within the regulatory agency itself, that the key issues guiding Ukrainian national policy in the nuclear arena have little to do with operational safety or environmental protection. The situation in Russia is more measured on all sides:

enforcement is pursued steadily, but less vigorously than in Ukraine. Moderation reigns in the attitudes of all concerned parties.

For instance, given the practical need to keep Chornobyl-type reactor units functioning despite the obvious inadequacies of the design, a decision was reached several years ago to install major safety enhancements. This is a slow and costly process that was begun in the early 1990s. For example, two of the four units at the Leningrad (St. Petersburg) nuclear station in Sosnovy Bor were substantially modernized by spring 1996, ten years after the Chornobyl accident. To provide a greater margin of safety during the continued operation of those RBMK units that have yet to be modernized, the Soviet government decided to limit their output to 70% of design capacity. This administrative decision— taken at the national level under urging by various international organizations—entails certain economic repercussions, but it dramatically increases the margin of operational safety at the units by increasing the time frames in which protective actions can be taken should another significant reactivity event occur in the future.

Furthermore, political issues are not etched as sharply, either. Judging by the unpublished results of a survey conducted during the summer of 1993 in St. Petersburg, Russia's second most populous city, there is little fear of danger from the power plant, which is located just 60 miles to the west—upwind; rather, here as elsewhere throughout Russia, people are much more concerned with their economic situation.[53] When the Yeltsin government announced ambitious plans to develop civilian nuclear power during the next two decades, there was no discernible negative reaction among the population. Site preparation for new, advanced reactor units has actually begun at Kola, although the plant manager there does not anticipate completion of the project until around the year 2005. Overall, to be sure, Russia has greater natural resources than Ukraine and, despite obvious technological difficulties, it exports significant quantities of natural raw materials. Foreign investment in Russia continues to increase—in sharp contrast to the situation in Ukraine. Thus, the hard currency exigencies faced elsewhere in the CIS are less pronounced in Russia.

In addition to, or perhaps as a result of, this situation, there seems to be much less conflict between the national nuclear operating agency in Russia, Rosenergoatom, and the regulatory body, Gosatomnadzor, than there is in Ukraine. This does not mean that disputes are non-existent, merely that there seems to have been developed over time a greater level of mutual understanding between these bodies. A good case in point may be the way in which new, American style emergency operating procedures are being approved for use at the power plants. As indicated, development of these procedures began in 1989 at Novovoronezh.

Although it was obvious to everyone involved that nothing could be implemented at the plant without regulatory approval, and that it was unclear what kinds of demands would be made by the regulator, still there was great reluctance within the production organizations to provide information or ask for input. As a result, when the whole package was ostensibly complete and the time had come to start training operators in the use of the new procedures, the process was stalled because the regulator believed, rightly, that it had to study the issues before allowing things to proceed. This caused a delay in implementation until January 1996, much to the dismay of the American side. By contrast, the regulator was brought into play at a much earlier time in the process with regard to developing EOPs for other reactor types, a program that has been underway for nearly four years. Rosenergoatom, which became frustrated with the slow pace of regulatory approval, finally saw the wisdom in the American approach, and the agency changed its confrontational policy.[54] Nevertheless, the Department of Energy, which had financed the development process for seven years, faced tremendous pressure from congressional staffers to produce some "scalps"—tangible proof that program funds were not expended in vain. When results did not materialize quickly enough, DOE diverted appropriations to other projects.

One can judge the different attitudes of the regulatory agencies in Russia and Ukraine variously. The primary function of the regulator, of course, is to regulate. By definition this is an adversarial stance, and many would castigate a situation in which the operators and the regulators collaborate to any great extent.[55] On the other hand, the regulator can insist on adherence to standards and procedures at a level that makes efficient operation of a facility virtually impossible. An example of such regulatory obstinacy can be seen in the U.S. at the present time. New technologies have been developed for detecting microscopic flaws in metals, and the existence of defective steam generator tubes is of great concern since they can lead to radiation releases. The new methods are so advanced, however, that they allow detection of some defects too small to be measured accurately, much less fixed. Naturally, it is within the authority of the NRC to require that any defective tubes be repaired or "plugged," which removes them from service and lowers the maximum energy output of the unit. This makes the unit less economical to run. Plug enough tubes and it no longer makes sense to keep the unit in operation. At least one American power plant is currently undergoing this intense scrutiny, and there is reason to believe that all others will soon face the same problem.

Should the regulator be faulted for enforcing regulations to the fullest extent possible? Can the utilities be trusted, in the absence of dogmatic regulation, to make wise decisions balancing their own economic interests with the public interest? Ultimately, in the long term, this is a decision for society to make. In the short term, however, regulatory practice can cause effects to occur that may or may not accord with social values or wishes—assuming that a consensus on such issues exists and that these values can be specified in any meaningful sense.[56] In the current U.S. situation, for example, there is no question that the essentially antipathetical attitude of the Clinton administration to future development of civilian nuclear power creates an atmosphere in which rigid enforcement thrives. On the other side of the coin, most Americans would deplore the opposite extreme, when a *laissez faire* attitude toward regulation in the White House leads to abuses of the market place by "Big Business." Of course, it is useful that the United States currently has a sizable surplus of installed electrical generating capacity in comparison to demand— partially the result of intensive efforts at energy efficiency and conservation throughout the economy. The choice of stringent enforcement is easier to make when there seem to be no compelling immediate drawbacks, such as the inability to adequately heat the nation's homes during the winter. Just ask the Lithuanians or Armenians.

Civilian Nuclear Safety in Russia and Ukraine

In the summer of 1989, Bill Lee—president of Duke Power Company, one of the largest nuclear utilities in the United States, and guiding force behind the creation of the Institute for Nuclear Power Operations almost a decade earlier—was sitting in a medium-sized conference room at the Chornobyl nuclear station outside of Kyiv listening to a discussion of plans to completely redesign the RBMK reactor protective systems. The World Association of Nuclear Operators had just been formed at a meeting in Moscow, and foreign participants were on a tour of the damaged power plant. Of particular interest, of course, were the control rods. They should have shut down the chain reaction when jammed into the reactor core, but instead they led directly to the terrible disaster.

An environment in which a chain reaction speeds up is said to be characterized by a "positive reactivity coefficient"; if conditions tend to slow down or stop a chain reaction, the system is said to have a negative coefficient. There are a variety of such coefficients that depend, for example, on temperature or pressure inside the reactor vessel. In some particularly abnormal situations, it is possible for steam bubbles—called "voids" because the space is devoid of fluid—to be formed in unanticipated areas of the core. In the Chornobyl accident, voids began to accumulate in the lower core region; the resultant positive void coefficient created a fantastic power spike, which in turn instantaneously produced pressures strong enough that they ripped open the reactor vessel and flipped the vessel head, weighing over one hundred tons, almost like the coin toss at the start of an American football game.[57]

Engineers at the Energy Technology Research and Design Institute in Moscow knew that this highly improbable scenario was theoretically possible, so they had provided operating instructions that should have made the occurrence of that scenario impossible. But just enough things went wrong in just the right sequence, and just the right safety systems were deactivated at just the wrong time.[58] So the 'impossible' happened, and Charles Perrow was proven correct: the statistically anticipated or 'normal' accident had occurred.

Not listening as the speaker's words were being interpreted into English, Bill Lee said, "Ask him if the void coefficient will still be positive." The answer, of course, was "yes." "Then there's nothing they can do to this reactor that will make it safe!," he exclaimed.

Bill Lee made one other salient pronouncement that day: there isn't a single reactor unit in the Soviet Union that could have been designed, built, licensed, or operated anywhere else in the world.

Much has changed in the world since that summer in 1989. To a large extent, those changes can be traced back to the accident three years earlier at Chornobyl. What happened there was not even a nuclear explosion, just a simple mechanical failure—too much pressure in the fuel channels—but it transformed the world in ways no one could ever have imagined. And the Soviet Union is no more. Nevertheless, all of those other Soviet designed reactor units are still operating (except, ironically enough, for Chornobyl Unit #2 that was destroyed by fire).

And what Bill Lee said back then is still true: only in the (post-) Soviet Union and the former satellite countries would these units still be in operation.

But we must be cognizant that these are not the same reactor units from an engineering standpoint. Improvements have been made in all of them, even in the pressurized water reactors that have little in common with the RBMK.[59] In addition, the governments running these plants know that at some level they will be held accountable if there is another terrible accident at a nuclear facility located on their territory. As a result, there now exists in all of these countries a functioning regulatory agency, not just a sham of an organization designed to convince the population that the government was looking out for their safety.[60] Granted it is hamstrung by inadequate resources, insufficient funding, and the political and economic factors described in this study; still it does regulate nuclear safety and it does look out for public safety in ways unheard of prior to Chornobyl.

Most importantly, the people who work in these facilities—people who have known all along how to operate nuclear power plants in a safe, responsible manner—are less under the compulsion to keep the plants running at all costs. Not completely free of that impulse, but freer to a remarkable extent. Yes, fulfilling production goals means everybody makes more money, through bonuses, just as in the old days of five-year plans. But nuclear safety, radiation safety, and environmental safety are all serious endeavors in the post-Soviet nuclear industry, whereas earlier the concepts barely existed. Operating procedures are being developed that will make a difference in the way emergencies are handled.

Are these power plants safe? By world standards, the answer must be "No." And it is not likely they ever will be. But are they safer than hitherto? By any standard, the answer must be "Yes." And as time goes on, particularly if stability and growth are established in the economies of these countries, the improvements in safety will continue.

Notes

1.   The total release amounted to less than 1×10^{-5} of the Chornobyl release. No one died, and it is difficult to believe that any one even suffered serious harm. Nevertheless, over $500 million in damages has been paid out as the result of civil suits brought against the operating company for putative harm caused by radiation in the aftermath of the accident.

2.   Ralph Nader, *Unsafe At Any Speed: The Designed-in Dangers of the American Automobile* (New York: Grossman, 1965).

3.   In the case of the Diablo Canyon power plant on the central California coast, scientists discovered a new fault line about three miles offshore *as the station was being built*. Diablo Canyon had been designed to very stringent seismic standards anyway, because of the proximity of the San Andreas fault; nevertheless, additional protection was designed and installed at a cost of several hundred million dollars.

4.   Marilyn J. Young and Michael K. Launer, "Redefining *Glasnost'* in the Soviet Media: The Recontextualization of Chernobyl," in Marsha Siefert, ed., *Mass Culture and Perestroika in the Soviet Union* (New York and Oxford: Oxford University Press, 1991), pp. 102-124 .

5.   Michael K. Launer and Marilyn J. Young, "Nuclear Power and Ecological Debates in the Soviet Press, Mid-1988 to Mid-1989," *Current World Leaders*, Vol. 35, No. 4 (August 1992): 695-716.

6.   Various Soviet sources indicate that some power units (for example, Zaporizhzhya No. 6) were as much as 80% complete. In reality, most were not nearly so far along. For instance, upon visiting a plant site in the Crimea last summer, one American observer guessed that capital construction had not reached the 40% level, and virtually none of the heavy equipment had been installed. Rather, it was all standing unprotected at the construction site, rusted

and useless. Soviet data in this area usually were based upon the percentage of initial estimated cost that had been expended by the moratorium date, but these figures did not generally correspond to physical completion levels.

7. For details, see David R. Marples, "The Decade of Despair," *The Bulletin of the Atomic Scientists,* Vol. 52, No. 3 (May/June 1996): 22-31; and David R. Marples, *Belarus: From Soviet Rule to Nuclear Catastrophe* (New York: St. Martin's Press, 1996), pp. 78-114.

8. Data regarding public opinion with respect to civilian nuclear power have been discussed at meetings of the Soviet Nuclear Society and successor organizations in Russia and Ukraine since 1990. Much of the work, which was performed by an institute in Kharkiv, Ukraine, was commissioned by power plant managers as part of an overall assessment of the political and ecological situation at their sites.

9. Vladimir Kramchenkov and Michael Launer, "Ukraine Nuclear Power Struggles to Survive," *FORUM for Applied Research and Public Policy,* Vol. 11, No. 1 (Spring 1996): 113-117.

10. The same message was widely disseminated in the West. Many Americans remember the horrifying covers of the news magazines after information regarding the accident was released. *Final Warning* by Dr. Robert Peter Gale with Thomas Hauser (New York: Warner Books, 1988) evoked this same apocalyptic theme. The book served as the basis of a popular made-for-television movie. See also two sensationalist diatribes published in England: Nigel Hawkes, et al., *The Worst Accident in the World. Chernobyl: The End of the Nuclear Dream* (London: Pan Books and William Heinemann, 1986), written by a team of writers from *The Observer;* and *The Chernobyl Disaster. The True Story of a Catastrophe—An Unanswerable Indictment of Nuclear Power* (London: The Hogarth Press, 1988) by Viktor Haynes and J. Marko Bojcun.

11. See Murray Feshbach and Alfred Friendly Jr., *Ecocide in the USSR: Health and Nature Under Siege* (New York: Basic Books, 1992).

12. See Murray Feshbach, *Ecological Disaster: Cleaning Up the Hidden Legacy of the Soviet Regime* (New York: Twentieth Century Fund Press, 1995); Ruben A. Mnatsakanian, *Environmental Legacy of the Former Soviet Republics* (Edinburgh: University of Edinburgh, Center for Human Ecology, 1992); and D. J. Petersen, *Troubled Lands: The Legacy of Soviet Environmental Destruction* (Boulder, CO: Westview Press, 1993).

13. The American position is viewed sardonically and somewhat contemptuously by Ukrainian government officials because it advocates such measures as replacing domestic light bulbs in halls, corridors, and exit signs with high-efficiency bulbs of Western manufacture. As if Ukraine has an abundance of lighted halls, corridors, and exit signs! As if the country could afford to purchase the bulbs in the first place or manage to distribute them throughout the country! As if people wouldn't immediately appropriate them or destroy them, as currently occurs! As if this would make a dent in the real problem even if the other difficulties were surmountable!

14. When operators at Soviet designed plants started to develop Western style emergency procedures (see below), a curious situation developed. For a particular accident scenario, the procedure writers proposed a response strategy that seemed contorted to the American experts participating in the activity: "Won't the RVLIS readout on reactor coolant level tell you what the situation is?," they asked. The answer was simple: Soviet plants do not have a reactor level sensor.

15. For a discussion of this problem as it applies to astronomy, see Michael K. Launer, "Russian Scientists Struggle to Survive," *FORUM for Applied Research and Public Policy*, Vol. 10, No. 3 (Fall 1995): 125-129.

16. Consider this cynical assessment of power plant systems by one American after his first exposure to a Soviet facility: "80% of the equipment works to 80% of spec approximately 80% of the time; that means it works right about half the time!" On a less facetious note, this situation greatly complicates the process whereby innovation is assimilated into the economy—whether that takes the form of new technologies or simply improving existing products.

17. One thing that is intuitively obvious to visiting Russians, but which dawns on Americans only after significant exposure to other cultures, is how expensive it is to make things pretty, easy, clean, or convenient.

18. Keep in mind that there have been repeated instances when fires have broken out at Soviet plants, but the local fire station could not be reached by telephone for several hours. Endemic problems relating to infrastructure and the economy impact all areas of life, not just nuclear power. We shall return to this problem below.

19. On-line refueling and, concomitantly, off-loading of plutonium made it extremely difficult for the respective intelligence services to determine exactly how much nuclear material was being produced by the other side. Prudence dictated assuming the maximum possible amount, which undoubtedly led to intensified efforts by both superpowers to maximize their own production, just to "keep up with the Joneses"—or Ivanovs, as the case might be.

20. An unfunny joke went as follows: Soviet power plants have two operating rules. Rule No. 1 states, "Operators shall not allow any accidents to happen." Rule No. 2 states, "In the event of an accident, re-read Rule No. 1." This is not all that far from the truth. In any event, to this day control room operators in Eastern and Central Europe bear criminal responsibility for accidents that occur. In one instance, a Czech shift supervisor told of an incident that happened several years ago: he was detained by the secret police, interrogated, and threatened with imprisonment because the unit he was working at tripped (shut down automatically due to some equipment malfunction) during a May Day celebration. The Soviet nuclear bureaucracy went to great lengths to convince Western governments that operator error was the sole cause of the Chornobyl disaster, including providing disinformation to the IAEA. They cleverly repeated some of the same justifications that were used by U.S. industry officials after TMI, and they found a ready, willing, and believing audience in some circles.

21. The new methodology, termed "symptom based," was developed in response to the lessons learned from the TMI accident.

22. Changing the mind set of American operators after the TMI accident so that they accepted the completely new symptom based approach to plant operations was an equally painful and slow process.

23. Congress and the bureaucrats in the Department of Energy who oversee the activities of the Lisbon Initiative, as this exchange program is called, have demonstrated continued impatience with the slow pace of tangible progress regarding emergency procedure development. Indeed this facet of the program was essentially terminated after fiscal year 1996. Nevertheless, in our opinion, changing "the hearts and minds" of these operators fully justified the time, effort, and expense of the program.

24. The Soviet government vigorously denied this allegation when it was raised at the time, but a highly placed plant official confirmed its correctness in a 1989 conversation.

25. If one compares exchange rates for the two currencies against the U.S. dollar, in January 1996 the Russian *ruble* was worth approximately 40 times the value of the Ukrainian *karbovanets*, but this is slightly misleading, because starting in mid-summer 1995 the Russian government began to hold dollar trading in an artificially narrow range—ostensibly for stabilization of the domestic economy, but more probably as an attempt to influence the outcome of the December parliamentary elections and the Spring 1996 presidential election. In July 1995 the *ruble* was worth approximately 32 times as much as the now defunct *karbovanets*— a more reliable comparative figure.

26. At an American power plant, operating shifts train together every fifth, sixth, or seventh week; the plants maintain at least one complete extra shift to make the scheduling of training an actuality. At a typical power plant in Eastern Europe, control room operators are unlikely to get more than two weeks of training annually.

27. It is important to remember, however, that one can never completely forget about cost/benefit ratios. At some level, some accidents are so unlikely, and the cost of protecting against them so great, that one decides to assume the risk. This, indeed, is the flip side of regulation. The calculus is very complicated because some of the variables, like public attitudes, are so indefinable, reminding one of Heisenberg's uncertainty principle.

28. Clever ideas such as irons that automatically shut themselves off and automobile air bags are examples of specific ways new or improved equipment can expand the envelope of design basis accidents—those events for which adequate protective measures are in place. They also show that to some extent ingenuity can overcome human factors of sloth, indifference, or carelessness, to say nothing of malice. But there are limits. The capacity of individuals to make fundamental blunders exceeds the resourcefulness and foresightedness of designers. Hence, nothing can be made completely foolproof.

29. It is now generally conceded that Soviet failure to share information regarding operating experience at nuclear plants within the industry itself was a prime contributor to the Chornobyl tragedy.

30. The Russian term for this policy is "khozrasschet." A similar situation obtains in the U.S. with regard to the Nuclear Regulatory Commission. The NRC generates most of the funds it needs to function from fees that the utilities pay for application reviews, operator licensing examinations, and other legislatively mandated services.

31. It is difficult to say for sure, however, since the Soviet economy, being orders of magnitude larger than the Polish economy, might not have responded in the same way. Be that as it may, Poland has witnessed steady economic growth recently after the three or four years of precipitous decline following the removal of the Communist Party from political control.

32. When employees finally do get paid, inflation may have eaten away 35-50 percent of their purchasing power.

33. Unfortunately, the government seems virtually powerless to halt the inflationary spiral. Moreover, the non-payment issue is fraught with dire consequences, whatever action might be contemplated. Perhaps the only solution would be to eliminate by governmental fiat all indebtedness (except back payment of wages) among governmental agencies and among domestic enterprises.

34. Vladimir Kramchenkov and Michael Launer, "Ukraine Nuclear Power Struggles to Survive," *FORUM for Applied Research and Public Policy*, Vol. 11, No. 1 (Spring 1996): 113-117.

35. In Armenia, the supply of heat and electricity to residents of Yerevan was reduced to two hours in every twenty-four because Azerbaijan had cut off the supply of oil and gas. Needless to say, this situation caused Armenians to change their attitude toward nuclear power, as a result of which the station that had been shut down after the 1988 earthquake is again up and running. Western experts believe that inadequate safety provisions and insufficient lead time before restart will cause serious operating problems in the future.

36. According to the director of the Kola nuclear power station, such funds as are collected in Russia get distributed first to the non-nuclear sector of the industry. This occurs for the simple reason that the agency which receives the funds is housed in the Ministry of Energy—not the Ministry of Nuclear Power—and that agency makes sure that its own organizations are paid first. Private conversation with Y. V. Kolomtsev, Polyarnye Zori, Russia, July 1995.

37. It takes a long time to bring a nuclear power unit on or off line. In the West, therefore, nuclear installations are considered base load, and the economics of the situation dictate that they run continuously if there is no technical reason for shutting them down. Peak demand is met using hydroelectric, fossil, or pumped storage sources. In Eastern Europe, however, competing ministerial priorities may take precedence, as indicated above, and technical considerations can be subordinated to bureaucratic imperative. [Kolomtsev interview.] Nor is the West immune from this problem: it appears, for example, that an analogous situation at NASA had a direct bearing on decisions leading to the 1986 Challenger disaster.

38. It is noteworthy that by late 1988, when the Armenian earthquake caused catastrophic disaster in that Soviet republic, the domestic political situation had changed considerably. Mr. Gorbachev not only cut short a visit to the United States in order to oversee rescue efforts, he publicly appealed to organizations such as the International Red Cross for assistance.

39. Marilyn J. Young and Michael K. Launer, "Redefining *Glasnost'* in the Soviet Media: The Recontextualization of Chernobyl."

40. This position, which makes a certain amount of sense in the context of Soviet government domestic propaganda, is encountered from unlikely sources, as well. For example, a 1993 book by a Ukrainian medical researcher considers Gale to be a dilettante who, "came, perhaps, with the best of intentions, but was not a specialist in radiation medicine, just a practicing physician who treated blood diseases." See L. V. Keisevich, *Zapiski vracha-likvidatora* [Notes of a Physician Who Participated in the Clean-Up] (Kyiv: VIPOL, 1993), pp. 15-16. What is remarkable here is that the author is virulently anti-nuclear: he spares the Soviet government and its nuclear lobby none of his wrath, but he also has little use for the Soviet doctors in Moscow who treated the radiation victims or for Robert Gale either.

41. In the fall of 1988 the Ministry of Nuclear Power requested, and was granted, an invitation for Deputy Minister Vladimir Lapshin to attend a conference of nuclear utility CEOs held in Atlanta at the Institute for Nuclear Power Operations, an industry supported organization created after the accident at Three Mile Island. Minister Lapshin called upon the West to participate in a Moscow conference the following summer and to create the World Association of Nuclear Operators.

42. For a survey of the early stages in the development of international programs to enhance civilian nuclear power safety, see Michael Congdon, "U.S.-USSR Nuclear Safety Cooperation: Prospects for Health and Environmental Collaboration," in John Massey Stewart, ed., *The Soviet Environment: Problems, Policies and Politics* (New York and Cambridge: Cambridge University Press, 1992), pp. 150-173.

43. It is impossible to prove, of course, but it seems likely that this experience contributed to political decisions, once freedom was attained, that made passing a language test in the vernacular a prerequisite to obtaining citizenship.

44. Of all Soviet designed reactors, only the VVER-1000 features a negatively pressurized, reinforced concrete containment structure similar to those in Western designs.

45. Central storage facilities that serviced the whole Soviet Union were situated in Western Siberia, deep inside Russia and surrounded by nuclear missile defenses. After dissolution of the union, all of these facilities were located outside the borders of the other former republics.

46. At the time, Zaporizhzhya had an installed capacity of 5,000 MW. A sixth unit, which had never been completed because of the Soviet moratorium, had been preserved through the clever ruse of declaring it a training facility. This

allowed station management to expend funds to maintain the construction site in reasonable materiel condition, thus preventing cannibalization of the unit for spare parts and enabling fairly rapid completion of equipment installation once the moratorium was lifted. Unit Six went critical in early August, 1995.

47. In addition to Lithuania's Ignalina station, Russia continues to operate eleven RBMK reactor units at three different sites—Sosnovy Bor (St. Petersburg), Kursk, and Smolensk. In addition, there exists a very low-power channel reactor serving the Siberian gold mines at Bilibino. See *Nuclear Power Reactors in the World*, IAEA-RDS-2/12 (Vienna: IAEA, April 1992), pp. 20-23.

48. Only Unit Three is currently in operation. A major fire—that had nothing whatsoever to do with the nuclear reactor itself—has put Unit Two out of commission for the past few years. On 2 December 1996, the Ukrainian State Nuclear Energy Committee ordered the restart of this unit by the fourth quarter of 1997. Though the first reactor was removed from the grid at the end of November 1996, its reconstruction was being discussed at the time of writing. See *Eastern Economist*, No. 437, 3 December 1996. The U.S., the Germans, and the French have been poring over Chornobyl for years doing safety assessments, upgrade evaluations, and cost analyses. As Michael Congdon notes in his contribution to this volume, restarting the Chornobyl units is not economically feasible without life extension, because the West wants to give credits, not aid, and the high cost of upgrading the units can not be amortized over the few remaining years of original service life. [Operable U.S. units have been shut down because the cost of mandated upgrades, like steam generator replacement, could not be recouped in the time remaining on the operating license and the political climate is such that the odds on getting life extension approval are very uncertain.] If the Ukrainians ever restart these units, then one can safely predict that they will not shut them down in the year 2000 or anytime soon thereafter.

49. One senior regulatory official, who requests anonymity, has argued in just this manner at official meetings with foreign delegations, but also has expressed his personal opinion that Chornobyl *should* be shut down. [Private conversation, Kyiv, Ukraine, July 1994]

50. The winner in this struggle proved to be the Zaporizhzhya plant manager. Just before New Year's Day 1996 President Kuchma traveled to the plant site to hand out medals commemorating the startup of Unit Six. Bronnikov was awarded the highest civilian honor the nation can bestow, and M.P. Umanets, Chairman of Goskomatom, was "advised" that he should retire to care for his health (Umanets does, in fact, suffer from heart disease, but in the summer of 1995 he had returned to work from a long convalescence and could be seen toasting foreign representatives into the night at a sanatorium outside of Kyiv). Umanets is a former director of the post-accident Chornobyl nuclear power plant.

51. This was far from a trivial matter. Absolving national authorities, the government, and the Communist Party of any responsibility for inadequacies in the system was always a cornerstone of Soviet society. After the Chornobyl accident, for example, only the plant manager was sent to jail, as the Ministry of Nuclear Power escaped all official censure. Soviet authorities did everything

possible to convince its citizens and the world at large that the cause of the accident was "operator error" and dereliction of duty at the plant level.

52. One suspects that the conditions would have mirrored those of 1989. Private conversation with Nikolay Shteinberg, Kyiv, Ukraine, January 1996.

53. The study was conducted by Marilyn J. Young and a team of researchers from Florida State University in conjunction with Alexander I. Yuriev, chair of the political psychology department at St. Petersburg State University.

54. The Ukrainian plant operators, it seems, have not reached the same level of understanding. At a meeting in July 1995 called to discuss regulatory concerns about the proposed dry storage project, V. Hryshchenko, a high ranking GAN official stated in his opening remarks that Zaporizhzhya would be forced to compare the analytical computer codes and industry standards used by the American consortium during the design process (codes and standards that satisfied the requirements of the U.S. Nuclear Regulatory Commission) to current Ukrainian standards in order to have them certified for use domestically—a costly and time consuming process which could delay construction by months, if not years. Later in the meeting, Hryshchenko indicated that perhaps one way to resolve the issue was for plant management to submit a formal request in writing that the foreign standards be accepted on an ad hoc basis, applicable to this particular facility only. Without promising anything, he nevertheless indicated that his agency could respond to an official request of this type in much less time than it would take to complete the required studies. But the plant representative thought that the regulator was being unreasonable, and it was only after several weeks of intense negotiating by the American consortium that the plant acceded to everyone else's position. Thus, when the regulator saw fit to be accommodating—having made its principled stand on the grounds of Ukrainian national sovereignty, but then recognizing the political and economic realities of the current situation—the operating organization chose to maintain an adversarial stance "on principle."

55. It is for this reason that resident inspectors at American plants are reassigned every five years, so that no "buddy-buddy" relationships can develop. In the CIS, on the other hand, the policy is to recruit regulators for work at a specific plant from local operations staff—the theory being that they will know the plant design better and will, therefore, be more effective regulators. As always, there is an economic side to this problem. While the family of an inspector is forced to undergo regular upheavals, at least they can buy a new house in their new locale. In Russia and Ukraine, housing is virtually impossible to obtain, and people can be recruited to ostensibly lower paid or lower prestige jobs by the promise of an apartment. Thus, since an organization such as a regulatory body does not control access to housing—the way a power plant used to, because it was the builder of all structures in the company town—it cannot entice people to work for them if that entails moving to another locale.

56. Moreover, what does one do as a national leader if one believes that the "nation" is wrong? Do you push for, e.g., civil rights legislation despite your personal beliefs and the beliefs of your peers (as Lyndon Johnson did) because of

a perceived greater good? Do you continue, e.g., to prosecute a war (as Lyndon Johnson did) long after most of the country has come to believe that it was a mistake even to have begun it? Or do you send out an army of opinion pollsters before deciding what policies you will advocate as best for the nation?

57. The reactor vessel head is still leaning at a strange angle against the rubble that was the reactor. All of this mass of twisted steel and magmatic nuclear material is covered by the Sarcophagus that protects the environment from the devastating effects of the radiation trapped inside.

58. The best general description of what actually caused the Chornobyl accident can be found in the introduction to David R. Marples, *The Social Impact of the Chernobyl Disaster*. "Introduction" by Victor G. Snell (London: Macmillan, 1988).

59. There are actually four different Soviet designed commercial reactor designs: the RBMK and three distinct VVER models—the first generation 440 MW (model 230), newer 440s (model 213—yes it makes no sense), and the 1000 MW units. Western experts believe that the older 440 MW VVER is actually a worse design than the RBMK. Kozloduy, a power plant in Bulgaria equipped with these old 440s, is generally considered to be the worst civilian nuclear installation in the world.

60. The obvious way in which the Soviet social contract was shredded by the cynical response of the government may have sounded the death knell to tottering socialist state.

4

The U.S.-Russia Joint Electric Power Alternatives Study: Nuclear Safety Implications

Michael B. Congdon

Wherever nuclear technology is employed, whether in Russia or Ukraine, in China or in Eastern Europe, or indeed in the United States, Japan or Western Europe, the safety of nuclear power plants will be best assured as much by sound economics and solid management principles as by competent operations and excellence in design.

Western countries have been working on these principles since the U.S. Three Mile Island accident in 1979. Unfortunately, because of the international political situation, similar attention to safety culture and effective management, to say nothing of sound economics, was not present in the former Soviet Union. And Chornobyl did not significantly change things in 1986. We are therefore engaged in a struggle for the future of nuclear energy, and the focus is in Russia and Ukraine. Unless there is a fundamental change in the way leaders in these countries think about nuclear safety, we are likely to see a repeat of past errors which, if serious enough, could turn global public opinion against nuclear power for the foreseeable future.

The Problem

The Chornobyl accident in 1986 alerted the world to a gross disparity in the attention given to nuclear safety in the Soviet Union and Eastern Europe, compared to what is minimally acceptable in the West. The problem, we learned, had three aspects:

1. There are critical design inadequacies in some key Soviet designed plants, particularly the graphite-moderated RBMK;
2. The Soviet Union exhibited substandard operational safety procedures and attention to detail in managing the production of electricity at all nuclear power plants; and,
3. There was an almost complete lack of independent governmental regulation of the state utilities, which were devoted to fulfilling the production requirements of the latest economic plan, often at the expense of safe operation.

Current Western Nuclear Safety Assistance

Since the late 1980's the United States and other western countries have engaged in an active program of nuclear safety cooperation and assistance, with the USSR and its successor states, and with the Central and Eastern European countries that employ Soviet designs. Assistance efforts have emphasized near-term technical upgrades to the highest risk plants, improvements in operational safety, and enhancement of regulatory structures. According to the G-24 in Brussels, these efforts total close to $1.5 billion in grants for safety enhancements. Much of the assistance has been bilateral or through the TACIS and PHARE programs of the European Union, with an increasing measure of coordination through the Brussels-based secretariat of the G-24. Also, a useful multilateral instrument for funding safety improvements was established in the Nuclear Safety Account at the European Bank for Reconstruction and Development.

Since 1992, the United States has engaged in a bilateral assistance program, under the Lisbon initiative for nucear safety, designed to improve regional nuclear safety training at sites in Russia and Ukraine, operational safety at all sites in these countries, and near term risk reduction measures for RBMK and VVER 440/230 reactors in Russia, Ukraine and Eastern Europe, as well as providing improved equipment and training for their nuclear regulatory authorities.

The United States Nuclear Regulatory Commission (NRC) has also dramatically increased its own bilateral efforts, focusing on helping these nations establish a nuclear safety culture based on a strong, independent regulator, in contrast to an approach motivated primarily by considerations of unimpeded energy production. In 1992 we joined with the other nations of the G-7 in Munich to emphasize to the leaders of Russia and Ukraine how important we believe nuclear safety is to the success of nuclear energy programs world-wide. And, in 1994, the G-7 launched an important initiative at the Naples Summit to provide assistance aimed at persuading Ukraine to shut down its still operating reactors at Chorno-byl—the unfortunate symbol of all that was wrong with the Soviet approach to nuclear power.

The Naples initiative was a comprehensive package of incentives designed to enable Ukraine to replace Chornobyl with a combination of efficiency measures, alternative power sources, and modern nuclear power plants. The G-7 committed to an initial grant package of $200 Million for this purpose, which, combined with additional grant and loan funds from the CEC Technical Assistance to the Commonwealth of Independent States (TACIS) program and European Investment Bank and possible EBRD loans, signals a significant commitment of western resources.

The Halifax Summit of June 1995 reiterated western support for the welcome closure commitment by Ukrainian President Kuchma. Ukraine's subsequent insistence on replacement power for Chornobyl, however, demonstrates a fundamental difference in perspective between countries schooled in the Soviet approach to electric power generation and western market economic approaches. We shall return to this point in addressing the Joint U.S.-Russian Electric Power Alternatives Study.

The United States has also been raising its nuclear safety concerns with Russia at the highest levels of government. In seven consecutive meetings between Vice President Gore and Russian Prime Minister Chernomyrdin, nuclear safety and the importance of a strong and independent regulator were firmly reinforced by the Vice President. This forum is also the venue in which the Joint Electric Power Alternatives Study was launched. The June 1995 meeting of the Commission approved both the text of the Study and the approach to a vigorous investment strategy for Russia's electric power (including nuclear power) sector.

Some of these efforts have begun to pay dividends in terms of enhanced operational safety and fixes to pressing near-term technical safety problems, particularly in Eastern Europe. Even in Russia and Ukraine, within the limitations of reactor design and construction quality, there have been some impressive technical improvements. But the basic "safety culture" in Russia and Ukraine has, in the opinion of many experts, not improved significantly. In fact, the limits on our success to date highlight both the importance and the difficulty of helping these countries move on to broader and more far-reaching efforts.

Achieving "Sustainable Safety" of Soviet-Designed Reactors

It is now eleven years since Chornobyl, and many in the west still lack confidence in the ability of Russia, Ukraine, Bulgaria, Lithuania, and

Armenia to manage their nuclear power systems with the same attention to safety that we take for granted in Western Europe, North America, and Japan.

While there are differing points of view about the intrinsic safety of Soviet-designed reactors, in the judgment of many the technical safety of these reactors is not the most serious safety issue facing the people of Russia and Ukraine. Nor does the problem lie in the technical competence of the operators and regulators, although the regulatory bodies in Russia and Ukraine are woefully under funded for the work they are asked to do. Almost seven years of cooperative work with these two states, part of which took place under the former Soviet Union, has shown that both the regulatory authorities and nuclear power plant operating personnel are well-trained and committed to doing a good job. And there is no question that the nuclear energy profession drew from the best of the former Soviet Union's massive scientific and engineering talent pool.

The nuclear safety problems in these countries are structural; having more to do with economics and sound management—and the difficulty these nations are having in making the transition to market economies. The term that best describes this, coined by former NRC Chairman, Ivan Selin, is "sustainable safety." The task is to transform patterns of conduct in the nuclear power sector of these countries from the old Soviet model of greater production at any cost to a system where current and future safety carries a higher value. The social, institutional, and economic transformation required, however, is likely to take decades, not years. Chairman Selin characterized "sustainable nuclear safety" as a three-legged stool. If all three legs are strong the chair will be stable. But if one leg buckles, the chair will tip over.

The first leg is technical and operational safety, which is the usual focus of safety and regulatory programs. The second leg is proper organization and good management, which includes self-regulation, adequate training, good personnel policies to attract solid operating staff, safety culture, standardization, responsible leadership, and realistic goals. The third leg is sound economics over the long term. A nuclear program, including its regulatory aspects, must be well-funded. It must be profitable enough to permit continued investment in maintenance and training. And, it must make good business sense. An uneconomic program will, among other things, eventually try to cut costs and thus compromise safety.

I wish to emphasize the third of these three aspects of sustainable safety in this paper—economic restructuring of the electricity sector, which was the topic of the U.S.-Russian Joint Electric Power Alternatives Study.

Joint Electric Power Alternatives Study

In June 1994, the U.S. NRC identified five issues which it saw as requiring continuing attention at the highest levels of the U.S. and Russian governments.

1. Shutdown of Plutonium Production Reactors.
2. Joint Electric Power Alternative Study (JEPAS).
3. Safety Assistance to Russia's Nuclear Program.
4. Material Control and Accounting/Physical Security.
5. Disposition of Weapons Material from Russia and Ukraine.

The second of these issues, the JEPAS, was considered fundamental to the effort to reform the entire energy system in Russia, with the aim of early closure of highest risk nuclear plants. The Study has proven to be extremely valuable, and it is linked analytically to efforts by the G-7, the EBRD, and the World Bank to financing energy projects in Russia.

The Joint Electric Power Alternatives Study was authorized at the second meeting of the Gore-Chernomyrdin Commission in December 1993, possibly the most productive of the GCC meetings from the nuclear safety point of view. The Study was motivated originally by our interest in demonstrating the economic importance of least cost energy analysis to Russian Energy officials and pointing out the extent to which nuclear power upgrades and new construction must be competitive with other forms of producing electric power, if Russia is to move toward a market economy in energy.

At the Russian Ministry of Atomic Energy's request a separate report called the Joint Parallel Nuclear Alternatives Study (JPNAS) was produced. This report provided the input to the main study on the costs of various options for the development and safety of Russia's nuclear power sector. By raising the Joint Electric Power Alternatives Study in the Gore-Chernomyrdin context, the U.S. hoped to increase Prime Minister Chernomyrdin's awareness of three major insights from the study, namely:

- that there are safety and economic reasons for early decommissioning of some of Russia's least safe reactors;
- that there is a clear need for institutional reform for the power sector to encourage external investor interest in the Russian energy sector; and,
- that there is a high-priority need for improving energy end-use efficiency in Russia's electric power sector.

The study received high-level Russian government concurrence (even from some former Minatom skeptics), and the final report was issued on June 6, 1995 to the U.S. and Russian governments. Both sides were eager to begin work on presentations of the study results to government officials, international financial institutions, and the private sector.

One measure of the report's balance is that various elements of its conclusions appeal to various Russian constituencies, but no Russian constituency likes all the recommendations. Minatom, for example, concurred on the report's conclusion that early closure of some of its least-safe reactors may be economical, because to meet adequate safety standards, the needed investment cannot be economically amortized over the reactors' remaining lifetime.

Russians involved in preparing the study were eager to begin publicizing it and implementing its recommendations, e.g., undertaking additional studies at the regional level to identify specific projects for investment aimed at improving energy efficiency, developing more modern and new power resources, and revamping Russian electricity transmission systems. The U.S. agreed to work on joint presentations of the report to the greater investment and business community. Support for specific projects will be targeted at bottlenecks and will press financing institutions such as the World Bank to undertake projects. One of the most important benefits Russia anticipates from the Joint Study is to enhance its ability to attract foreign financing to its electric power sector.

The U.S. NRC had supported a comprehensive, economic approach to the Russian energy sector since 1993 and were strong proponents of the electric power alternatives study as a way to convince the Russians of the need to use economic criteria to justify their nuclear power program, vis a vis competing sources of electric power. NRC Chairman Ivan Selin was instrumental in pressing the potential benefits of the study, and he remained a strong proponent throughout his tenure as Chairman (through June 1995).

This support was motivated by the conviction that only a solid economic basis for nuclear-generated electric power, in which the operators and regulators are paid a reasonable, and market-based, price for their service, can insure the long term safety of the program. This is true not only in Russia but in any nation that wishes to invest in nuclear power over the long term—which is the only sensible and responsible way to invest in nuclear power. As it has turned out, the results of the study are not anti-nuclear, and actually recommend several nuclear safety upgrades as being justifiable from an economic point of view—upgrades that had earlier been undertaken for purely nuclear safety reasons.

The study was a key accomplishment of the GCC in the energy field. It is now important to market the study to the international financial community to solicit investment financing in Russia for energy over the next decade. I would like to summarize some of its key aspects in the remainder of this paper.

The Goals of the JEPAS were:

1. To make an objective assessment of Russia's electric power sector alternatives through the first decade of the next century (2010);
2. To provide a time-phased investment program for Russian power sector for the balance of the present decade (1995-2000);
3. To identify projects for possible financing; and,
4. To interest western financial institutions in the Russian energy sector.

Methodology

Energy officials from the two countries decided to use projections of future electricity demand to gauge investment needs. Accordingly they constructed two scenarios, one of somewhat higher growth, the Russian preferred case, and a second that the U.S. considered more realistic. We then sought to identify the most cost-effective options for meeting demand under these two scenarios. Based on these findings, by technology sector (e.g., efficiency, fossil, nuclear, hydro, and transmission) we developed an overall power investment strategy through 2005, and estimated financing requirements from domestic and international resources, considering key factors affecting capital mobilization and investment in Russia. An intermediate goal was to determine what role nuclear energy and nuclear safety upgrades should play in the mix of technologies that should attract investment.

The two governments formed five joint working groups to carry out the analytical work. These were supervised by an inter-governmental steering committee comprised of concerned ministries and agencies. I was privileged to serve on this committee for the U.S. Nuclear Regulatory Commission. The study used two electric power integrated planning models which complemented each other.

The Russian simulation model incorporated 1) detailed expert knowledge of the entire Russian power system; 2) screening analysis of the cost-effectiveness of supply and energy efficiency options; and 3) fuel supply constraints and environmental impacts.

The American integrated resource planning model uses least-cost optimization techniques to analyze the same set of issues as the Russian model. The Joint Study used the technical flexibility of the American model to study the sensitivity of answers to a wide range of economic uncertainties and policy questions raised by the Russian model. While few concerned with the study believe the models can determine an investment plan for Russia, both agree they will be an important aid to formulating such a plan. The data generated by the working groups were used in the two models to identify the mix of technologies needed to meet Russia's electricity demand under two scenarios through the year 2010. The two demand scenarios described above were based on two views of Russian economic performance and electricity demand—set out in the Energy Strategy for Russia (Main Directions), and on a set of assumptions regarding the pace and degree of success of measures to control inflation and reform the economy. Time phased investment and fuel requirements were estimated using the two planning models. Financing requirements were calculated from the total costs of the investments, and potential domestic and foreign sources of finance were identified.

Since all the scenarios and financing requirements are based on assumptions about future developments of the Russian economy that are subject to uncertainties, the team prepared an investment strategy that addresses the main elements of uncertainty. As the future direction of reform and the rate of evolution to a market economy become clearer, it will be necessary to undertake periodic reevaluations of investment priorities.

Study Conclusions

The study shows significant reductions in the need for investment in the electricity sector over what had earlier been thought necessary, as a result of the economics of plant life extension.

It is extremely important for the Russian Government to attract foreign and domestic investment into its oil and gas sector for domestic electricity production to make most efficient use of its resources.

Russia needs to improve inter-regional transmission in order to integrate its electricity sector and obtain the benefits of evening out peak load in different regions at different times.

The first real lesson in the nuclear area lies in the need to incorporate decommissioning costs into the cost of nuclear generation of electricity. The second lesson is that even with this additional cost, nuclear power is still competitive.

The study also shows the economic benefit of safety upgrades to nuclear power plants. This is important for enticing western investments in nuclear power.

Key Findings

The study indicates that it would be important for Russia to undertake certain high priority projects on a time-phased basis over the next 10-15 years to maximize the effectiveness of its power sector and energy efficiency investment decisions. The amount of financing required would range from $12 to $43 billion, depending on the demand for electricity. Short-term support from the international community during the next two years 1995-1997 are required in the amount of about $2 to $4 billion.

Priorities for the Next Five Years (1995-2000)

The priorities for the next five years are as follows:

1. Promotion of and investment in improvements in electricity end-use efficiency;
2. Rehabilitation and nuclear safety upgrades for 1st-generation nuclear power plants;
3. Construction of inter-regional and intra-regional transmission between surplus and deficit areas;
4. Fossil thermal plant modernization and rehabilitation; costs and benefits of life extension should be considered as a way of deferring major expenditures;
5. Completion of nuclear power plants in advanced stages of construction,
6. Construction of new gas-fired simple cycle and combined cycle plants; and,
7. Completion of the detailed design for new generation nuclear power plants to enable their certification by regulatory authorities.

Priorities for 2001-2005

The longer-term priorities can be summarized as follows:

1. Complete large under-construction hydroelectric plants;
2. Commercialization of clean coal generation technology;
3. Construction of clean coal generation plants and new generation nuclear power plants (and development of the new generation NP 500 and NP 1000 plant designs);
4. Re-assess the promise of extending transmission lines both east and west of Siberian hydro power plants to demand centers, based on development of the wholesale market for electricity.

The amount of electricity generated from natural gas is expected to rise significantly under both demand scenarios, because generation from natural gas using combined cycle and simple cycle technologies is economically competitive in many regions. Hydroelectric power generation is also expected to increase in both demand scenarios, but by a much smaller amount. Nuclear power generation is also expected to increase in both demand scenarios until the year 2000; whereupon in the higher demand case nuclear is expected to increase slightly, and in the lower demand case it will decline slightly. Use of coal for electricity is expected to decline in both scenarios.

Recommendations

The study makes a number of recommendations worth summarizing.

Energy Efficiency

Russia needs to introduce market oriented incentives to improve end-use efficiencies, and it should encourage the development of energy service companies to provide equipment management techniques and financing for improving efficiency.

Nuclear Safety

The study recommends performing "economically justified" safety upgrades of RBMK and first generation VVER nuclear power reactors. This is estimated to cost about $1.0 billion between 1995 and 2000. Both Russian and international financial support should be used.

Fossil Plant Life Extension

RAO EES Rossii and the AO Energos are advised to rehabilitate and modernize their older thermal plants to extend their operating lives and improve their efficiency and environmental performance. 79 gigawatts of power should do this, 39 in the next five years.

Gas Turbines

Russia should give high priority on technology and investments into simple cycle and combined cycle gas turbines, installing from about 40 to 80 gigawatts by the year 2010; about 5 to 20 by the year 2000.

Sectoral Least Cost Planning

Russia should do detailed studies of the electrical energy needs of the North Caucasus, Urals, and TransBaikalia, using least cost planning tools and local supply factors. The areas are expected to require from 24 to 36 gigawatts of new capacity and strengthened transmission and inter-ties among regions.

Expanded Transmission Lines

Russia should also perform feasibility studies on extending transmission of Siberian hydro power capacity both to the east and to the west. The Russian authorities should also look into interconnecting the grid with the other republics of the former Soviet Union as well as with China and Central Europe.

Russia also needs to secure from $30 to $80 billion in investments into capacity replacements and additions, as well as improved efficiency and transmission. The breakdown is in the attached table.

Economic Reform and Western Investment

The Russian Government needs to reform its economy and create conditions to attract investment from abroad. It needs, for example, an improved state system for regulating natural monopolies as well as appropriate laws and standards to guarantee foreign investors that they are a reasonable risk. The market is there; the social and legal infrastructure is not. Mechanisms are needed, for example to make energy self-financing, in order to increase the internal cash generated and improve the efficiency of allocating the funds through depreciation and retained earnings of the operating entities.

TABLE 4.1. INVESTMENT REQUIREMENTS IN $ BILLIONS

	High Demand	Low Demand
Generation		
1995-2000	21-26	9-10
2001-2005	25-34	14-20
Subtotal	**46-58**	**23-30**
Energy Efficiency		
1995-200	3-4	2-3
2001-2005	5-11	3-8
Subtotal	**8-15**	**5-11**
Transmission		
1995-2000	2-3	1-3
2001-2005	5-5	3-5
Subtotal	**7-8**	**4-8**
All Requirements		
1995-2000	26-34	12-16
2001-2005	35-48	20-33
Total	**61-81**	**32-40**

Allocation of Investments

As a transition to a more modern regulatory system, Russia should establish a better mechanism to allocate investment funds between federal and regional levels; also, it should try to create incentives to attract funds from both domestic and foreign sources on both an equity and a debt basis. One way to do this would be to make the part of retained earnings that is directed into investment tax deductible, including the part collected through centralized investment funds.

Assure Reasonable Rates of Return

Russia should institute government guarantees to assure reasonable levels of return on investment. As an interim measure, funds should be generated at the federal level to finance modernization and rehabilitations, and a mechanism must be developed to allocate these between federal and regional levels.

Make Nuclear Energy More Competitive

Russia should develop a mechanism that can be applied to the nuclear energy sector, to set electricity prices high enough to generate funds internally, including for decommissioning, but without pricing nuclear energy out of the market. Some of these funds should be placed in a national reserve to finance safety upgrades, plant completions, decommissioning, and new plant construction.

Market Pricing and Privatization of Nuclear Energy

Russia needs to privatize the nuclear sector—converting it into stock companies—and provide guarantees to private and foreign investors. A more competitive environment should be set up to allow producers to charge market prices for electricity, rather than subsidize its use, thereby increasing the cost to the consumer of wasting energy.

Finally, the government needs to develop a program for the public sale of government-held power sector stock at reasonable prices for acceptable values. The funds from these sales should be reinvested in the power sector. Economic stability and market pricing of energy are fundamental to the development and maintenance of a safe and sustainable nuclear power program. Ukraine has made strides toward this goal, and one is encouraged by the dedication of the President and his key nuclear safety advisors to take a comprehensive look at the total electric power sector in the context of shutting down the Chornobyl nuclear power plant by the year 2000. While progress in Russia toward restructuring of the energy economies seems slower, because of the enormous challenges that country confronts, the JEPAS was a major achievement towards orienting

Russia's leadership to an integrated national electric power perspective—and away from regionalism and fuel-based sectoralism.

One of the assumptions of the JEPAS was that certain conditions must be met for nuclear power to be both economically sound and physically safe. Energy tariffs need to be based on the market price of supply, including all the hidden costs such as eventual decommissioning of nuclear power plants, in order to fund the maintenance and investment resources needed for technical excellence. Western investments are now beginning to gravitate to the Russian non-nuclear energy sector, which will make it far more competitive than the nuclear power sector. We believe these conditions also need to be satisfied in the nuclear power programs of Russia and Ukraine before they will be able to attract significant investments, whether domestic or international, to assure safety.

This is illustrated by a more fundamental point. Truly "sustainable" efforts to improve nuclear safety must emerge from within these societies themselves. This is not yet happening. Plant operators and regulators in Russia and Ukraine are not receiving adequate pay for their work. Utilities are still not receiving payment for the electricity they produce. Regulators face bureaucratic and legal impediments to their ability to do their jobs right. Plant operators are very well educated and well trained, and they operate with considerable individual responsibility and discipline. But because of a traditionally centralized management philosophy which compartmentalized functions and inhibited horizontal communication, there has been a tendency for individuals to view responsibility in the very narrowest sense.

For nuclear safety to be sustainable, each worker's view of responsibility must expand. The safest and most efficient plants are those where people take responsibility not only for their individual contributions to safety and efficiency, but also for the safety and efficiency of the entire plant. Pride and sense of ownership of this caliber do not arise by accident. They are the result of management actions to create a supportive, questioning environment. And this is very hard to do when you don't have the resources to pay your employees.

As in the rest of their industrial sectors, these countries must find ways to pay adequate salaries, provide funds for necessary maintenance and improvements and, in general, support their nuclear infrastructures in a way which assures a high priority to safety over time. This task will require a major and persistent effort on the part of the energy ministries and the commitment of substantial resources for upgrades, spare parts, maintenance and effective regulation. Such efforts can not be financed by western governments. They must originate within the societies themselves, and they must increasingly draw on commercial lending through international financial institutions and involvement by the private nuclear industry worldwide.

Thus, progress on nuclear safety will depend increasingly on economic reforms; on the willingness of western commercial interests to invest in these economies; and on the willingness of the operating organizations of Russian, Ukrainian and certain Eastern European plants to invest in their people.

Annex I: Safety Upgrades and Cost Estimating Methodology

The JPNAS did not address quantitative levels of safety for nuclear power in the traditional sense. Because of limited time and resources, no PRA's or PSA's were performed. However, existing safety studies were used to identify the set of upgrades for use in the JEPAS and JPNAS. The safety upgrades for operating RBMK's, VVER 440's, VVER-1000's and partially completed VVER-1000's were identified as:

1. Upgrades that are already being implemented as part of the existing Russian upgrade program. Upgrades in this program that are either partially complete or not yet implemented were costed on a percent complete basis.
2. A selected subset of the safety related upgrades for the International Users Group (IUG) of Soviet Designed Reactors and published in a March 1994 reports prepared for the World Association of Nuclear Operators (WANO).
3. Engineering studies that will lead to detailed upgrades in addition to those identified in 1 and 2 above.
4. Several possible confinement/containment systems for RBMK and first generation VVER-440's, including a full U.S. style containment retrofit.

The upgrades identified in 1 and 2 above would have the effect of narrowing the gap between the existing level of safety at Russian plants and current Russian safety standards. The inclusion of the upgrades that would result from 3 and the confinement/containment upgrades from 4 would have the effect of narrowing the gap between the existing level of safety at Russian plants and current Western standards. However, in every case, full containment for older reactors turned out to be too costly.

The cost estimating process began by selecting U.S. based reactor templates to represent Russian designs. All of these cost estimates were converted from a U.S. basis (*U.S. dollars for materials purchased in and labor performed in, the U.S.*) to a Russian basis (*U.S. dollars for materials purchased in and labor performed in, Russia*) by applying a series of conversion factors provided by the Russian Energy Research Institute (ERI) for use by the JEPAS. For the purposes of this study these factors are:

TABLE 4.2.

Conversion Item	Factor
Equipment	0.50
Construction Materials	0.70
Metals	0.75
Labor	0.10

The specific parameters used to modify and complete these templates (including design details, mass, size, capacity, etc.) were provided by Russian experts. The cost estimation of the system/facility was computed on the basis of the corrected parameters.

Annex II: Ukraine's Energy Sector: Negotiating the Group of Seven (G-7) Comprehensive Program

At the Naples Summit and the European Union's Corfu meeting in July 1994, the G-7 proposed a cooperative Action Plan for assisting Ukraine's energy sector for the purpose of obtaining early closure of the RBMK reactors at Chornobyl. The plan was submitted to the President of Ukraine by the Prime Minister of Italy, that year's G-7 chairman. Laborious negotiations followed, which bore little fruit between the Naples and Halifax Summit Meetings. Accordingly, the G-7 put together a new package, based in large part on a much more comprehensive action plan for restructuring the Ukrainian energy economy. It was this Action Plan that led to conclusion and signature, on December 20, 1995 of an MOU with the Ukrainian Government that pledges both sides to "...a Comprehensive Program to support the decision of Ukraine to close the Chornobyl Nuclear Power Plant by the year 2000 as formulated by President Kuchma in his statement of April 13, 1995 and in his letter of August 8, 1995, to G-7 leaders. The Program will thus implement the commitments of the leaders of the G-7, made in Naples, Italy in 1994 and Halifax, Canada in 1995."

Chornobyl is not just one of the reactors that has certain physical characteristics that led to a devastating nuclear accident in 1986. Rather, Chornobyl is the single most dangerous nuclear power reactor site in the world; not just because of its design, but because the Ukrainian government can't afford to operate it any more with any degree of safety. Operators are not being paid and have been leaving for better paying jobs elsewhere; fuel is being scavenged from the closed second unit—fuel not at currently specified levels of enrichment—and this is admitted to be dangerous by the operating organization; the site remains contaminated; storage of spent fuel is inadequate; one could go on and on. This is why the Group of Seven nations agreed to offer to help shut it down.

The Comprehensive Program with Ukraine is a commitment to close this site while setting up an energy plan for Ukraine that emphasizes economic and energy efficiency, conservation measures, signature of the NPT, western assistance in safety assessments and a least cost approach to energy development, and a package of western investment assistance to help the Ukrainians recover their economy from the reeling inflation it now faces.

5

Nuclear Power and Civil Society in Post-Soviet Russia

Gert-Rüdiger Wegmarshaus

The theoretical framework of this paper follows, as the title may suggest, a dual approach: it attempts to converge two different and still mostly separated strains of argumentation, two distinct fields of inquiry. On the one hand, it examines the social studies of science and technology, and on the other, the political studies of post-communist, transforming societies.

1. The first line of argumentation I will draw on are the debates on the social conditions (including cultural settings, economic constraints and political processes) of science and technology and the assessment of their likely consequences. These debates, within the sociology of science and technology, provide strong evidence against the so called "technological determinism." Recent sociological reflections as well as studies in the history of science and technology reveal a complex picture of the interconnections between science, technology and society. Although the advancement of modern technology influences and shapes the society and the ways in which people produce goods and communicate with each other, it hardly makes sense to regard technology as the ultimate driving force of human development. There is a remarkable influence on technology exerted by society, i.e., by the accepted value system, by the people's perception of benefits and dangers involved in new technologies, by the legal framework regulating scientific inquiry, by political strategies and even military goals and options.[1]

Strongly connected to these questions are the theoretical discussions on and the empirical investigations into the various kinds
of risk perception, risk evaluation and risk communication in
general and in particular concerning risks involved in new
technologies.[2]

2. The second line of argumentation on which this paper will draw
are the debates on the nature of the Soviet system, including its
political order, its economy and its social psychology. There have
been various theoretical attempts to interpret the Soviet reform
movement from above: "Perestroika." These investigations include
the consideration of its goals, its achievements and its unintended
results. The most recent studies on Post-Soviet realities are
focussing on the probability of genuine reform and real progress
toward parliamentary democracy and market economy in the
successor republics of the USSR.[3]

Considering the case of nuclear power in the late Soviet Union as well
as in Russia today I intend to converge these two different fields of
analysis: Science and Technology Studies (STS) and Soviet Studies. If the
theoretical assumption of STS, that the genesis of new technologies as
well as ways and methods of assessing their impact is largely determined
by society (its values, economic factors and political institutions), is true
in general, then this thesis should be applicable to the study of technology in Communist and post-Communist societies as well.

The assumptions of Soviet- and post-Soviet studies on the nature of
the Soviet system and the process of democratization and Westernization
in the post-Soviet republics, the achievements and the obstacles on that
way shall be proved in the particular field of science and technology
studies and the case of nuclear power.

Whether Russia is becoming a country following in its development
the western model of society is today still an open question. Theoretically, the question may be raised: should Russia become a western-type
country? This question is based on the assumption that there is a
historical significance and a universal applicability of the western model
of society combining democracy with a market economy. Empirically: can
Russia become a western type society? The underlying assumption of this
question is that one can distinguish at least some features of (western
type) modernity in Russia, serving as a starting point for post-Soviet
developments. This empirical part of the question, i.e., the indispensable
preconditions for the transformability of post-Soviet Russia is being
addressed (at least partially) by examining the ways Russia is handling
the nuclear power complex.

Questions such as: What regulating bodies exist or will emerge?, what legal frameworks are being used?, what forms of lobbying for and against nuclear power have been established?, how strong are environmental groups and what are the attitudes of the population towards the risks of nuclear industry?, may guide further investigations. Hence the focus of this article is the necessary circumstances for creating institutions of a civil society in post-Soviet Russia capable of running its nuclear power complex at internationally acceptable risk levels. But before turning to the topic, it is worthwhile to recall the social and the technical revolutions as well as the military dilemmas and purposes posed by nuclear development to humanity.

Nuclear Power: Necessity or Contingency?

There is an often repeated historical statement, that two events have largely shaped the course of the 20th century: the Russian Revolution of 1917 and the explosion of the atomic bomb at Hiroshima in August 1945. History surely is not pre-determined by single events, but the long-lasting significance of these two dates can hardly be denied. Needless to say, both events had similar effects imposed on politics at a very different velocity. They shocked, changed and altered the world dramatically, but—to use a metaphor—what the Bolshevik political revolution needed 10 days to accomplish took the scientific-technical revolution, embodied in the American bomb, only 10 seconds.[4]

Both events, although seemingly different in origin, must be regarded against a larger, common background. The Bolshevik revolution, having been prepared by deep, strong currents of social unrest in the first decades of the 20th century, materialized in a political explosion, smashing not only the shaky, unfinished building of democracy in Russia, but threatening the very foundations of the libertarian and constitutional societies in the West. The political history of the 20th century appears in retrospective largely as a battle between Totalitarianism and Democracy. This clash of ideologies: Marxism against Liberalism (a Closed Society versus an Open one) shaped international politics for more than 70 years.[5]

The explosion of the American atomic bomb in August 1945 marked a technical revolution, shaping the world politically and economically until today. But it is inadequate to judge the atomic bomb as a scientific achievement in itself. The atomic project in its technical dimensions and in its military applications had become possible because of the political situation of that time. The initial creation of the American bomb can be regarded as an act of self-defense, can be seen as a scientific and technological shield against the expansionism of totalitarian regimes. It is a well known and documented fact in the history of science that the fear of a possible Nazi-bomb triggered the Manhattan-Project.[6] Furthermore, growing suspicion of Soviet military power and political influence after the victory over Germany and Japan contributed more than any strategy of avoiding allied casualties in the Pacific theatre of war to the actual dropping of "Little Boy" and "Fat Man" in August 1945.[7]

Although the atomic thunder over Japan did finalize the war, its hidden message and its strategic significance became obvious only during the famous Fulton Speech of Winston Churchill, in which the former British wartime prime minister remarked that the totalitarian system of Soviet Communism imposing an "iron curtain" on Eastern Europe had to be stopped by any means including diplomatic influence, political pressure, economic incentives and military deterrence.

Efforts by the U.S. and the UN to keep the nuclear weapons under international control ended in vain. The logic of the Cold War resulted in the arms race between the United States and the Soviet Union. As predicted by physicists and feared by politicians, within a few years the USSR had become a nuclear super power as well, challenging the West politically and technologically. For the West the nuclear arms race in the 1950s posed a certain dilemma in handling and justifying the huge nuclear complex, for no one could anticipate that ultimately it would surpass the communist adversary in stockpiling annihilation power. The arms race seemed to be prolonged ad infinitum, causing a public image of the "atom" as an agent of death and destruction.

Fortunately, the speedy economic recovery in the United States and in Western Europe at that time made it possible to fill the "Nuclear Legitimation Gap" by civilian application of specially designed nuclear installations: the nuclear power stations.[8] To meet the growing demand of electricity by producing it seemingly out of nothing (excluding "a few pounds" of Uranium) was a challenging prospect. It helped to sustain economic growth by offering cheap and available electricity to virtually every household, creating incentives for widespread use of modern technical appliances like TV sets, washing machines, air-conditioners etc. Thus in the West, the general economic and social up-swing after the war produced a remarkable side effect: the closing of the "legitimation gap" in nuclear matters by promising general wealth and universal health by forcing the hidden energies of nature to serve peacefully mankind.

Nuclear Power in the Soviet Period

It is not surprising that the debates in the Soviet Union over the specific issues of developing nuclear physics and using its results for the build-up of a huge nuclear industry beginning at the end of World War II can properly be understood only if one pays attention to the more general patterns of policy, politics and ideology of the Communist Party ruling the country. These general patterns throw light on the specific traits and forms of nuclear power discourse within the Soviet system as well as on the lack and the shortcomings of that discourse in political and public terms (both in style of argumentation and structure of public discussion).

It is sufficient to recall two major structural political and economic decisions made by the Soviet government under Lenin in the early 1920s. The combination of these two decisions predetermined more or less the character, scope and possible impact of discussions on energy policy in general and nuclear power issues in particular. These two decisions are well known. The first was the adoption of the ambitious GOELRO Plan, elaborated by a team of Russian scientists and engineers headed by Krzhizhanovsky.[9] This plan had been personally approved by Lenin, who hoped that by putting this blueprint into practice Soviet Russia would eventually overcome its industrial backwardness and become a wealthy nation. Expectations rose even higher than that. Taking into consideration the vast energy resources of Soviet Russia and envisaging the prospects of building a socialist society in a single country (at least for the time being), Lenin pointed out his ideas for the Soviet future in his famous formula: Communism=Soviet power+Electrification of the entire country.[10]

The fate of this formula is well known. The somewhat ludicrous expectations and hazardous promises of the late Khrushchev era, when the power engineering program, including nuclear power build up, was well on its way, that the next generation of Soviet people would be living under Communism[11] should be explained not only simply by referring to the revolutionary pathos but by considering the scientific and technical nature of the entire political and social life under the Soviet system.

This brings us to the second major decision: Having gained power in the wake of the successful military coup on October 25, 1917 (what was later called in a self-laudatory manner "The Great October Socialist Revolution") the Bolshevik Party abolished in three steps the structural prerequisites of political, and eventually social modernity in their country. First, the Bolsheviks dissolved the National Assembly, resulting from the February Revolution. The abolition of the Parliament proved fateful. Second, during the Civil War and finally after the abortive uprising at Kronstadt in 1921, they prohibited the existence of all political parties with the exception of their own. Third, in 1921 Lenin imposed a ban on all intra-party factions or wings with the result, that the ultimate power of obtaining relevant information (*Herrschaftswissen*) and making decisions (*Entscheidungskompetenz*) was transferred to the inner circle of the Politburo.[12]

These decisions resulted in the creation of a society in Russia that departed from the road of democracy, parliamentary decision-making process and a gradual evolution toward a free market economy and the rule of law.[13] By establishing an authoritarian, Party-autocratic type of statehood the revolutionary expectations of the poor and underprivileged classes in the Russian society had been turned into the grotesque reality of Byzantinism, self-sacrifice of the individual and the nightmare of the Gulags. Thus the Soviet Union evolved in manner, best described by Hannah Arendt as Totalitarian Society.[14]

Although there were some significant achievements in Industrialization, including power engineering, during the years before and after World War II, Soviet society was modernized in a peculiar fashion.[15] The clear progress, achieved in the fields of industry, science and technology has to be assessed against the background of fundamental shortcomings in public participation and public involvement in the decision-making process at the governmental, administrative, and strategic levels. These shortcomings determined not only the basic scientific and technical approach to society as a whole but shaped the science and technology policy as well. Strategic planning and implementation of decisions in these fields were entirely concentrated in the hands of party and state political bureaucrats, scientific administrators and technocrats.

Science and technology policy in the Soviet Union in general and nuclear policy in particular have been performed in a technocratic manner, giving a considerable degree of influence to nuclear physicists and engineers in matters concerning the planning and performing of an energy program.[16] In the 1950s and 1960s the use of nuclear power in the Soviet Union was regarded as a necessary prerequisite for attaining the goals of Communist society. According to the official Leninist ideology, Soviet nuclear armament should provide an offensive "umbrella" against a hostile "bourgeois" environment, should foster the revolutionary process all over the world, while the "peaceful" use of nuclear power should provide abundant energy, indispensable for an affluent communist, egalitarian society."[17]

This rather naive confidence in nuclear power as an ultimate benevolent technological agent reflected the prevailing scientific paradigm in Soviet social thought, thus revealing hidden positivist currents in the

Marxist-Leninist *Weltanschauung*. There is obviously no need here to draw a general picture of the Soviet nuclear power program, beginning after World War II, nor is it necessary to mark the various stages, ups and downs in the implementation of the nuclear power program, depending on the availability of gas and oil resources, the development of fuel prices and longer lasting trends of investment in capital and labour in the Soviet economy.[18]

It will be sufficient to mention here the heavy nuclear power build up program, commencing in the early 1970s. The major reasons for this program, as far as the Soviet Union is concerned are easily recalled to mind: Despite the discovery, the rapid exploration and the increasing exploitation of the vast west Siberian oil fields and the huge resources of natural gas and coal, there still remained a dual gap between energy supply and energy demands: a dual gap because not only did the supply fall steadily behind the ever increasing demands of industry and households, but there was also the traditional geographic imbalance between the energy supply regions east of the Urals and the heavily industrialized and densely populated regions in the European part of Russia and Ukraine. For these reasons it was decided to meet the energy demands in European Russia and Ukraine by speeding up the construction of nuclear power plants at a wide range of locations: from the north near Leningrad to the South near Odesa and in the Crimea.[19] The goals were ambitious: the power plants were designed not only to serve the needs of industry and households in supplying electricity. Additionally some of these stations were designed to produce energy for heating official buildings as well as hundreds of thousands of apartments in the residential areas of major industrial cities.

In the 1970s, the nuclear power program of the Soviet Union also had an international dimension: the COMECON adopted far-reaching plans for the construction of several nuclear power plants in each European COMECON country. Moreover, it was decided to create a COMECON-based reactor building industry with a high degree of specialization in the production of parts and components. These joint efforts, it was hoped, would result in the construction and production of reactors at a high rate of output at the Volgodonsk reactor building plant. Because of the traditional shortages in the centralized planned economies of the COMECON countries these high goals were never attained.

What were the specific traits of nuclear power discourse in Soviet society?

1. According to the structure of political power in the USSR the principal decisions about the use of nuclear energy as well as about timing and scope of a nuclear energetics build up had to be

made at the highest level of the Communist Party hierarchy: the Politburo of the Central Committee of the CPSU. This does not mean that these decisions have been totally involuntary, unbalanced or not well grounded. On the contrary, within the logic of the administrative bureaucratic system of power much was done to reach economically balanced and technologically grounded decisions: a number of departments of the Central Committee prepared internal reports on a wide variety of related issues as well as departments in the Council of Ministers (Soviet government), the State Committee for Science and Technology and the Academy of Sciences. The usual means of releasing information about nuclear energy plans was the Party Congress and the announcement of a new Five-Year Plan. Needless to say, neither the economic and technological planning in general nor the nuclear power program in particular faced open criticism or were even questioned at official State or Party rallies.[20]

2. The Research and Science system including the Academy of Sciences and its research centers, institutes of the Ministry of Defence, institutes related to ministries of the industry and some special establishments of higher technological education (*Tekhnicheskie vuzy*) have been playing an important role in developing and checking various scientific and technological blueprints. The R & D work done by these scientific and technological institutions led to some different types of graphite moderated and water pressurized reactors. According to western specialists the common features of the R & D efforts in Soviet reactor construction program have been the pushing of larger and larger single units (for the sake of economy of scale) to a degree, that never would have been licensed in the West and with significantly lower safety standards than the West (especially the lack of reactor containment).[21] These two areas of discourse (the internal political and the internal scientific technological) have been described by Joan DeBardeleben as the "esoteric nuclear power discourse" in the Soviet Union.[22]

3. The Legislature did not play the role in these sensitive questions it plays in the West. The Supreme Soviet of the USSR as well as the soviets at the republican and local levels have been totally subordinated to the Party hierarchy. No general open or even controversal debates in the Parliaments were reported. No special sessions of parliamentary subcommittees (Science and Technology, Environmental Protection) led to critical or controversial public statements with regard to the nuclear energy program.

4. No independent judiciary existed. For this reason neither officials at the republican or local level or private persons could defend their legitimate interests against an overriding Party and State bureaucracy putting into practice largescale scientific and techno-logical projects, afflicting the lives of hundreds of thousands of people. The whole process of choosing appropriate building sites for nuclear power stations (ecological, seismic, economic dimen-sions) as well as the erection and exploitation of nuclear power stations appeared to have taken place in a manner free of law, if not to say in an unlawful manner.[23]

5. The lack of an independent and free press, unable and unwilling to report on difficulties and contradictions within the nuclear power program and incapable of reflecting the attitudes, fears and concerns of scientists, engineers and the ordinary people in these sensitive questions resulted in an uninformed, manipulated public, mostly uncritical and unaware of the dangers and risks inherent in nuclear technology.

6. Not surprisingly, the task of critical reflection of the direction and dimensions of scientific and technological progress with regard to Soviet society in general and to ecological hazards in particular were fulfilled, at least partially, by novelists and free lance writers. The writings of Aitmatov and Rasputin come to mind in this respect.[24] In summary, one can say that the way nuclear technol-ogy was pushed forward in the USSR illustrates the general thesis of the social conditioning of technological change: Military ambitions, political prestige, economic constraints and social utopianism shaped the Soviet nuclear power program itself as well as the climate of secrecy and the official and public neglect of the dangers inherent in nuclear technology.[25]

Perestroika and the Nuclear Issue

Perestroika, the reform process initiated by General secretary Gorbachev was a unique, far-reaching attempt to modernize Soviet society which, in spring 1985, was in a state of economic stagnation, political alienation and psychological depression. For several reasons Perestroika failed to reach the intended objectives, and ultimately produced quite unexpected results.[26] But Perestroika showed that a society in motion is changing the set of social, political and even psychological factors, regulating the usage of science and technology. The case of the nuclear industry during Perestroika, especially after Chornobyl, is a good illustration of how the development and the use of technology is shaped by social factors.

There is a close interconnection between the general process of democratization, public involvement in political and economic affairs started in 1985 and the Chornobyl accident one year later. Perestroika and Glasnost gradually made possible a more open discussion about the ecological hazards in nuclear technologies. The Chornobyl catastrophe itself reinforced the already developing process of democratization, and gave an additional impetus to the people's demand for Glasnost, political pluralism and participation.

The Chornobyl accident of April 1986, which placed in severe doubt the future success of Perestroika, was the starting point for terminating the technological determinism in social thought as well as the catalyst of a vigorous grass-root environmental movement. Chornobyl and its aftermath had a twofold effect: It triggered an unprecedented ecological awareness among the Soviet people and it effectively undermined the already waning confidence in Soviet authorities and the Party state.

What were the main features of change in the political, scientific and public discussion of nuclear power in the Soviet Union during Perestroika? It can be shown, that the degree of open and free discussion about nuclear power during Perestroika depended almost entirely on the degree of political freedom achieved within the process of Glasnost. Despite the emergence of a new style of politics by Gorbachev beginning in March 1985, despite all his public statements and speeches at public meetings and Party conferences, the accident at the Chornobyl nuclear power plant and the information released about it, showed how little had changed in practice at that time.

The shameful story of the official Soviet news coverage of the Chornobyl accident is well documented in both the West,[27] and also in contemporary Russia and Ukraine itself.[28] A detailed inquiry into the news coverage about Chornobyl and its consequences (print media, radio and TV) proves that the amount of critical information about the seriousness of the accident, the possible ecological and health risks had been restricted as long as the Party had been able to put pressure to bear on the media. With the waning of the Party's influence and power critical articles increasingly appeared, not only about the true dimensions of the Chornobyl catastrophe but also about the background of the atomic program of the Soviet Union, about failures and shortcomings in reactor design, and lack of public participation in the decision-making process.

In the period prior to 1988, the year when the 19th Party Conference took place (this event was a watershed within Perestroika) publications on Chornobyl and related nuclear power issues were prepared in the usual Soviet manner, i.e., playing down the scale of the accident and denying major ecological or health hazards for the population; focussing on the heroic work of the Soviet rescue workers (mainly firemen, servicemen, physicians), praising the supervision of the rescue operations by Party and Soviet officials as well as by leading scientists and engineers, flown in from the major scientific centers, dealing with nuclear matters, showing gratitude for international help and opening at the same time a fierce propaganda battle against the alleged Western "Anti-Soviet Chornobyl Campaign." The only exception to this rule during that time was the appearance of theater play named *The Sarcophagus*, dealing in a more open manner with the moral dimensions of man's failure to make use of the forces of nature in a cautious and solicitous way.[29] This highlights once more the important role, played by novelists, writers and artists in filling the gap left open by the daily press, TV and scientific publications.

Beginning in 1989 with the open political battle between the reformers and the Communist hardliners within the Party, with the diminishing of the Party's influence in Soviet society and with the emerging of first sign of the establishment of a multiparty system, the discussions in the press and in the electronic media about Chornobyl and the Soviet atomic program as a whole, including military aspects (weapon development, testing sites) gradually became more open, and free of pressure from the higher ranks of Party and State bureaucracy. In 1990 and especially in 1991, when the Soviet Union was beginning to break apart and the real powers in the republics had been transferred to the newly elected parliamentary bodies, the full impact of the Chornobyl tragedy on the Ukrainian and Belarusian people was revealed. On the fifth anniversary of the Chornobyl accident at the end of April 1991, conferences were held in both Kyiv and Minsk on the consequences and the various ramifications of the Chornobyl disaster.[30]

Eventually critical comments began to appear about major short-comings and even defects in the design of the RBMK (Chornobyl type) reactor, thus highlighting that not only the irresponsible behaviour of the technical and engineering staff at the Chornobyl station is to blame for what occurred, but that some inherent weak spots in the very constructon of the reactor have to be regarded as the main contributor to that catastrophe. Moreover, articles appeared in the press and television programs featured aspects of the military use of nuclear energy, including the radioactive contamination of large areas in the Urals and in Kazakhstan, through either accidents that occurred in the past and were kept secret by the military, or as a result of the testing of nuclear warheads in the "Semipalatinsk Polygon."

Triggered by these publications concerned citizens in many of these afflicted regions (Kazakhstan, the Urals region, northern and central Russia, Ukraine, Belarus, the Baltic Republics) came together and founded either movements in protection of the environment and defying nuclear technologies (both military and peaceful) or Green or Ecological Parties. One of the influential movements, which played a significant role during the political struggle for Ukrainian independence was the Green Movement of Ukraine.[31]

Post-Soviet Russia and the Nuclear Power Question

There is general agreement among political scientists that the end of the Soviet Union in 1991 and the foundation of democratic republics within the CIS has in many respects paved the way for the transition of Russia to a western type parliamentary democracy. It remains an open question, however, whether Russia will succeed on its quest for democratic rule. The establishment of democratic institutions and procedures in Russia after 1991 (a presidency and Parliament elected under competitive conditions; the division of power between legislative, executive, and judicial authorities; the existence of a pluralistic media system encompassing a wide range of political and ideological positions) is a particular development similar to the waves of democratization after 1945 throughout the world.

Nevertheless some researchers maintain that the process of establishing democracies in Eastern Europe is not to be confused with the simple installation of parliamentary institutions. The problem is much deeper. Real progress in matters of East-European democratization depends on institution-building as well as on the emergence of structures and behavioral patterns of a "civil society." In using the term "civil society" the author is aware of the vagueness and even ambiguity of this concept: whether civil society encompasses the institutions of the democratic state or not is an issue of contention among scholars. But having in mind the historical evolution of the civil society in Western Europe with its emancipation from the *ancien regime*, it is clear that the introduction of the concept "civil society" during the 1980s within the Communist states of Eastern Europe was either a matter of dissident circles (Poland, Czechoslovakia, Hungary) opposing the existing state,[32] or owed more to reform oriented intellectuals within the higher ranks of the ruling parties desiring to improve the state (notably and most influentially in the Soviet Union under Gorbachev).[33]

Assuming for historical and methodological reasons that the civil society exists independently from the insitutions of the democratic state, it is hard to deny that in the case of Russia, as well as in the other East European countries, we face the problem that the social traditions in these countries are lacking a great deal of "civilian elements."

Most of the societies of Central and Eastern Europe which were later to find themselves with the communist bloc, and are currently in the process of systemic transformation, did not experience this (western) path of development: "...their peripheral character and backwardness were not conducive to the development of civil society.... Thus there was no mass socialization culminating in the acceptance of the institutions of the state, familiarity with their structure, and assumption of responsibility for them."[34]

Hence the survival of the democratic state in Russia today depends to a large extent on the emergence of a civil society, its mentality, its patterns of action and standards of behavior. In this respect there is a peculiarity in post-Soviet Russia and a specific difference from Western Europe. In Western Europe civil society developed prior to the structures of the democratic state; in Russia today one can distinguish structures of parliamentarism, but there is no civil society comparable to that in the West. Hence the emergence of a civil society is to be fostered by the state itself, not to gain more power over the people, but on the contrary, to become less powerful and yet more stable, as the people begin to take care of themselves and their lives. If there is no progress in creating a civil society in Russia, then the republican institutions in that country will remain little more than a mere "facade": vulnerable, weak and fragile.

Having noted this relationship between institutions of democratic statehood and civil society in Eastern Europe, let us consider the question what has changed in the Russian civil nuclear complex since independence in 1991? How can these changes can be interpreted in terms of the concept of a civil society?

The Political Perspective

After the collapse of the USSR in late 1991 the Russian Federation as well as the other successor republics with nuclear power installations (Ukraine, Lithuania, Armenia) had to come to terms with the Soviet nuclear legacy from scientific, technological, economic, ecological and psychological perspectives. The dissolution of the Soviet Union had a negative impact on the functioning of the nuclear energy facilities in each republic: the once highly centralized unified power system had been split, impeding the flow of necessary technical information as well as the circulation of nuclear fuel.

The process of dividing the bodies of state supervision and regulation into independent agencies (begun already in the late Soviet period) had been continued at the level of the national republics. In Russia and Ukraine different state organizations began to operate independently, entrusted with the supervision or operation of nuclear installations.[35] Both the Russian and the Ukrainian Parliaments have passed legislation regulating the clean-up operations in the afflicted Chornobyl regions and the ways of compensating the victims and the damage caused to the local population.[36] State-financed scientific, technical and medical centers have been set up for gathering information about the extent of environmental pollution, the state of public health in the contaminated regions and for oncological treatment of severely irradiated patients.[37]

The established multi-party-system reflects the growing concern over environmental issues within the population. The programmatic statements of almost every political party or grouping contain segments or passages concerning the protection of the environment.[38] Having played a prominent role in unveiling the damage caused by Chornobyl and having mobilized the population against nuclear installations, local environmental movements have remained active. As a result of the influence of protest movements the build-up of new nuclear power plants has been brought to a virtual standstill.

The Economic Perspective

The dissolution of the Soviet Union has led to the disruption of the economic ruble-zone and to the introduction of national currencies. Hence the formerly united nuclear power complex in Russia and Ukraine has been split up financially and economically. For Ukraine nuclear fuel supply and waste disposal is now a matter of foreign trade with Russia. Russia is the only succesor republic of the USSR enjoying the benefits of a self-sufficient national atomic energy complex.

The painful process of economic transformation from central planning to free market competition put severe strains on the governments in Russia, Ukraine and even Lithuania, preventing them from closing down the inherently unsafe RBMK and early VVER reactors. In both Russia and Ukraine the attempts during recent years to introduce a market economy and to privatize large stocks of capital have led to huge inflation. Subsequently a massive disruption of mutual payments between enterprises has occurred, afflicting the state-owned nuclear power stations as well. Workers and technicians at the power stations are not being paid regularly. On several occasions the personnel has threatened to go on strike in order to demand regular payment of salary.

Because of poor working conditions and dramatically reduced salaries—both in relative and absolute terms—for the staff in the nuclear complex a portion of the younger, ambitious engineers and workers is leaving the enterprises opening up a security gap. Nevertheless, Russia and Ukraine are still forced to rely heavily on nuclear energy production: Russia for reasons of the traditional geographical imbalance of energy supply and demand, Ukraine because of an absolute shortage in national oil and gas reserves.[39]

The Scientific-Technological Perspective

There is a continuing discussion in the scientific community of nuclear physicists and technicians about the possible future of the civil nuclear program in Russia. This discussion is being publicized in general and special scientific journals.[40] The main topics of that discussion are the improvement of safety at existing nuclear facilities, possible traditional and non-traditional alternatives to nuclear power, economic and safety features of new reactor designs, problems of waste disposal and reprocessing. A special center to inform the general public about nuclear technology questions has been established. Its publications are aimed at a Russian audience, critical about the alleged benefits of nuclear technology.[41]

In summarizing the outlined features of nuclear policies and nuclear power debates in the post-Soviet era it is fair to conclude that the structural and institutional changes in the atomic complex as well as the relative opennness of the political and scientific debate on nuclear power demonstrate a certain progress of Russia and Ukraine toward the model of a democratic society. The least one can say is that structural foundations for a democratic and pluralistic discourse on science and technology in general and the utilization of nuclear power in particular have been laid. This does not mean, however, that one can expect in the near future a comprehensive or even sound Russian or Ukrainian strategy on how to use the existing nuclear facilities, how to improve their safety, how to succeed in designing new types of reactors and where to place them.

Conclusion: The Dilemmas of Russian and Ukrainian Nuclear Policy

The first dilemma is based on economics. It is a result of the so far painful and not very successful shift to market economy in Russia and in Ukraine. In both republics, notwithstanding the sharp decline in GNP, there exists a shortage of energy supply mostly as a result of the use of old energy wasting technologies. This creates a need to generate electricity from insecure nuclear reactors. In Ukraine, given the absence of domestic oil and gas reserves the need for electricity generated in insecure nuclear power stations can hardly be denied. This explains, but does not justify the strange politics of the Kyiv government concerning the promised shut down of the Chornobyl station.

In Russia the situation is quite different: the country possesses huge natural ressources of oil, gas and coal. But the need for nuclear power in the European part of Russia, especially in the big cities of Moscow and St. Petersburg is a matter of fact. An additional factor behind the domestic use of nuclear power is the traditional structure of Russian exports: The main source of hard currency revenues is the export of crude oil and natural gas to the West. This export strategy imposes limitations on alternatives using gas turbines for power generation instead of nuclear reactors.

The second dilemma is of a scientific-technical nature, but related to economics. The existing Russian civilian nuclear complex, consisting of dozens of scientific and technical institutions with thousands of highly qualified scientists and engineers, is able to design and produce new, safer types of pressurized water reactors. In order to improve—wherever feasible—the safety of the existing reactors, Russian scientists are willing to cooperate with the West. The scientific discussions in Russia reflect the need for safer reactors as well as the ability to achieve that goal. But unfortunately at that rather abstract point the consensus and the capacity in Soviet nuclear science ends. Given the economic situation in today's Russia, no one can offer a clear-cut realistic strategy for a renewed nuclear power program.[42] Furthermore, any prolonged economic crisis in Russia will certainly weaken the scientific and technical basis for innovations in the nuclear industry and therefore damage the capability of Russia to modernize or replace its aging nuclear reactors.

The third and most powerful dilemma is a political one. The existing political institutions and governing bodies in Russia and Ukraine (Presidency, Parliament, independent Judiciary) are being legitimized by the will of the people expressed in free elections. In that respect any parliamentary decisions or presidential *ukazy* enjoy a political legitimacy much greater than the decisions of the "people's assemblies" in Soviet times. But this is a rather formalistic statement, true only in principle, for a given moment of time. The political legitimacy of any institution and its decisions is derived from the existence of democratic procedures and adherence to democratic rules.[43]

In this respect the political institutions in Russia and Ukraine today can be regarded as democratic ones. But once the democratic rules of the political game are given, then the legitimacy of decisions is self-asserting or self-denying for pragmatic reasons: The legitimacy of political decisions is also dependent on how these decisions are being put into practice and to what extent they are being honored by the various political actors. If parliaments are producing legislation nobody cares about, then the legitimacy of these laws is being undermined. Many parliamentary and governmental decisions in Ukraine and Russia have at least doubtful practical relevance in daily politics. Clearly the Russian and Ukrainian population have little respect for parliaments that indulge in idle, vain and fruitless debates.

Under these circumstances neither Russia nor Ukraine is to be expected to develop and implement a sound, technically and economically grounded as well as a politically legitimate nuclear energy program in the near future.

Notes

1. Everett Mendelsohn and Peter Weingart, eds., *The Social Production of Scientific Knowledge* (Dordrecht and Boston, 1977); Bernard Sciele, ed. *When Science Becomes* (Ottawa: University of Ottawa Press, 1994); Wojciech Gasparski and Timo Airaksinen, eds., *Science in Society* (Warsaw, 1995); Peter Weingart, *Wissensproduktion und Soziale Struktur, stw 155* (Frankfurt/Main, 1976); Peter Weingart (Hrsg.), *Technik als sozialer Prozess, stw 795* (Frankfurt/Main, 1989).

2. Mary Douglas and Aaron Wildavsky, *Risk and Culture* (Berkeley, CA, London, 1982); Wolfgang Krohn and Georg Krücken (Hrsg.), *Riskante Technologien: Reflexion und Regulation. Einführung in die sozialwissenschaftliche Risikoforschung, stw 1098* (Frankfurt/Main, 1993).

3. Stephen White, *Gorbachev and After* (Cambridge, 1992); Rachel Walker, *Six Years that Shook the World. Perestroika—the Impossible Project* (Manchester, 1993); Amin Saikal and William Maley, *Russia in Search of its Future* (Cambridge, 1994); Karen Dawisha and Bruce Parrot, *Russia and the New States of Eurasia* (Cambridge, 1994); Klaus von Beyme, *Reformpolitik und sozialer Wandel in der Sowjetunion (1970-1988)* (Baden-Baden, 1988); Meinhard Miegel (Hrsg.), *Das Ende der Sowjetunion* (Baden-Baden,1994); Klaus Segbers (Hrsg.), *Perestroika. Zwischenbilanz* (Frankfurt/Main, 1990); Klaus Segbers (Hrsg.), *Rußlands Zukunft: Räume und Regionen* (Baden-Baden, 1994); Klaus Segbers and Stephan de Spiegeleire, eds., *Post-Soviet Puzzles* (Baden-Baden, 1995).

4. See Hannah Arendt, *On Revolution* (New York, 1963), Introduction; Michael Salewski (Hrsg.), *Das Zeitalter der Bombe. Die Geschichte der atomaren Bedrohung von Hiroshima bis heute* (München, 1995).

5. Karl R. Popper, *The Open Society and its Enemies* (London, 1945); Hannah Arendt, *Elemente und Ursprünge totaler Herschaft* (Frankfurt/Main, 1955); Irving Howe, ed., *1984 Revisited. Totalitarianism in Our Century* (New York, 1983); Zbigniew Brzezinski, *The Grand Failure: The Birth and Death of Communism in the Twentieth Century* (New York, 1989); Abbott Gleason, *Totalitarianism: The Inner History of the Cold War* (Oxford, 1995).

6. Gideon Heimann, "Oppenheimer bekam sofort Skrupel," *Der Tagessiegel*, July 16, 1995, p. 23; Hermann Jensen, "Warum Hitler die Bombe nicht baute," *Die Zeit*, May 1, 1992, p. 13.

7. Gar Alperovitz, *The Decision To Use The Atomic Bomb* (New York, 1995); Thomas B. Allen and Norman Polmar, *Code-Name Downfall* (New York, 1995); Robert J. Lifton and Greg Mitchell, *Hiroshima in America. Fifty Years of Denial* (New York, 1995).

8. Boyd Norton, "The Early Years," in Michio Kaku and Jennifer Trainer, eds. *Nuclear Power. Both Sides* (New York, London, 1982), pp. 15-28; Joseph G. Morone and Edward J. Woodhouse, *The Demise of Nuclear Energy?* (New Haven, London), 1989, esp. Chapter 2: "Origins of the Light Water Reactor."

9. *Plan electrifikatsii RSFSR* (Moscow, 1920), 2d ed. 1955; G. Krshishanowski, *Die Hauptaufgaben der Elektrifizierung Russlands* (Moscow, 1920).

10. W.I. Lenin, *Werke* (Berlin, 1959), Vol. 31, pp. 414-415; ibid., pp. 278-279, 513.

11. N.S. Chrustschew, *Bericht des Zentralkommittees an den 22. Parteitag der KPdSU* (Moscow, 1962).

12. See Wolfgang Engler, *Versuch über den Staatssozialismus* (Frankfurt/M., 1992), pp. 26, ff.

13. Andrzej Walicki, *Marxism and the Leap to the Kingdom of Freedom. The Rise and Fall of the Communist Utopia* (Cambridge, 1995).

14. Hannah Arendt, *Elemente und Ursprünge totaler Herschaft* (Frankfurt/Main, 1955).

15. The proposed notion "Half-Developed Modernity" (in German: "Halbierte Moderne") may be instrumental in describing the peculiarities within the modernizing Soviet Union: tremendous progress in science, technology and industry against a background of political repression and ideological indoctrination. The question though, how to assess the modernization (industrial, social, scientific) of non democratic, totalitarian or authoritarian societies requires further investigation. Parallels between modernizing processes in Nazi Germany and the Soviet Union during the thirties may be drawn. In particular the question of social mobility and technological modernization in totalitarian societies needs to be analyzed.

16. Paul R. Josephson, "Atomic Culture in the USSR: Before and After Chernobyl," in Anthony James, Walter D. Connor, and David E. Powell eds., *Soviet Social Problems* (San Francisco, Oxford, 1991), pp. 57-77.

17. On the official Soviet line toward nuclear power, "the taming of the atom for peaceful and defensive purposes," see *Science in the USSR* (Moscow, 1973), p. 26. See also *Atomnoy energetike XX let* (Moscow, 1974).

18. David R. Marples, *Chernobyl & Nuclear Power in the USSR* (London: The Macmillan Press, 1987), pp. 37-70.

19. Ibid., pp. 71-93.

20. See *Proceedings of the 24th, 25th, 26th and 27th Party Congresses of the CPSU* (Moscow, 1971, 1976, 1981, and 1986).

21. On the Soviet nuclear program, see A.M. Petrosy'ants, *Problems of Nuclear Science and Technology. The Soviet Union as a World Nuclear Power* (Oxford, New York, 1981).

22. Joan T. DeBardeleben, "Esoteric Policy Debate: Nuclear Safety Issues in the Soviet Union and in the German Democratic Republic," *British Journal of Political Science*, 15 (1986): 227-253.

23. Donald D. Barry, "Political and Legal Aspects of the Development and Use of Nuclear Power in the USSR and Eastern Europe," in Peter Maggs, Gordon Smith, and George Ginsburgs, eds., *Soviet and East European Law and the Scientific Technical Revolution* (New York, 1982), pp. 159-180.

24. See V. Rasputin, *Abschied von Matjora* (Berlin, 1979); D. Aitmatov, *Der weisse Dampfer* (Berlin, 1974).

25. Zhores Medvedev, *Nuclear Disaster in the Urals* (New York, 1979); Zhores Medvedev, *The Legacy of Chernobyl* (Oxford, 1990); Victor Haynes and J. Marko Bojcun, *The Chernobyl Disaster: An Unanswerable Indictment of Nuclear Power* (London, 1988).

26. Hans Wassmund, *Die gescheiterte Utopie. Aufstieg und Fall der UdSSR* (München, 1993); Stephen White, *Gorbachev and After* (Glasgow, 1992); Rachel Walker, *Six years that Shook the World. Perestroika the Imposssible Project* (Manchester, 1993).

27. Marples, *Chernobyl & Nuclear Power in the USSR*, pp. 1-35.

28. See *I vpade zvezda polin* (Kiev, 1991). See also the book by Andrey Illesh, a Russian journalist, working with *Izvestiya: Chernobyl* (New York, 1987).

29. *The Sarcophagus* by Vladimir Gubarev was published in excerpts in *Sovetskaya kultura* in September 1986. See also the eyewitness accounts in Yuri Shcherbak, *Chernobyl: A Documentary Story* (London, 1988), and the novel by Volodymyr Yavorivsky, *Maria z polinom u kintsi stolittya*, published in the journal *Vitchyzna* in 1987.

30. David R. Marples, "Chernobyl: Observations on the Fifth Anniversary," *Soviet Economy*, Vol. 7, No. 2 (April-June 1991): 175-178.

31. David R. Marples, *The Social Impact of the Chernobyl Disaster* (New York, 1988); See also "Report on Tatarstan Anti-Nuclear Society's efforts to call for an All-Russian Referendum on nuclear power plants," *Postfactum* (Moscow), No. 10 (May 1992).

32. On Poland, see Piotr Ogrodzinski, "For Models of Civil Society and the Transformation in East-Central Europe," in Edmund Wnuk-Lipinski, ed., *After Communism* (Warsaw, 1995), pp. 183-184.

33. The concept of "Civil Society" was discussed during the 1980s by Soviet social scientists and philosophers, who maintained that "Democratic Socialism" should be based on the rule of law and on open discussions on the existing contradictions within society. On the former Soviet Union, see Gail W. Lapidus,

"State and Society: Toward the Emergence of Civil Society in the Soviet Union," in Seweryn Bialer, ed., *Politics, Society and Nationality Inside Gorbachev's Russia* (Boulder, Co., 1989). See also Anatolij Butenko, "Zum Verlauf der Perestroika," in Klaus Segbers, ed., *Perestroika. Zwischenbilanz* (Frankfurt/Main, 1990), pp. 367-383.

34. Jadwiga Stanizkis, "In Search of a Paradigm of Transformation," in Edmund Wnuk-Lipinski, ed., *After Communism* (Warsaw, 1995), p. 43.

35. The national bodies of supervision of the nuclear complex in the USSR were the Committee for the State Supervision of Safety in Industry and Nuclear Power, and the Ministry of Nuclear Energy and Industry. In Russia since 1992 there has operated the Russian State Atomic Safety, The State Committee for Extraordinary Situations, the Russian Committee for Hydrometeorology, the State Sanitary-Epidemiological Inspection, and the Russian Ministry of Ecology. In this same period, Ukraine has had the Ukrainian State Committee for Nuclear and Radiation Safety.

36. Legislation on Chornobyl includes the Law concerning the social protection of citizens suffering from the influence of radiation as a result of the catastrophe at the Chornobyl nuclear power plant, cited in *Rossiskaya gazeta*, August 5-6, 1992; and *Zakonodatel'nye akty Ukrains'koi SSR svyazannye s Chernobyl'-skoi katastrofy* (Kyiv, 1991).

37. Chornobyl study and treatment centers include the Russian State Chornobyl Committee; The Russian Institute for the Problems of Safe Development of Atomic Energy; the Center for Radiation Medicine in Kyiv, Ukraine; and the Institute of Radiation Medicine in Minsk, Belarus.

38. Concerning political parties, the programs of which pertain to nuclear power and the environment, see Galina Luchterhandt, ed., *Die politischen Parteien im neuen Russland* (Bremen, 1993).

39. In Russia, nuclear power accounts for only 11% of the total electricity produced, but in St. Petersburg the share is 33%, and in Moscow, 22%. In Ukraine, the share of nuclear power in the overall production of energy is currently between 35 and 42%.

40. The Commission for Atomic Energy of the Russian Academy of Sciences has led these discussions. See, for example, "Bezopasnost' yadernoy energetiki. Diskussiya v Prezidiume RAN, *Vestnik Rossiyskoy Akademii Nauk*, No. 9 (1992): 3-39.

41. Information Bulletin of the Center for Public Information About Atomic Energy.

42. On scientific debates on the future of nuclear power in Russia, see the following: L.A. Bol'shov, chief editor, *Problemy bezopasnogo razvitiya atomnoy energetiki* (Moscow, 1993); V.N. Abramova and A.I. Abramov, *Nuzhna li nam yadernaya energetika?* (Moscow, 1992); I.I. Novikov, G.N. Kruzhilin, and E.P. Anan'ev, "Atomnye elektrostantsii i vozmozhnye alternativy," *Vestnik RAN*, No. 6 (1993): 498-502; K.N. Semenenko, "Vodorodnaya energetika: mif ili real'nost'?," *Vestnik RAN*, No. 10 (1993): 885-888.

43. Niklas Luhmann, *Legitimation durch Verfahren* (Frankfurt/Main, 1983), p. 443; Bettina Westle, *Politische Legitimaet. Theorien, Konzepte, empirische Befunde* (Baden-Baden, 1989).

6

Ukraine as a Nuclear Weapons Power

Roman P. Zyla

It is absolutely fundamental for a nation to arrive at a clear conception of its place in the society of nations, to develop its international relations accordingly, and to augment its military establishment in order that it retain a respectable position in that society.
—Stuart Portner, "Militarism and Politics"

As the results of the December 1, 1991 referendum on Ukraine's independence were tabulated, foreigners gathered at the Hotel Lebid' in Kyiv wondered what the new state would face in the coming era. Across town at the Supreme Soviet, that question was already being debated by political pundits from both extremes of Ukraine's newly independent political spectrum. The new state faced many monumental issues, the most complicated and contentious however, was how to deal with its inherited nuclear status.

In the early post-referendum era, Ukraine was viewed as an irresponsible nuclear weapons wielding power by some Western observers.[1] This viewpoint, it will be held, was mistaken. In reality, Ukraine was never a force to be feared as it did not have positive control of the weapons on its territory. Furthermore, since independence Ukraine has always had the second move in the negotiation process. Paradoxically this also signified that the country never had the opportunity to allay global fears of its new-found nuclear status. Furthermore, Ukraine was thrust into a difficult situation with little or no experience and personnel who could contend with the nuclear issue. Ukraine was also a political neophyte. Its president, Leonid Kravchuk, a wily campaigner, assigned top priority to national survival and it was within that context that the country formulated its initial policy on nuclear weapons. Essentially it placed Ukraine on the defensive.

Overview

Mikhail Gorbachev's ascension to power in 1985 signalled a new era for the USSR. This period was marked by major changes in the Soviet military and in politics. The western media considered Gorbachev a modern Soviet leader with vision, who saw a need to fundamentally change the way the Soviet Union operated. The changes he tried to implement proved to be more than the archaic state was able to bear, and soon the peripheries began to seek their own directions, tearing the empire apart.

Ukraine declared its independence on August 24, 1991. The first assertion made by the new republic was its desire to become free of nuclear weapons. The Supreme Council of Ukraine adopted a decree claiming sovereignty over military units and equipment based on its soil, which included 1800 nuclear warheads.[2] It further proposed the creation of a Ukrainian Ministry of Defence, a National Guard, National Security Forces and Ukrainian Armed Forces.[3] By this decree, Ukraine had become *de facto* the world's third largest nuclear weapons power.

Four months later, on December 1, 1991, Ukrainians voted overwhelmingly in favour of independence in a national referendum. This vote was seen by many as the 'death knell' for the Soviet Union and thus an end to Mikhail Gorbachev's desire for a reformed Union. The margin and composition of the majority of those who voted in favour of independence surprised even the most optimistic observers in the West.[4] Having achieved complete independence and concomitantly having been elected Ukraine's first president, Kravchuk again announced that one of his main priorities was to see Ukraine become nuclear weapons free.

On December 8, 1991 three independent nations, Russia, Ukraine, and Belarus formed the Commonwealth of Independent States (CIS).[5] The Commonwealth was forced to deal with a number of issues which resulted from the break-up of the USSR, including the nuclear weapons question. Claims on the weaponry were made by the four nuclear inheritors: Russia, Ukraine, Belarus and Kazakhstan. The CIS faced great uncertainty regarding who controlled the weapons of the dismantled empire. Following initial talks, Ukrainian President Kravchuk, Belarusian Parliamentary Chairman Shushkevich and Russia's President Yeltsin together announced that control over all weapons of the former USSR would be held jointly by these three founding states of the CIS.[6]

Interpretations of the agreements were varied and almost immediately the differences strained the CIS. In its understanding of the agreement, Russia maintained that the former Soviet air force, air defence, space, navy, and strategic and tactical nuclear forces would fall under central-ized control (CIS) and that individual republics would create their own ground forces. Russian officials, including President Yeltsin and Chief of the General Staff, General Vladimir Lobov, had insisted that the weapons of the former Soviet Union be transferred to the Russian Republic, where they could remain under centralized control.[7] Ukraine on the other hand, proposed a "three button" mechanism to control the launch of nuclear weapons, ensuring that no one country could set a launch without the full authorization of the other two members of the joint control.

On December 18, 1991, Russia announced that all former Soviet ministries' functions were to be transferred to Moscow's jurisdiction by the new year (1992), including control over nuclear weapons and strategic military services. Obviously feeling threatened by this pronouncement, Ukraine claimed control over all troops and equipment on its territory including the Black Sea Fleet, and three military districts in Ukraine established by the Soviet Union.[8] Further, in an effort to win recognition from the West and in particular, from Washington, Ukraine pledged to destroy or remove all nuclear weapons from its territory. President Kravchuk pursued plans to remove all tactical nuclear weapons from its territory by July 1, 1992. This promise was kept: the last tactical nuclear weapon was shipped from Ukraine to Russia on May 6, 1992.[9]

The successful removal of tactical weapons from Ukrainian territory offered Ukraine an opportunity to show its willingness to cooperate with global powers. According to Colonel-General Kostiantyn Morozov, the Pentagon recognized Ukraine's important role in the region.[10] Ukraine's independent nuclear policy began with Kyiv leaving the command structure of the CIS on May 4, 1992. At this point Ukraine emerged as a new nuclear power, independent of the former USSR and Russia, and linked only loosely to the CIS.

Over the next three years, negotiations regarding Ukraine's signing of the START-1 treaty and the NPT were marked by Ukraine's change in strategy on the weapons issue. Ukraine began to seek compensation for weapons disarmament (and environmental problems resulting therefrom) and for strategic materials and tactical weapons already taken from Ukraine. The U.S. and Russia dominated the dialogue, leaving Ukraine to react to the positions set out by Washington and Moscow. The change in Ukraine's position was coupled with the demand for security guarantees and financial compensation. Eventually a trilateral agreement was reached between Ukraine, Russia and the U.S. on January 14, 1994. It offered Ukraine partial assurances that the U.S. and Russia would recognize Ukraine as a legal, sovereign, independent territory, the borders of which were inviolable. This latter point was critical for Ukraine which, until that point had never had such assurances from either the U.S. or Russia.[11] Ukraine's signature on the agreement was the beginning of the end of Ukraine's nuclear weapons era. My goal in this paper is to examine the factors behind the actions of the U.S. and Russia, as well as the motives behind Ukraine's apparent nuclear weapons posturing. Let us examine each of the relevant parties in turn.

The United States

The U.S. hesitated before recognizing Ukraine as an independent country, largely because of fears that the newly emerged republic posed a threat to the security of the former Soviet Union, to Europe as a whole and most importantly, to the United States itself. Buoyed by Ukraine's rhetoric on the nuclear weapons issue, however, Secretary of State James Baker "said he was satisfied with the former Soviet republic's assurances on nuclear security and disarmament...".[12] Baker was also concerned with the other new weapons powers: Belarus and Kazakhstan. The delicate East-West balance established through years of the Cold War, was now teetering because of the emergence of fifteen countries from the former Soviet republics, four of which possessed nuclear weapons.

Some analysts have examined the psychological effect the break-up of the Soviet Union has had on the United States.[13] When American President George Bush announced to the world that the West had won the Cold War, it was implied that the victors would dictate the rules of the new order. The reality of the new world order however, was that the West had become responsible for expanding the disarmament dialogue with these new nuclear states.

The republic of Belarus, like Ukraine, was quick to renounce nuclear weapons in the pursuit of an independent security policy. However, in contrast to Ukraine, at no time did Belarus make a serious claim over the nuclear weapons on its territory. The West understood that although Belarus's leadership advocated neutrality with its non-nuclear status, the *realpolitik* of Eastern Europe meant that Belarus was obliged to retain close links with Russia. In the early stages of the new world order, this was seen as a positive reality. Kazakhstan, like Ukraine and Belarus, also pledged to become nuclear free. Although it took time to accede to the NPT, most analysts agreed that Kazakhstan was not a serious contender for nuclear weapons stewardship. With few expert political analysts and fewer nuclear weapons specialists on its territory, "Kazakhstan had never been a nuclear republic. It was merely a testing site and a launching pad for the military elite in Moscow."[14]

Ukraine however, proved to be a more difficult case for the United States' leadership. American interests did not include ensuring that nuclear weapons were removed quickly from any of the inheritor republics so long as the weapons were under Moscow's control, and therefore under the scrutiny of international agencies.[15] When Ukraine began to make claims to the weapons and moved to gain at least administrative control over them, the U.S. felt it lost control, vital interests were threatened and Ukraine thus became a problem for the West.

As debates continued between Moscow and Kyiv over the ownership of the weapons and their eventual removal or dismantling, the U.S. at least tacitly supported the Russian position. To some extent this attitude was inevitable given the predominance of Moscow in the Super Power relationship during the Soviet period. The White House thus became concerned that Ukraine was impeding its goal of restricting the proliferation of nuclear weaponry. The potential hazards of the disarmament process also worried the United States. Washington had spent many years establishing a dialogue and developing measured progress in negotiations with Moscow. Initially it did not recognize that Ukraine had quite a separate agenda, outside Russia's sphere or proposed sphere of influence.[16]

For some U.S. observers therefore, Ukraine was a country with an uncontrolled and unstable nuclear arsenal on its territory, with no proven record of political leadership or negotiation. Ukraine's government had made promises of nuclear disarmament but to many analysts appeared to be behaving irresponsibly on the weapons issue. Lending credibility to this analysis were the differing positions espoused by Ukraine's polarized political spectrum, with nationalists at one extremity and "accommodationists" on the other. The latter, whose stronghold was in eastern Ukraine and counted in their numbers current President Leonid Kuchma, as well as the bulk of those involved in the military industrial complex, generally supported the CIS concept and were oriented toward closer economic ties with Russia. On the issue of nuclear arms, this group openly supported returning the nuclear warheads to Russia. Although the accommodationists viewed the disarmament issue as important to Ukraine's survival, this group expected some degree of compensation and the resolution of other issues. Among these additional issues were participation in U.S.-Russia space exploration and some efforts that would permit Ukraine to maintain its missile, defence and industrial sectors intact, most of which lay in this geographical region.[17]

The nationalists, on the other end of the spectrum, have always been based in western Ukraine, a more nationally conscious region which fell under Soviet authority during the Second World War, much later than the eastern regions. In general, the nationalists felt that historically throughout the Russian-Ukrainian relationship, Russia has been the aggressor. They perceived Russia as a threat to Ukraine's national survival.[18] The nationalist camp was divided into several political parties, including Rukh (Popular Movement), the Ukrainian Republican Party and the Social-National Party of Ukraine. The divisions in the nationalist platform were between those "who advocate the primacy of the state against those who see as the first task the necessity of economic and political reform."[19]

The West's worries stemmed from the various nationalist camps advocating the slowdown, halting and in some cases, the reversal of the nuclear disarmament process. Rukh and other nationalist parties initially supported the pronouncement of a nuclear-free Ukraine. However, even by 1992 they had changed their thinking on this matter and pushed the government to focus on Ukraine's security needs and national interests. Based on these perceived needs, they moved away from a position that supported a simple divestiture of nuclear weapons. Their influence was such that the Ukrainian leadership also began to question its initial policy, i.e., that all weapons should be given up to Russia as soon as possible.

Consequently, Ukraine halted shipments of warheads to Russia in March 1992. The leaders justified their action by arguing that they would encounter difficulties in shipping nuclear weapons to Russia for destruction because "technical, environmental and maybe political uncertainties may interfere with the completion of the plan."[20] The West reacted swiftly to Ukraine's actions and warned it would freeze aid unless the shipments were resumed. Ukraine was forced into complicity but decided to develop a new and more assertive foreign policy. The new strategy was revealed on November 8, 1992, shortly after President Kravchuk affirmed Ukraine's intention to speedily negotiate with the other CIS nations a way to dispose of the strategic nuclear weapons. Deputy Prime Minister Dr. Ihor Yukhnovsky announced that Ukraine would seek compensation for dismantling nuclear weapons on its soil. Yukhnovsky announced that "Ukraine should benefit from its non-nuclear status. Ukraine should sell its warheads to the highest bidder among the nuclear states, first of all to Russia. We want to be paid for dismantling [the nuclear weapons]."[21] Ukraine's new approach, compounded with Kyiv's recalcitrance in signing and complying with the NPT and START-1 agreements heightened the West's concern about Ukraine's policies.

During discussions in Massandra (Crimea) on September 3, 1993, Russia and Ukraine agreed on the details of the withdrawal of strategic nuclear warheads from Ukraine to Russia.[22] This agreement, however, only partially concluded the matter: a hand-written addendum stipulated that the agreement would involve only those weapons encompassed by the terms of the START-1 Treaty. The addendum was subject to wide interpretation by all parties involved.

Once again, Washington was frustrated by Ukraine's continued stewardship over strategic nuclear weapons. By the end of 1993, the U.S. had earmarked $175 million in aid for Ukraine to assist in the disarmament process but none of the committed funds were delivered. Delegations from the West came to Kyiv as frequently as they went to Moscow, thus they were fully aware of Ukraine's economic predicament and knew Ukraine could not afford to maintain the weapons.[23] The U.S. observed Ukraine's poor economic performance and used it to pressure Ukraine to comply on the weapons issue by linking monetary aid to compliance with nonproliferation and the signing of the START-1 Treaty. The United States announced that "Washington would not engage in a bargaining process with Ukraine over ratification of the START-1 and NPT agreements."[24]

The Bush administration also had little sympathy with Ukraine's demands for adequate compensation for the removal of weapons. The United States had offered $175 million for assistance in disarmament, but Ukraine argued that the full cost of disarmament was closer to $3 billion.[25] However, without positive control over the weapons and lacking the funds for disarmament, Ukraine had only two options. Either Kyiv could keep the weapons to "protect" its new found independence and face an economic collapse, or it could give up the weapons and receive the promised economic assistance, in the process gaining international support. In effect, the West had established an aid and assistance blockade on Ukraine.

The "blockade" was lifted in 1994 with Ukraine's signing of the Trilateral Agreements in Moscow as Ukraine had agreed to the conditions of disarmament and weapons transfer set by Russia and the U.S. In essence, the Agreement committed Ukraine to the "elimination of all nuclear weapons, including strategic offensive arms, located on its territory in accordance with the relevant agreements and during the seven year period as provided by the START-1 Treaty."[26] As a result of the signing, the U.S. pledged to increase economic assistance to Ukraine. In March 1994, the assistance package from the U.S. was doubled to $340 million and in July, the G-7 announced a $4 billion aid package for Ukraine.

Ukraine was on its way to divesting itself of nuclear arms in earnest: by October 1994, Ukraine had rid itself of 90% of the nuclear arsenal from its territory. Although Ukraine had improved its international standing, by October 1995, a number of G-7 nations still had not provided the promised credits to Ukraine.[27] From the Ukrainian perspective, it appeared that the country was still some way from earning the complete trust of the Western industrial countries. Why was this? One reason appears to have been the Russocentric nature of the western media, which had long relied on Moscow as its official source for the non-Russian republics. The unfortunate effects of such a policy had been made evident four years earlier when U.S. President Bush delivered his "Chicken Kyiv" speech in the summer of 1991, warning of the dangers of "suicidal nationalism" in Ukraine.[28] It took time therefore for Ukraine to cast off an image of a strongly nationalist country that posed problems for the stability of the Eurasian region. In addition, Ukraine's economic predicament compounded the nuclear weapons question from Washington's perspective.

Russia

The historical relationship between Russia and Ukraine has been a complex one. The post-independence era has proved no different. Russia and Ukraine remain divided over several issues, and at the time of writing a Treaty of Friendship and Cooperation, initialled as long ago as February 1995, has still to be officially signed. The nuclear weapons issue was the first of the major hurdles to be crossed in the period of post-Soviet relations.

Ukraine's independence has been fragile from the outset, and clearly some prominent Russians, particularly in the Duma, have had problems reconciling themselves to the fact of Ukraine's independence. Ukraine's claim to the nuclear weapons on its territory compounded the difficulties between the two major Slavic countries of the former USSR. Russia's policy toward independent Ukraine was described in a *Financial Times* as an attempt to isolate Ukraine and bring the country ultimately under Russian hegemony. One Russian official tried to convince Western European nations not to open embassies in Ukraine, since they would soon become unnecessary.[29] While such viewpoints did not necessarily emanate from the Russian presidency they clearly influenced public opinion in Ukraine.

At a seminar devoted to Ukrainian security questions, Dr. Vladimir S. Shekhovstov[30] maintained that the hostile attitude of some Russians toward Ukraine was a psychological reaction to the break-up of the USSR. While psychological factors—as well as the historical role played by Moscow in the region—cannot be ignored, the more critical reason for Moscow's involvement in Ukraine was the West's offer to help pay for the dismantling of the weapons and offers of compensation for nuclear materials. The triangle between Ukraine, Russia and the United States pitted two economically devastated countries against each other, each trying to woo and impress Washington to gain a greater share of the proposed disarmament package.

As Ukraine and Russia both face difficult economic futures, the key to survival is to improve their respective economic standings. Moscow's traditional contacts with the West arguably benefited the Russian republic more than the others of the former USSR. With the break-up of the USSR, Kyiv attempted to make inroads into well established Russian-Western ties by taking advantage of the weapons issue. These efforts raised the ire of Russia. Some Russian statespersons also noted that the "loss" of Ukraine had thrown the manufacturing process into chaos. A large proportion of the USSR's industrial and manufacturing centres were in Ukraine and thus both economies had suffered accordingly from the dissolution of the Union.

Ukraine's independence separated Russia from access to Crimea: a strategic military zone, the base of the Black Sea Fleet and less important-ly, a traditional resort area for the nomenklatura. Ukraine is also a vital "buffer zone" separating Russia from Europe and the South. Of concern to Russia therefore was the fact that independent Ukraine made overtures to the European Union as well as to NATO about possible alliances. Such agreements would bring NATO threateningly close to the Russian border and Russia's role as an arbiter in the region would therefore be signifi-cantly diminished. These issues struck at the heart of the relationship Russia believed it had with Ukraine. Russia viewed these issues as threats to its own vital interests.

Russia's positions toward Ukraine appear to come from both official and non-official sources, the most reactionary of which are non-official. The rhetoric of Russian nationalists has gained significant influence and often seems to override official policy and attain wide publicity.[31] Such rhetoric has not been confined to the nondemocratic camp. Mikhail Gorbachev said on October 21, 1991 that Ukraine was "irreplaceable" and that a Union without Ukraine was "unimaginable."[32] Shortly after Ukraine had declared independence, a report out of Moscow cited Boris Yeltsin as inquiring of his Russian military command if a nuclear strike against Ukraine was possible.[33]

Nuclear weapons in the former Soviet Union were always controlled by Moscow-based decision makers and the responsibility for negotiation and maintenance of the arsenal was, in reality, theirs alone. However, the international disarmament process severely diminished Moscow's role, as portions of the arsenal were on the territory of Ukraine and that of the other newly independent nuclear successor states. There is evidence to suggest that the West's somewhat jaundiced view of Ukraine on the nuclear weapons question was heavily influenced by Russia. Information about Ukraine in the past had often been solicited directly from Moscow, where contacts were stronger, rather than Kyiv. In 1993, according to one source, western information about Ukraine's nuclear capability was tenuous at best and derived mainly from "Russian sources eager to display to the West why Ukraine should be forced into giving up its arsenal."[34] It has been suggested that information coming out of Russia on nuclear and other matters relating to vital interests was used to serve Moscow's own purposes.[35]

Ukraine's Options

Ukraine used the nuclear weapons on its soil as a tool to raise its status on the world's political stage as well as to try to improve its economic standing. A former U.S. Secretary of Defence, Robert S. McNamara, once wrote that the essence of security is "to maintain in constant readiness the military forces necessary to protect the nation from attack, keep its commitments abroad and support its foreign policy. Beyond that central mission of combat readiness, however, security is a broad concept. [The state must be prepared to focus its resources] both supporting our basic mission and adding to the quality of our national life."[36] Ukraine's actions in the early days of its independence were possibly the best option available to the nation to fulfil what McNamara termed "adding to the quality of [their] national life."

There is no evidence to suggest that Ukraine was attempting to gain positive control over the nuclear weapons on its territory. Martin Dewing suggests that potentially Ukraine could have gained control over the arsenal but goes no further than that inconsequential statement. In his view Ukraine was "increasingly likely" to seek nuclear capability.[37] In September 1995, however, Ukrainian government officials and security advisors assured their Canadian counterparts that Ukraine's nuclear era was indeed coming to an end.[38]

A balanced analysis of Ukraine's inheritance of nuclear weapons and subsequent pressures from the West and Russia for Ukraine to disarm, must be accompanied by an understanding of Ukraine's prime objective: to achieve and maintain independence. In the early post-independence period, Ukraine's leaders saw the road to achieve this end as "to deter Russia and to obtain U.S. guarantees and attention."[39] In pursuing its prime objective, Ukraine sought administrative control over the nuclear arsenal on its territory. This control, albeit limited by technical constraints, was sufficient to alarm the U.S. and Russia. For Ukraine, the question of removing the weapons ultimately was never at issue: the country had already pledged to do so from the outset. The government's goal was to secure American and Russian agreement to several preconditions.

Ukraine's main preoccupations in the immediate post-Soviet era were to maintain statehood, and to gain international stature as a European nation. Ukraine's initial position—to rid itself of nuclear weapons—was well received by the international community. However, it soon became clear to the Ukrainian leadership that its sovereignty, economic stability, and territorial integrity were being threatened and the prompt disarmament policy was shelved. Ukraine was concerned, for example, that in the period prior to and during the Clinton-Yeltsin Summit in Vancouver, Russia and the U.S. appeared to define their respective spheres of influence. Ukraine undoubtedly fell under that of Russia as part of what the Russians have termed "the Near Abroad."

Ukraine undertook a policy to keep the remaining strategic weapons on its territory until certain conditions were agreed to by the international community. These conditions included compensation for disarmament as well as compensation for the strategic materials being transferred to and those already transferred to Russia, and perhaps most importantly, Ukraine's security was to be guaranteed by the U.S., Western Europe and Russia. Above all, Ukraine sought to convey its security fears to the United States, even though it was evident that Russia would eventually acquire the weapons.

Perceived Threats to Ukraine

The most imminent external threat to Ukraine's independence appeared to come from Russia. Three factors played a role in Kyiv's change of attitude toward disarmament: Russian-Ukrainian relations; Russia's internal instability; and Ukraine's economic predicament. Kyiv's security concerns ranged from real defense questions and external factors to territorial integrity and economic disintegration. Relations between Moscow and Kyiv had been strained over several issues. For example, Russia had assumed the leadership of the CIS in what was initially structured to be a union of equal partners, particularly in the sphere of military co-ordination. Further, CIS policies appeared to be increasingly driven by Russia's domestic needs. Transferring launch codes from Soviet military structures to Moscow was one way that Russia was able to use the CIS to its advantage.

The dispute over Crimea also highlights the problems of Russian-Ukrainian relations. Russia's evident assumption of the mantle of the Soviet Union prompted some truculent statements and demands, including the right of Russia to speak out on behalf of Russian minorities outside its borders, whether or not these people were citizens of Russia (the vast majority were not).[40] Russia's 1993 military doctrine anticipated interventions by its army in the event of "peripheral conflicts and the protection of the rights of Russian minorities in neighbouring states."[41] Crimea, with a majority Russian population, was always an area of particular interest to Moscow. In addition to and superseding Russian interest in Crimean Russians (though sometimes veiled by the latter) was the desire to maintain control over the Black Sea Fleet naval bases in Sevastopol.

Crimea typifies Ukraine's security fears elsewhere in the republic. If Russophone populations wanted to separate from Ukraine and join Russia, Moscow had suggested that it would assist with the secession. Secessionist or autonomist movements in the eastern regions of Ukraine and regions bordering Romania and Slovakia were supported to some extent by Moscow. Russian policy was elucidated by Vice-Premier Shokhin, who stated that the status and rights of Russian minorities in former Soviet republics would be linked to any negotiations with the former republics, including in economic talks. According to one analyst, these comments were slowly being accepted within the Russian government as normal diplomatic procedure. The Russian election in December 1993 of a "still more aggressively imperialist-minded coalition," further raised Ukraine's anxiety.

Some Russians have taken chauvinistic attitudes to new heights, and have gone so far as to deny Ukraine's right to exist as an independent state. Russian Foreign Minister Kozyrev has called Ukraine a mythical state. Russian diplomats have argued abroad that Ukraine will not be a state for long, attempted to isolate Ukraine from Poland in particular, and frustrated any attempt to create a Baltic-Black Sea bloc in Eastern Europe. They also have worked to prevent Ukraine from joining any Western security system that Russia is not a part of. Russia thus seeks a veto over Ukraine's freely chosen entry into NATO or the European Union.[42]

The question in the minds of Ukrainian leaders was: What if proto-imperialist or expansionist forces come to power in Russia? Such an eventuality led Ukraine's leadership to seek some means of protecting its vital interests. Russian guarantees of Ukraine's borders were made only in the context of the CIS, without a bilateral agreement. In 1993, Russia released its military doctrine within which Russia claimed a Monroe Doctrine-type policy over the CIS region, stating that Russia alone could guarantee the security of the region. Ukraine felt especially threatened during the period when the United States appeared to stand behind Russia and opposed to or, at the least, ambiguous toward the interests of Ukraine.

Russia also had a major influence on Ukraine's economy, particularly within the energy sector. Ukraine had been reliant on Russian energy exports since its independence, without much hope for a change for the status quo in the near future. This interconnection with Russia allowed Moscow to withhold delivery of fuel, or to charge higher rates for delivery of oil and gas, bringing its own sector close to world prices. This development put a severe strain on Ukraine's economy and paradoxically led Ukraine to increased dependence on nuclear power to meet urgent energy needs.[43]

The second issue, and one which increased Ukraine's anxieties and compelled it to change its attitude toward disarmament was Russia's internal instability. In Russia, President Yeltsin's task in the early post-Soviet period was to balance the interests of reformers and conservatives. The undemocratic military attack on the Russian White House in October 1993 and the subsequent election of a conservative government in November of the same year, brought to parliament individuals such as Vladimir Zhirinovsky, again raising the possibility that a self-acclaimed Russian expansionist could eventually succeed to the presidency.

One observer notes that during the communist era, the economic needs of the Soviet Union were often secondary to those of security and strategy demands. In his view, Yeltsin changed the system from one in which the domestic needs played no role in the formation of foreign policy to one in which domestic political needs were co-ordinated with those of the national security policy.[44] The threat to a country like Ukraine was made worse by the latter policy. The economic needs and the security needs Russia must satisfy for itself are often predicated on Ukraine being a buffer between Russia and Western Europe, on its being an agricultural and industrial center and on providing access to the Black Sea and to Crimea. These factors all play an important role in Russia's domestic political needs.

Russia's own internal situation was declared to be "catastrophic" at this time. In early 1993, Foreign Minister Andrey Kozyrev said that "no foreign policy can be successful without the establishment of order—new order of course, not the old one—democratic and market order in our own house."[45] The underlying premise was that Russia's house was not in order. Russia's new foreign policy was being determined by Russia's domestic situation, which was reportedly in crisis.

The third issue affecting Ukraine's decisions regarding its weapons arsenal was Ukraine's poor economy. Lack of economic reform and limited privatization had prevented any real economic growth. In 1994, the volume of industrial output fell by 28.3%, continuing a trend established in the year following independence.[46] The alarm created by an ever falling economy prompted Ukrainian leaders to demand compensation for its nuclear weapons. Ukraine was "now counting every kopeck and every dollar and could not give up its nuclear stock without compensation. The United States and Russia are rich. They must help Ukraine in this terrible situation."[47]

Finally, Ukraine's own domestic political divisions complicated the leadership's ability to reach a concordant position on the nuclear weapons issue. After the 1991 referendum and President Kravchuk's claim to the role of defender of Ukraine's sovereignty, many nationalist parties were left without an issue to pursue. The nuclear weapons question gave these parties the opportunity to influence the political agenda of the country. Nationalists have been the backbone of the anti-Russian sentiment, and their position demanding the retention of the nuclear weapons was effective in swaying national policy regarding the weapons. The nationalist parties were also instrumental in countering the Russian propaganda campaign. Through escalating rhetoric, Ukrainians undoubtedly increased the uncertainty of which country was the greater threat.

Conclusion

Ukraine was considered in the early post-Soviet period as an irresponsible state because of its change in stance on disarmament. The U.S. believed that with the Cold War over, it faced a severely diminished threat from the former region of the Soviet Union. In its place however, emerged four republics with nuclear weapons on their territory. The United States regarded this new situation in Ukraine with alarm, particularly since the new state appeared to be on the verge of economic collapse. The image of instability was also perpetuated by Russian officials, particularly Russian nationalists. As the center of power during the Soviet era, Moscow occupied a privileged place in international discourse. With the emergence of newly independent states, however, Russia had to compete for Western attention and economic assistance, and particularly with Ukraine and its 52 million strong population. Furthermore Ukrainian independence deprived Russia of most of its warm water ports and access to the bases of the Black Sea Fleet.

Ukraine emerged from the rubble of the USSR with one primary interest: to survive as an independent nation. Confronted with threats from Russia and abroad, and facing economic collapse and the spectre of national oblivion, Ukraine had few options. The nuclear arsenal was used as a bargaining chip, eventually winning much of the compensation and security assurances it sought from the U.S. and from Russia. Ukraine's stewardship over the strategic weapons had more to do with gaining security, economic assistance and higher international status than it did with Ukraine becoming a nuclear military power. Ukraine's prime objective was to maintain independence: from Moscow, from economic collapse and from political oblivion. This could only be achieved by deterring Russia and by obtaining U.S. guarantees of security as well as its attention. While Ukraine was a major country simply in terms of size and natural resources, it lacked Russia's clout with the industrialized nations. From the Ukrainian perspective therefore the presence of the nuclear weapons guaranteed that Ukraine would be included in any international assistance efforts.

Notes

1. See, for example, David R. Marples, "Ukraine's Relations with Russia in the Contemporary Era," *The Harriman Review* (Spring 1996): 105-107.

2. The claim to sovereignty over nuclear warheads was a symbolic one. Ukraine never possessed "positive" control over these weapons. Its negative control was based on administrative power over the units and the bases on which the weapons were maintained. Kyiv was also capable of preventing Russia from simply ordering troops to load the warheads on trains and head for Russia. For a detailed discussion of the issue of control of the weapons on Ukrainian territory, see Martin J. Dewing, "Ukraine: Independent Nuclear Weapons Capability Rising," MA thesis, U.S. Naval Postgraduate School, Monterey, CA, 1993, Chapter 3.

3. *Literaturna Ukraina,* August 29, 1991.

4. In the December 1991 referendum in Ukraine, over 90% of the population ratified the declaration of independence. Of the 11-million strong Russian minority, a significant percentage is said to have voted in favor of independence. See Peter J. Potichnyj, "The Referendum and Presidential Elections in Ukraine," *Canadian Slavonic Papers,* Vol. 23, No. 2 (June 1991): 123-138.

5. Kazakhstan chose not to join the CIS structure, but weapons on Kazakh territory were considered as part of the CIS structure by its founders.

6. *The Washington Post,* December 17, 1991.

7. Roman Solchanyk, "Ukraine, the Kremlin and the Russian White House," *Report on the USSR,* Vol. 3, No. 44 (November 1, 1991): 13-16.

8. V. Litovkin, "Politicians Have Set Army and Navy in Ukraine a Difficult Choice," *Izvestiya,* January 4, 1992, p. 2.

9. *Izvestiya,* May 6, 1992.

10. Interview with Col. Gen. Kostiantyn Morozov, Boston, Mass., December 28, 1994.

11. Petro Matiashek, "Yaderna spadshchyna," *Polityka i Chas,* No. 2 (1995): 15. The exception is the Ukraine-Russia Treaty of November 1990. Many in Kyiv argued that this treaty did not go far enough to assure Ukraine's sovereignty.

12. Cited in *The Ukrainian Weekly,* December 22, 1991, p. 1.

13. Morozov (December 28, 1994) made a comparison between the Russian

psychological reaction to its loss of an empire to that of the United States, which claimed to have won the Cold War but in reality had won nothing at all.

14. Mikhail Ustiugov, "A Temporary Nuclear State," *The Bulletin of the Atomic Scientists* (October 1993): 34.

15. *Atlantic Council of the United States Bulletin*, Vol. 5, No. 9 (Washington, D.C.: Atlantic Council of the United States), September 9, 1994.

16. Both Belarus and Kazakhstan indicated in the early post-Soviet period that they would be giving up any claim to Soviet nuclear weapons. NATO was thus less occupied with planning for nuclear strategic talks with these countries and was able to focus its attention on Russia and Ukraine.

17. Sherman Garnett, "Ukrainian Nuclear Policy: Sources, Conduct and Future Prospects," draft paper, August 1994, p. 5.

18. On the political differences between East and West Ukrainians, see, for example, Dominique Arel and Valeri Khmelko, "Ths Russian Factor and Territorial Polarization in Ukraine," *The Harriman Review*, Vol. 9, No. 1-2 (Spring 1996): 81-91.

19. Garnett, "Ukrainian Nuclear Policy," p. 6.

20. Jeffrey R. Smith, "Ukraine Plans to Speed Removal of A-Weapons to Russia Within Year Envisioned," *The Washington Post*, December 20, 1991, pp. A1, A41.

21. Boris Klymenko, "Ukraine May Seek Financial Compensation for Nuclear Warheads," *The Ukrainian Weekly*, November 8, 1992, pp. 2, 4.

22. The Massandra Protocol, signed by the prime ministers of Ukraine and Russia on September 3, 1993, agreed on the "withdrawal of all nuclear warheads of the Strategic Nuclear forces deployed in Ukraine to the Russian Federation." See, for example, *Nezavisimost'*, September 24, 1993, p. 1.

23. Morozov, December 28, 1994.

24. Don Oberdorfer, "Bush Details Assurances for Security of Ukraine," *The Washington Post*, January 9, 1993, p. A18.

25. Dewing, "Ukraine," p. 97.

26. *RFE/RL Research Report*, January 28, 1994, p. 14.

27. Open Media Research Institute, "Nuke Deactivization Proceeds," cited in *Ukrainian News*, October 11-24, 1995, p. 16.

28. See, for example, Alexander J. Motyl, *Dilemmas of Independence: Ukraine After Totalitarianism* (New York: Council on Foreign Relations, 1993), p. 81.

29. Eduard Lysyshyn, "Pro deyaki aspekty yadernoi polityky Ukrainy," *Polityka i chas*, No. 9 (1993): 31.

30. Interview with Dr. Vladimir S. Shekhovstov, Deputy Director of the National Institute for Strategic Studies, Dnipropetrovsk branch, Kingston, Ontario, September 19, 1995.

31. Lysyshyn, "Pro deyaky aspekty," p. 312.

32. Solchanyk, "Ukraine, the Kremlin and the Russian White House," p. 2.

33. Ibid.

34. Dewing, "Ukraine," p. xi.

35. Interview [by telephone], Sherman Garnett, Senior Associate, Carnegie Endowment for International Peace, November 23, 1995. Garnett said that the same was likely to be true of information emanating from Kyiv. Ukraine placed a Ukraine-oriented spin on its information.

36. Robert S. McNamara, *The Essence of Security* (New York: Harper and Row, 1968), pp. 122-123.

37. Dewing, "Ukraine."

38. Information provided by Ukrainian military and national security officials at the Canada-Ukraine Seminar, "Ukraine at the Strategic Crossroads," Department of National Defence, Kingston, Ontario, September 19-21, 1995.

39. Stephen Blank, *Proliferation and Nonproliferation in Ukraine: Implications for European and U.S. Security* (Carlisle Barracks, PA: U.S. Army War College, July 1, 1994), p. ix.

40. Colonel Stephen D. Olynyk has described this scenario in a recent article. It has also been brought up by ultra-Russian nationalist Vladimir Zhirinovsky and more moderate leaders seeking to gain popular support by calling for the protection of Russian minority rights abroad. Stephen D. Olynyk, "Emerging Post-Soviet Armies: The Case of Ukraine," *Military Review*, No. 3 (1994): 9.

41. Ibid.

42. Blank, *Proliferation and Nonproliferation*, p. 12.

43. See, for example, David R. Marples, "Ukraine, Russia, and the Current Energy Crisis," in George Chuchman and Mykola Herasymchuk, eds., *Ekonomika Ukrainy: mynule, suchasne i maybutne* (The Economy of Ukraine: Past, Present, and Future) (Kyiv: Naukova dumka, 1993), pp. 313-324.

44. Nikolai Andreyev, "From 'Nyet' to 'Don't Know'," *The Bulletin of the Atomic Scientists* (January/February 1993): 21.

45. Ibid., p. 25.

46. *Pravda Ukrainy*, February 3, 1995, p. 1.

47. Sergei Kiselyov, "Ukraine: Stuck with the Goods," *The Bulletin of the Atomic Scientists* (March 1993): 30.

7

Nuclear Smuggling from the Former Soviet Union[1]

William C. Potter

The West—until recently—has been extremely lucky regarding nuclear leakage from the former Soviet Union. Despite frequent sensationalist headlines to the contrary, for over two years it avoided an influx of militarily significant nuclear goods from the ex-USSR. This luck, however, has run out.

In at least four cases during the past year, there have been seizures outside of Russia of weapons-usable material of probable Russian origin. Additional quantities of highly-enriched uranium (HEU) were diverted from Russian nuclear facilities, but were seized prior to their export.

Senior Russian officials continue to deny publicly that any diversion of weapons-usable material has taken place. Many Western analysts and government officials, on the other hand, maintain that the recent seizures of HEU and plutonium are but the first wave of the long anticipated flood of nuclear contraband. Some also see the fingerprints of organized crime and the KGB in everything from nuclear material trafficking to assassinations using the equivalent of radioactive bullets.

Given the intense, albeit unsustained, media interest in the subject and the parallel focus on the part of many Western governments, it is surprising how few efforts have been undertaken to analyze systematically the record of FSU-origin nuclear related diversions and exports.[2] Even fewer attempts have been made to look for patterns of behavior with respect to suppliers, end-users, and supply networks; to analyze seriously the evidence linking organized crime to nuclear trafficking; or to differentiate between the myriad of reported cases of nuclear smuggling and those for which there is corroborating evidence about their proliferation significance.[3]

Proliferation Significant Diversions

Until last year, there was little apparent correlation between the frequency of reported efforts to smuggle nuclear material from the former Soviet Union and proliferation-significant exports. According to a recent West European intelligence report, for example, in 1992 and 1993 there were a total of 109 cases of actual or attempted nuclear smuggling from former Communist states.[4] During this same two-year period, there were no confirmed cases in which more than minuscule quantities of HEU or plutonium were exported beyond the borders of the former Soviet Union, and only three confirmed instances in which such material had been diverted (but not exported) from nuclear facilities in the newly independent states.

By 1994, the number of confirmed instances of significant illicit nuclear exports had grown to four, and the size of the individual material seizures also had increased considerably. In 1994, therefore, one moved from the realm of hypothetical threats of nuclear leakage to actual cases involving the illicit export of kilogram quantities of weapons-usable material.

Important characteristics of the significant cases of diversion and/or export of probable FSU-origin HEU and plutonium are summarized in Appendix A. Here it is sufficient to highlight those aspects of the cases relevant to the issue of establishing patterns of behavior with respect to the suppliers, the traders, and the end-users.

Luch Scientific Production Association, Podolsk (1992)

The first confirmed case involving the diversion of HEU or plutonium from nuclear facilities in the former Soviet Union occurred at the Luch Scientific Production Association in Podolsk, a town approximately 40 kilometers southwest of Moscow. Between late May and early September 1992, Leonid Smirnov, a chemical engineer and long-time employee of the plant, stole approximately 1.5 kilograms of weapons-grade HEU. He accumulated this quantity by some 20-25 different diversions, taking the material in the form of $UO2$ powder from the facility in 50-70 gram glass jars and storing it on his apartment balcony, initially in a half-liter jar wrapped in a plastic bag and then, when it became nearly full, in a larger metal container.

Smirnov had no accomplices and appears to have been motivated by an article he read in *Komsomolskaya pravda* about the fortune to be made by selling HEU. He was apprehended at the Podolsk Railroad Terminal on October 9, 1992, along with most of the HEU concealed in three lead cylinders. He had planned to travel to Moscow for the purpose of selling the nuclear material. Although Smirnov initially confessed to having a specific customer from the Caucasus in mind, the official investigation concluded that there was no concrete buyer who had been contacted.

Smirnov was convicted under Articles 223.2 and 223.3 of the 1988 Penal Code for stealing and storing radioactive material, and could have received up to ten years of imprisonment. Instead, on March 11, 1993, he was sentenced to three years on probation and was released from prison. The Ministry of Atomic Energy (Minatom) continues to deny publicly that a diversion occurred at Podolsk despite public testimony to the contrary by the thief, the criminal investigators in the case, and the director of the Luch plant. Indeed, the diversion is acknowledged in internal Minatom documents and, in fact, led to decrees adopted by Minatom to tighten physical protection at its nuclear facilities. Minatom, however, has been slow to implement the decrees due to financial constraints and organizational politics.

Andreeva Guba, Russia (1993)

One of the earliest confirmed thefts of HEU occurred in late July 1993 at a storage facility of the Northern Fleet naval base at Andreeva Guba, 40 kilometers from the Norwegian border. Two naval servicemen were arrested in the case and accused of stealing 1.8 kilograms of HEU from two fuel assemblies. The material, which was recovered, was enriched to approximately 30 percent uranium-235 (U-235) and used as fuel for third-generation naval reactors. The men said they were operating under instructions from two naval officers—both of whom continue to deny involvement in the theft. At the trial of the four suspects, which concluded in November 1995, the two naval servicemen were sentenced to prison terms of five years and four years. The two naval officers were found not guilty due to lack of evidence. Additional suspects associated with a Murmansk-St. Petersburg criminal ring are still under investigation.

Sevmorput Shipyard, near Murmansk (1993)

On November 27, 1993 Captain Alexei Tikhomirov and Oleg Baranov slipped through an unprotected gate and into the Sevmorput shipyard near Murmansk—one of the Russian navy's main storage facilities for nuclear fuel. Captain Tikhomirov, a retired naval officer whose brother Dmitry still worked at the shipyard, climbed through one of many holes in the fence surrounding "Fuel Storage Area 3-30," sawed through a padlock on the back door, and pried open the door with a metal fire pole he found next to the building. Once inside, he located the containers of fresh submarine fuel, broke off parts of three assemblies from a VM-4-AM reactor core, stuffed the material containing 4.5 kg of uranium (enriched to approximately 20 percent U-235) into a bag, and retraced his steps.

The theft was soon discovered because the perpetrators carelessly left the back of the storage building open. The culprits, however, were only apprehended and the material recovered from Baranov's garage six months later when Alexei Tikhomirov told a fellow officer about the theft and asked for help in selling the stolen merchandise. The parties to the crime, it appears, had not figured out a way to dispose of the material despite having carefully planned the operation for months prior to its execution.

In early 1994, the three defendants—all past or present naval officers with no prior criminal records—were tried for the theft of naval fuel. Two received prison sentences of three and one-half years; the third was freed.

According to the military prosecutor who investigated the case, at the time of the theft, potatoes were guarded better than naval fuel, despite the fact that most of the fuel was highly enriched and some of it was weapons-grade.[5] The first and last time the contents of most of the fuel canisters were checked, the prosecutor contends, was at the fuel fabrication plant. As a consequence of inadequate material control and accountancy, he argues, the diversion at Sevmorput "could have been concealed for ten years or longer" had the open door of the storage building not attracted the guard's attention.[6]

Tengen, Germany (May 10, 1994)

The first known case in which more than minuscule quantities of HEU or plutonium were illegally exported occurred in 1994.[7] It involved the inadvertent discovery by German police in Tengen (Baden-Wuertemberg) of a vial containing 5.6 grams of nearly pure Pu-239. The weapons-grade material was found on May 10, 1994 in the garage of Adolf Jaekle who was under investigation for counterfeiting.

Although the origin of the material has not been determined definitively, there are indications that it was produced for non-weapons purposes at the Soviet nuclear weapons laboratory Arzamas-16 (recently renamed Kremlev). According to the prevailing U.S. Department of Energy thesis, the amount found in Germany was part of a total inventory of no more than several kilograms of very pure plutonium used as a "standards sample" to measure fission cross-sections and the energy levels of nuclei.[8] Samples similar to the amount seized in Tengen, it is hypothesized, may have been distributed by Arzamas-16 to dozens of nuclear research laboratories in the former Soviet Union, as well as in Eastern Europe. An alternative explanation about the source of the material, provided by a German plutonium specialist with unusual contacts in the Russian nuclear industry, is that the plutonium was produced at a special centrifuge facility in Central Asia (most likely Chkalovsk, Tajikistan).

At the present time, many important questions about the Tengen case remain unresolved, especially regarding the plutonium supply route and the intended end-user, if any. The case, however, clearly is significant if for no other reason than the fact that it was not a sting operation. Indeed, there are tantalizing reports—but no hard proof—of end-user customers who may have been interested in the contraband. Most frequently mentioned in press reports as likely customers are Iraq and North Korea. The evidence linking these states to the Tengen plutonium relates primarily to classified testimony attributed to Western intelligence agencies, statements reportedly made by Jaekle shortly after his arrest, names of individuals found among Jaekle's papers, and the prior trading partners of a Bulgarian firm that is alleged to have been involved in the supply of the plutonium. Leads once thought to be promising about the end-users, however, have yet to yield more than speculation.

Little progress also has been made in establishing more than a circumstantial case for the linkage between organized crime and the traffickers of the Tengen plutonium. The most intriguing thesis in this regard is that Jaekle was part of a transnational KGB-Bulgarian-Iraqi nuclear supply chain.[9] According to this view, representatives of a Bulgarian trading company, Kintex, were the likely agents involved in procuring the plutonium from Russia and organizing its shipment, from the Bulgarian port of Varna to Athens, and from there to Zurich. This interpretation is consistent with Jaekle's testimony that he received the sample from a Swiss contact. Its implication of Kintex, a licensed arms trafficking firm with close links to the former KGB and one that was involved in a variety of illicit smuggling activities under the old Communist regime, also has a certain face validity. That is, Kintex, by virtue of its contacts in Russia and the international arms trade netherworld and its prior smuggling record, is a plausible conspirator in a transnational nuclear supply chain. No hard evidence, however, has yet been produced to substantiate this hypothesis or to corroborate the assertion that the tiny sample of very pure plutonium found in Tengen is part of a much larger shipment of up to 150 kilograms of the material already in Switzerland.[10] The extraordinary costs associated with the production of such pure plutonium make it unlikely that more than a few kilograms of the material was ever produced, much less stolen and exported.

Landshut, Germany (June 1994)

In August 1994, Bavarian authorities reported that on June 13, 1994 they had seized 800 milligrams of HEU enriched to 87.7 percent U-235. This material was recovered in Landshut, Bavaria. Subsequently, on August 8, a German real estate dealer was arrested as the central figure in a group accused of illegal commerce in and possession of nuclear material. Also arrested as part of a sting operation were five men from Slovakia and the Czech Republic. Based upon spectrometric analyses of the HEU and its enrichment level, Euratom authorities believe the material did not come from weapons stocks, but rather was likely produced for use as naval reactor or research reactor fuel. Although only a small quantity of HEU was seized at Landshut, the case is potentially significant because the material is identical to the much larger seizure made in Prague six months later.

Lufthansa/Munich (August 10, 1994)

The last of the significant German smuggling cases occurred on August 10, 1994 when the Bavarian Landeskriminalant (LKA) seized a suitcase from luggage being unloaded from Lufthansa Flight 3369 from Moscow at Franz Jozef Strauss Airport in Munich. Inside the suitcase were a plastic bag filled with several hundred grams of lithium 6 (used to make tritium) and a metal container holding 560 grams of mixed oxides of uranium and plutonium. This seizure, the result of a sting operation, was by far the largest quantity of weapons-usable material (363 grams of Pu-239) recovered in the West. Justiniano Torres Benitez, a Columbian national, and Spaniards Julio Oroz and Javier Bengoechea Arratibel were arrested at the airport in connection with the smuggling operation.

German authorities initially asserted that the plutonium seized in Munich was produced in Russia for use in weapons. Russian officials not only denied those charges, but maintained that the material did not originate in Russia. From Moscow's vantage point (or at least that of Minatom), the entire operation was staged to try to embarrass the Russian nuclear industry and undercut its international competitiveness. Some Minatom spokesmen went so far as to accuse German intelligence agents of placing the plutonium on board the Lufthansa flight. German authorities now concede that they knew in advance that the plutonium would be on board the Lufthansa flight from Moscow. They justify their failure to notify Russian officials, however, because of concern about links between Russian criminal groups and security personnel.

Today, Western authorities are convinced that the plutonium seized in Munich, like that recovered in Tengen and Landshut, was not produced for weapons purposes. Although strong circumstantial evidence suggests that the plutonium is of Soviet origin, as Mark Hibbs points out, the absence of a catalog of signatures from Soviet fissile material production facilities makes it impossible to conclude on technical grounds that the plutonium—possibly from a batch of experimental reactor fuel—comes from a Russian reactor fuel depot, as opposed to one in Kazakhstan, Ukraine, or Eastern Europe.[11]

The Lufthansa case was significant in demonstrating the existence of an international nuclear supply network. The demand in this instance, however, appears to have been artificially created by German intelligence and security service officials. This possible violation of German law by the German foreign intelligence agency (BND) and its head Bernd Schmidbauer was the subject of an investigation launched in April 1995 by the Parliamentary Control Commission. Reportedly, as much as $276 million was made available to the smugglers as a bank credit for the purpose of purchasing the material. The BND and the LKA also are accused of offering their undercover operative in the case a cash bonus of 300,000 DM ($215,000) if he succeeded in obtaining plutonium from a smuggler.[12]

Largely because of the method by which the parties were enticed to commit the crime and the absence of evidence demonstrating the involvement of any buyer other than the BND or LKA, in July 1995, the Munich District Court handed out light sentences to the three confessed smugglers. Although the men might have received prison terms of up to 10 years under the Federal Weapons of War Control Act, the most harsh sentence handed out was only four years and ten months (Benitez). The others received jail terms of three years and nine months (Arratibel) and three years (Oroz).

Prague, Czechoslovakia (December 14, 1994)

On December 14, 1994, Prague police, acting on an anonymous phone tip, seized 2.72 kilograms of HEU from the back seat of a car parked on a busy street in the Czech capital. The HEU, enriched to 87.7 percent U-235, was in the form of uranium dioxide (UO2) powder. It was contained in two cylindrical metal canisters. Police arrested the car's owner, 54 year old Jaroslav Vagner, from the Czech Republic, and his two companions in the car from Belarus and Ukraine. All three had backgrounds in the nuclear industry. Vagner had worked for many years at the Nuclear Research Institute at Rez and at nuclear power stations at Dukovany and Temelin, reportedly leaving the latter plant in frustration over poor wages. According to Czech police, the individuals from Belarus and Ukraine also were "nuclear workers" who had come to the Czech Republic in the past year.[13] Media reports in March 1995 indicate that Czech police arrested two additional individuals in connection with the case, one allegedly a Prague police officer.

The seized material—the largest quantity of weapons-usable nuclear contraband seized to date—appears to be identical to the 800 milligrams of HEU recovered in Landshut, Germany in June 1994. As in the Landshut case, there is no consensus as to the origin of the material, which consists of 11% U-238, 87.7% U-235, just under 1.1% U-234, and 0.2% of U-236. Czech officials originally claimed that the material had been irradiated in a reactor, separated in a reprocessing plant, and then re-enriched. Some analysts believe the material may be a "cocktail" consisting of uranium from several sources—perhaps designed intentionally to mask the production site(s). Still others believe the material has been reprocessed from spent RBMK fuel or may be a blend of reprocessed uranium and other stock. Experts agree, however, that the material did not originate from weapons stocks and was more likely produced for use as fuel in naval or research reactors. Consistent with this interpretation, Mark Hibbs reports that Czech police believe the HEU seized in Prague may have been provided by criminals who supply stolen submarine or icebreaker fuel from Russia's Northern Fleet.[14]

Additional Cases of Proliferation Concern

The seizures of nuclear material in Podolsk, Andreeva Guba, Polyarny (near Murmansk), Tengen, Landshut, Munich, and Prague are singled out as proliferation of significant because, unlike other reported cases of nuclear diversion, they involved more than minuscule quantities of either HEU or plutonium and also indisputably occurred. There are at least three more cases that are of probable proliferation concern, but which do not as clearly meet the standard of unambiguous evidence with respect to either independent sources of corroboration of the diversion or the size and/or enrichment level of the material involved. These cases involve: (1) the seizure of a large cache of beryllium, including a much smaller quantity of a beryllium and HEU alloy, in the basement of a bank in Vilnius, Lithuania in May 1993; (2) the reported recovery in St. Petersburg in June 1994 of 3.05 kilograms of weapons-usable HEU in the form of uranium dioxide powder, allegedly stolen from a nuclear facility (most likely Electrostal) near Moscow in March of that year; and (3) the seizure of six kilograms of enriched uranium (probably 20 percent U-235) in March 1995 in Kyiv, Ukraine.

Potentially the most serious diversion of the lot in terms of the reported quantity and enrichment level of material involved is the St. Petersburg case. Initial Russian press accounts, however, have not been followed by the release of more detailed information by other media sources or from a criminal investigation or trial, if any took place. Continued interest in the episode derives mainly from its inclusion in a list of possible nuclear thefts cited by FBI Director Louis Freeh in testimony before Congress in May 1994 and speculation that it may be part of the same stockpile of HEU from which the Landshut and Prague material were supplied.

The Vilnius case, discussed in more detail below, is intriguing mainly because of the possible complicity of government authorities. At issue in the March 1995 Kyiv seizure is the level of enrichment of the six kilograms of uranium. Although the U.S. Energy Department is inclined to categorize the fuel as low-enriched uranium for power reactors—based upon the cylindrical shape of the pellets in which it is contained—analysis of the material by the Kyiv Institute for Nuclear Research indicates an enrichment level of 20 percent, consistent with much naval reactor fuel.

Under the heading of "cases of proliferation concern" one also should highlight the flourishing, but largely unnoted trade in nuclear-related dual-use materials and technologies. These are 65 items such as beryllium, zirconium, and hafnium that have both civilian and nuclear weapon uses and are subject to the Nuclear Suppliers Group (NSG) export guidelines. Russia, Ukraine and Kazakhstan are major producers of dual-use nuclear goods, and the Baltic states have served as principal transshippers of them, especially rare-earth metals. The seizure by U.S. Customs agents in June 1995 of over seven tons of Ukrainian-produced zirconium is only the most celebrated case. Five of the tons, produced at the Pridneprovsky Chemical Factory in Dniprodzerzhinsk, were trucked from Ukraine to Germany in 1993 or 1994. Two additional tons of the contraband, also produced in Dniprodzerzhinsk, were recovered in Cyprus. U.S. customs officials report that subsequent to the seizures in the June 1995 sting operation, they learned that another 45 tons of zirconium had been stored in Cyprus for two years, ten tons of which were transferred recently to Vienna. They also corroborated an earlier published report that at least 45 tons of Ukrainian-origin zirconium still sit at docks in Antwerp and Rotterdam.[15]

Patterns of Behavior

An analysis of the confirmed cases of theft and/or diversions of HEU and plutonium reveals a number of interesting, if not statistically significant, patterns of behavior. It is apparent, for example, that although the number of proliferation-significant instances of nuclear material theft remains small, it is increasing, as is the quantity of material offered for sale.

Most of the material recovered to date has been enriched uranium, usually in the form of uranium dioxide powder. If one includes in the sample of cases those of "probable proliferation concern," the preponderance of seizures involving definite or possible fresh fuel for propulsion reactors is striking. The remaining cases involved nuclear material similar to that found in many of the more than 50 sites in the former Soviet Union at which HEU and plutonium are present.[16] Although a number of these facilities in Russia are engaged in both civilian and military-related nuclear activities, none of the seizures to date provide any evidence of having a nuclear weapons' origin.

It is difficult, based upon the available information, to make generalizations about the initial procurers of proliferation-significant nuclear material. Most of the reliable information we do have, moreover, is limited to those parties who did not succeed in selling the material. Nevertheless, from what is known, many suppliers appear to have been "insiders," working at nuclear research institutes or naval bases, or having previously worked at such facilities. Most of the perpetrators do not appear to have had customers in hand (other than perhaps German intelligence authorities) at the time of the diversions. Rather, evidence suggests that the thieves—especially those who were apprehended— generally were ill-informed novices in the business of nuclear trafficking who were disaffected with their economic lot, looking to make a quick profit. This finding applies even more clearly to traffickers in nuclear material of no proliferation significance, some of whom have perished through careless handling of their radioactive contraband.[17]

Most analysts believe that an "end-user market" exists for weapons-usable nuclear material. The most likely end-users—those who desire the material for actual use, as opposed to resale for a profit—are perceived to be rogue states with nuclear weapons ambitions. Terrorist groups and even transnational criminal organizations also have been identified as potential customers for weapons-grade material, if only for extortionist purposes. A review of those cases in which HEU and plutonium actually have been diverted, however, does not reveal reliable evidence that end-users have been active in the illicit Russian nuclear marketplace to date.

To be sure, one legitimately may ask, "How confident should we be that proliferation significant exports of FSU-origin nuclear material have simply escaped detection?" It is known, for example, that after the collapse of the Soviet Union, Iran became particularly interested in Kazakhstan's nuclear-related assets, including those present at the Ulba Metallurgy Plant in Ust-Kamenogorsk.[18] Some media reports also suggest the possibility that prior to his arrest, Adolf Jaekle might have had discussions with representatives of a nuclear weapons aspirant.[19] This nuclear supply chain thesis, however, is not yet borne out by the available data. Instead, there are indications that some states may be seeking to exploit imprudent but state-sanctioned nuclear exports from Russia to meet their nuclear weapons aspirations.

New and Old Nuclear Threat

If at the present time most evidence indicates a slow, but growing, increase in the rate of proliferation significant diversions, it also suggests the existence of conditions conducive to an exponential rise in the rate of nuclear leakage from the former Soviet Union. These factors include enormous inventories of weapons-usable materials, underdeveloped safeguards, inadequate export controls, a rise in political instability and corruption, and a corresponding decline in the perception of national (as opposed to individual and organizational) interests.

Nuclear Plenty

Although material shortages were commonplace in the Soviet Union, they did not apply to nuclear weapons or weapons-usable material. It is estimated, for example, that Russia's nuclear material inventory—distributed over more than 50 sites—consists of approximately 1100-1300 tons of highly-enriched uranium and 165 tons of weapons-grade plutonium.[20] The bulk of the ex-USSR's nuclear assets are concentrated in Russia. One should not discount, however, proliferation significant quantities of weapons-grade material in Belarus, Kazakhstan, and Ukraine. Although there are unlikely to be any more hidden caches of the magnitude of that discovered—and removed—from Ust-Kamenogorsk, it would not be surprising to see the declared nuclear material inventories in a number of post-Soviet states increase as IAEA inspections take place. Indicative of this phenomenon was the five-fold increase in weapons-grade uranium reported to the IAEA this year at Ukraine's Kharkiv Physical-Technical Institute (from 15 to 75 kg of HEU enriched to 90 percent U-235), and the IAEA's discovery during its February 1995 visit to Sevastopol of a previously undeclared research reactor at the Navy Academy of the Ukrainian Ministry of Defense.[21]

Underdeveloped Safeguards

International safeguards are designed to deter national governments from diverting nuclear material from peaceful to military purposes and to detect diversion if it occurs. Since the collapse of the Soviet Union, all of the non-Russian successor states have acceded to the NPT as non-nuclear weapon states and many (Armenia, Belarus, Estonia, Kazakhstan, Latvia, Lithuania, Ukraine, and Uzbekistan) have concluded safeguards agreements with the IAEA. Although safeguards agreements are currently in effect for only Armenia, Latvia, Lithuania, and Ukraine, there is no longer much worry that any of the post-Soviet states will attempt to divert nuclear material for indigenous weapons programs.

Of far greater concern is the prospect that the post-Soviet states with nuclear assets will be unable to meet reasonable standards for national safeguards that are directed at non-state actors. These safeguards emphasize the provision of physical security, material control, and accounting (MPC & A) and refer to measures undertaken by national governments "to detect, deter, prevent, or respond to the unauthorized possession or use of significant quantities of nuclear materials through theft or diversion and sabotage of nuclear facilities."[22]

According to conventional wisdom, the Soviet nuclear fuel cycle was very secure from penetration by outsiders because of the country's authoritarian political system, its pervasive network of internal security, and the close integration of its civilian and military components. The vulnerability of the most sensitive nuclear facilities—uranium enrichment and conversion plants and plutonium reprocessing and storage facilities—also was reduced by their location in relatively remote and stable regions of Russia.

Physical protection probably remains better today at Russian uranium enrichment and plutonium production sites than at research institutes, fuel storage facilities for propulsion reactors, and non-standard fuel cycle facilities. An underdeveloped physical protection culture, along with declining resources for workers in the nuclear sector, however, combine to undermine the security of all Russian nuclear installations. This is apparent even at those sites where large quantities of weapons-grade uranium and plutonium are present. Although security against external threats (i.e., penetration from outside) generally is high, until recently little attention has been given to the threat of diversion by insiders. The threat is a function of both inadequate physical security and the remnants of the Soviet approach to material control, which emphasized centrally-planned production targets and personal responsibility, rather than facility-specific inventory accounting. Especially prone to neglect in terms of measurement and reporting, and a point of diversion vulnerability now recognized by Minatom, were fissile material waste streams and scraps that did not count toward the production quota. This less than systematic approach to material accounting may explain in part the extraordinary recovery by members of the Project Sapphire team of more HEU than Kazakhstan thought was in its Ulba Plant inventory.[23] Progress now is being made to provide Western assistance in upgrading MPC & A at key Russian nuclear facilities, but a tremendous gap remains between the magnitude of the national safeguards problem and the effort that has been directed toward its resolution.[24] Among those nuclear sites identified by the U.S. government as most in need of safeguards improvements are fuel cycle facilities at Tomsk-7, the Mayak Chemical Combine, Krasnoyarsk-26, Sverdlovsk-44, the Electrostal Machine Building Plant, and the Novosibirsk Chemical Concentrate Plant. The following research centers also are targeted for priority MPC & A assistance: Kurchatov Institute (Moscow); the Institute of Physics and Power Engineering (Obninsk); the Scientific Research Institute for Atomic Reactors (Dmitrovgrod); the Luch Scientific Production Association (Podolsk), and the Bochvar Institute of Non-Organic Substances (Moscow).[25] Until recently, it generally was assumed in the West that notwithstanding possible shortcomings in the civilian nuclear sector, physical security was high in the military domain. Although security at military facilities probably remains much higher than at civilian nuclear sites, the situation may be less sanguine than previously recognized.

Ironically, one new problem has arisen from progress in implementing START I and from the successful redeployment onto Russian territory of the tactical nuclear weapons previously scattered throughout much of the former Soviet Union and Eastern Europe. It concerns the lack of adequate storage facilities in Russia for the influx of nuclear warheads. According to one recent report, "many nuclear warheads are now being stored in facilities constructed for the storage of conventional munitions under less than adequate physical security."[26] These warheads may be particularly vulnerable to theft by disgruntled past or present Russian Special Operations (Spetsnaz) soldiers who are trained to use atomic demolition weapons and may have special knowledge of and even access to nuclear weapons storage depots.

On occasion, Minatom officials themselves have acknowledged that interim storage facilities from dismantled weapons are "not very safe" and "are not adequately guarded."[27] Among specific safeguards deficiencies noted by Minatom in internal directives are the shortage of trained personnel and modern equipment, inadequate transport control procedures, and the lack of storage facilities. Russian officials also have privately confided that security is particularly suspect at warhead disassembly facilities in Zarechny (formerly Penza-19), Trekhgorny (formerly Zlatoust-36), and Lesnoy (formerly Sverdlovsk-45), as well as at certain weapons component facilities at Kremlev (formerly Arzamas-16). Although there are not yet any confirmed cases of warhead diversion from these or other sites, there is at least one instance in which a fissile material component from a warhead may have been lost and then recovered.

In another alarming case, inspectors from the Ministry of Defense are reported to have discovered a temporarily deserted SS-25 nuclear missile battery, its crew having left the site for several hours in pursuit of food.[28] Although one would hope that these stories were apocryphal, the general state of disarray and economic malaise in the Russian military and nuclear weapons complex argues against dismissing them out of hand.

Nuclear Terrorism

The risk of nuclear terrorism in the Soviet Union was minimal because of the extraordinarily centralized and regimented nature of the state and the pervasiveness of internal security measures. Although still low, the probability of non-state actors resorting to nuclear violence has risen with the fracturing of the Soviet state, ethnic upheaval, and the location of nuclear assets proximate to regions experiencing organized violence. The probability is likely to increase further if political turbulence in the newly independent states grows, economic chaos ensues, ethnic violence escalates, and central authority and control diminish.

Nuclear terrorism subsumes a variety of threats.[29] The one most often discussed in the Western press involves the seizure of nuclear weapons by a renegade military movement. This possibility was reduced, but not eliminated, by the transfer of all tactical nuclear weapons to Russian territory. Weapons from the tactical nuclear arsenal are apt to be the preferred target for terrorist seizure because of their relatively small size and the absence on the older weapons of "permissive action links" (PALs) to protect their unauthorized use.

A second potential terrorist threat concerns the possible use of conventional weapons against a civilian nuclear power facility. Although the probability of successfully implementing such a strike is not high, Russian officials take seriously the possibility of terrorist attacks by Chechen commandos against nuclear power installations. At least some nuclear power facilities, for example, reportedly are now guarded by rapid reaction troops as well as police units.[30] Armenian authorities also are alert to the potential terrorist risks posed by the restarting in 1995 of the Metzamor Nuclear Power Plant that had been shut down since 1989.

Implementation of the planned physical protection upgrades at nuclear sites in Russia and the other Soviet successor states will go a long way toward reducing the danger of nuclear terrorism in the former Soviet Union. The vast stocks of weapons-usable material in Russia and the difficulty at the present time of distinguishing between "material unaccounted for" (MUF) and material that has been stolen, however, enhances the credibility of extortionist threats by terrorists—even if they are unfounded. Illustrative of this dilemma was the decision taken by Lithuanian authorities in November 1994 to shut down temporarily the Ignalina nuclear power plant in response to a terrorist threat by local organized crime figures. The threat had to be treated as credible, especially in light of a case two years earlier when an employee at Ignalina was found to have sabotaged the plant's computer system by introducing viruses.[31]

Organized Crime

There is broad agreement among analysts that crime is mushrooming in the ex-USSR. Most observers also discern rampant organized criminal activity, although they may differ on what constitutes "organized crime."[32] Little agreement—and even less reliable information—exists, however, on the extent of organized criminal activity (or interest) in nuclear material trafficking.

To date, most evidence linking organized criminal groups in the post-Soviet states and nuclear material smuggling is anecdotal in nature and is not well-documented. U.S. government officials, therefore, continue to maintain that there is no solid evidence that organized criminal groups—as distinct from individuals who may have had ties to organized crime—have been directly engaged in the theft or trafficking of sensitive nuclear materials. This finding is consistent with a careful analysis of the open-source literature on nuclear smuggling, although the definitive study on the topic has yet to be written.[33] Less reassuring, however, are indications that a blurred line separates legal and illicit nuclear trade and criminal and state-sanctioned activities in the former Soviet Union.[34]

The ambiguous divide between the criminal and official worlds is illustrated by the May 1993 Vilnius case, cited previously. It involved the discovery in the basement of the Innovation Bank of 27 wooden boxes containing approximately four tons of beryllium pieces, some of which had been mechanically implanted with HEU. It was only the presence of a small amount of U-235—probably no more than 150 grams—that enabled authorities in Vilnius to seize the cache, since Lithuania had no laws or regulations governing the possession of/or commerce in dual-use nuclear-related material.[35]

A team of U.S. reporters that has investigated the case concludes that the material found in Vilnius probably originated at the Institute of Physics and Power Engineering at Obninsk and was shipped to Vilnius by a firm from Sverdlovsk. Also reportedly involved in the deal were officials from the Sverdlovsk region.[36] Despite the fact that Russia, unlike Lithuania, has regulations governing the export of beryllium and notwithstanding the use of improperly documented export papers by the Russian shippers, Russian government authorities chose not to treat the transaction as an illegal export. As a consequence, the beryllium—minus those pieces contaminated by HEU—has been returned to the Innovation Bank where it now stands as collateral for a loan, presumably made by its Russian owners. Under such circumstances of underdeveloped law and governmental acquiescence in questionable nuclear commerce, it is hard to say what constitutes organized criminal activity in the nuclear realm.

One can, however, think of a number of reasons why organized criminal groups might rationally decide to shy away from the nuclear smuggling sector. As Rensselaer Lee has noted, "few other activities seem as likely to arouse the interests of Western security services and to generate international pressure for a Russian government crackdown on the organized crime sector."[37] Moreover, as Lee points out, unlike narcotics, no mass market for sensitive nuclear materials exists, buyers may be hard to locate, and special precautions must be taken in handling the contraband.

These are persuasive disincentives. They may not always prevail, however, especially among high-risk-taking criminal groups that seek short-term profits rather than long-term extortion relationships. In this respect, it is interesting to note the finding that in the revolutionary economic and social conditions of post-Soviet Russia, criminal groups appear to be less inclined than their counterparts in the United States and Western Europe to seek "long-term relationships that allow both organized crime groups and businesses to prosper."[38] It also should be anticipated that organized criminal activity will gravitate toward nuclear smuggling if it is demonstrated that: (1) weapons-usable material is accessible in quantity; and (2) real end-users become active in the nuclear marketplace. Regrettably, the sting operations of 1994 have confirmed the former of the two conditions, and in so doing also may unintentionally stimulate end-user activity.

Export Controls

Most nuclear material, as well as related technology and equipment that leaves the former Soviet Union, is exported through official channels. Foreign access to nuclear supplies from the ex-USSR, therefore, depends upon both national export policy and the effectiveness of export controls. As the inheritor of the well-developed Soviet export control structure, the Russian system from the outset possessed considerable technical knowhow. Most of the formal changes that have been introduced since 1992, consequently, have involved efforts to reorganize the existing bureaucracy and to make the prior system more compatible with the rise of nongovernmental exporters and more market-based activities.[39]

One of the major organizational innovations was the creation in April 1992 of an intergovernmental Russian Federation Export Control Commission, that was supposed to coordinate state export control policy in pursuit of Russia's nonproliferation objectives. In order to facilitate this mission, the Commission was given formal responsibility for granting final approval for exports of nuclear and other specified material, equipment, technology and knowhow. In practice, however, export decisions involving nuclear material and technology increasingly have been taken by Minatom and the Ministry of Foreign Economic Relations with little input by either the Ministry of Foreign Affairs or the Export Control Commission. This fact, together with the difficult economic and political constraints under which the Russian export control system functions, helps to explain a number of recent and imprudent Russian nuclear export initiatives.[40] They include contracts to provide nuclear assistance to Iran (involving completion of the Bushehr nuclear plant, the supply of a gas centrifuge facility, and training for Iranian nuclear scientists); to assist the development of China's nuclear program, including provision of reactors and a uranium enhancement plant; and to build two 1000 MWe VVER-type reactors at Koodangulan in India. The Indian deal, if implemented, is particularly serious as it would appear to be at odds with Russia's pledge to insist upon full-scope safeguards (i.e., international safeguards on all facilities) as a condition of nuclear export. These state-sanctioned nuclear initiatives that subordinate nonproliferation objectives to those of economic gain also send the wrong signals to private nuclear entrepreneurs within Russia and to other Soviet successor states.

Unlike Russia, the other post-Soviet governments inherited little in the way of export control structures or expertise. Although some progress recently has been made in developing new export control procedures in Belarus, Kazakhstan, and especially Ukraine, high-level political commitment to stringent export controls in these states is not apparent.[41]

The effectiveness of Russian export controls also is undermined by the absence of effective custom controls between Russia and the other post-Soviet republics. The lack of controls on intra-CIS trade, combined with the underdeveloped state of export controls outside of Russia and a lack of equipment for monitoring illicit nuclear trade means that sensitive defense goods—including nuclear material and technology—can pass readily from Russia or Ukraine to other post-Soviet states, and from there to countries of major proliferation concern. If anything, this problem of the "weakest link" will increase if recent agreements to establish custom unions and unregulated trade between Belarus and Russia, and Russia and Kazakhstan, are implemented.

Corrective Measures

The West no longer can rely on luck to prevent nuclear leakage from the ex-USSR. Proliferation-significant cases of diversion and export of weapons usable material have occurred, and it is counterproductive to deny the existence of the problem. It also is true, however, that a nuclear deluge is not inevitable and may be averted if a combination of short and longer terms corrective measures are undertaken.

U.S.-Russian Cooperation

U.S. denuclearization assistance through the government-to-government Cooperative Threat Reduction Program and the lab-to-lab effort have contributed significantly to safeguarding Russia's nuclear assets, especially in the past nine months. The potential impact of U.S. assistance, however, has been diminished by the asymmetry in the donor-recipient relationship and by perceived differences in the program objectives of the donor and recipient states. CIS officials particularly have resented the CTR legislative requirements regarding stringent audits and the purchase of U.S. equipment.[42]

In order to minimize these impediments and expedite improvements in national safeguards, the United States and Russia must move from a donor-recipient relationship to one of true cooperation in which both countries work together to promote nonproliferation objectives at home and abroad. As Graham Allison and his colleagues at Harvard University point out, this means forging a "shared sense of mission" between the former Cold War rivals, and also introducing a greater degree of reciprocity in MPC & A activities, even when the problems of safeguards may not be perfectly symmetrical.[43]

A serious obstacle to greater collaboration is resistance within both countries by institutions whose organizational interests may not correspond to national ones. The U.S. Navy, for example, has been unenthusiastic about Russian proposals to extend MPC & A cooperation to naval fuel because of a concern about demands for reciprocal access and transparency that it might entail.

Minatom, for its part, understandably is wary of assistance efforts that have the potential both to discredit its past operations and to undermine its present dominance in the nuclear sector.[44] U.S. offers of financial assistance for purposes of inventory accounting and material control, therefore, may be resisted if they are judged to threaten Minatom's institutional power, even if such assistance may serve other institutional objectives.[45] An effective, joint program for securing Russian nuclear stocks, consequently, must include appropriate incentives to ensure Minatom's cooperation. Probably the most financially lucrative incentive is the timely implementation of the 1992 U.S. agreement to purchase 500 tons of surplus Russian weapons HEU for $12 billion. The United States should seek to accelerate the HEU deal, which has moved at a very slow pace, and to purchase additional weapons usable fissile material—from both dismantled weapons and non-weapons stocks. It may be possible, for example, to purchase up to 100 tons of surplus Russian weapons plutonium for fabrication into reactor fuel at the nearly completed Siemens plant at Hanau, Germany.[46] A portion of the payments could be earmarked for MPC & A improvements, and also to assist in the conversion away from plutonium activities of Russia's three "plutonium cities"—Tomsk-7, Krasnoyarsk-26, and Chelyabinsk-65.

Expansion of Safeguards Effort

The Department of Energy has an extremely ambitious program which, if implemented on schedule, should go a long way toward stanching the illicit flow of sensitive nuclear materials from the former Soviet Union. Under current plans, by the end of 1996, the United States hopes to have provided the resources to: (1) upgrade MPC & A at all sites in the non-Russian successor states at which weapons-usable material is present; (2) upgrade MPC & A at all of the major civilian sites in Russia that handle weapons-usable material; (3) initiate MPC & A upgrades at a wide range of additional Russian sites, including those throughout the Minatom weapons complex; (4) establish the basis for MPC & A cooperation at all Russian nuclear material sites, including those in the weapons complex and both civilian and naval propulsion reactors; (5) facilitate the development of a national nuclear material accounting system; (6) foster the growth of an effective national regulatory program in Russia[47]; and (7) facilitate the development of a sustainable, indigenous Russian MPC & A program. These all are vital steps, which deserve the highest level of political support in both countries. The estimated cost of approximately $100 million to implement the program through the end of the 1996 calendar year is a modest amount to pay for improved physical protection and material control.

Not all safeguards' problems, however, are amenable to "technical fixes." Probably most difficult to correct, but also significant for the long-term security of Russia's nuclear assets, is what may be thought of as an underdeveloped physical protection culture among the staff and custodians of the post-Soviet nuclear industry. In part, this undervaluation of physical protection rules and regulations is the product of the Soviet political and economic system which bred work and management practices, such as an avoidance of individual initiative and responsibility and the neglect of employee safety. These habits persist today, despite the acknowledgement by many officials in the Russian nuclear industry that improvements need to be made regarding plant security and material control. Illustrative of the gap that remains between formal recognition of the problem and internalization of new physical protection precepts was the initial inclination of staff at the Kurchatov Institute to disassemble parts of the new physical protection equipment shortly after its installation and demonstration at Building 116 in late 1994. This reaction at perhaps the most forward-looking nuclear facility in Russia with respect to physical protection should serve as a useful reminder that providing portal detectors, two person access controls, personnel identification equipment, and motion-detection alarms is a necessary, but not sufficient condition for the enhancement of physical protection. Those in charge of the equipment must be predisposed to turn it on and use it as intended.

Changing attitudes and instilling a new philosophy cannot be accomplished easily or quickly. Nor will an influx of money alone solve the problem. What is required is a sustained educational effort. The planned creation of an MPC & A training center in Obninsk, proposed by Russia and agreed to by the United States, is a step in the right direction. It is intended to reinforce indigenous MPC & A efforts by educating a new generation of specialists who will serve both as practitioners and instructors in the field.

New Directions and Long-Term Solutions

Most of the nuclear security problems in the former Soviet Union are inextricably linked to the region's troubled economic, political, and social conditions. As such, they are unlikely to be completely resolved in the absence of substantial progress toward stabilizing the economy and renewing public trust in governmental institutions and law. These developments are not apt to occur soon, and the United States, therefore, will continue to face at least some threat of nuclear leakage from the ex-USSR for the foreseeable future.

The precise nature of the threat will be determined by a combination of factors including the pace with which the aforementioned corrective actions are implemented, national decisions regarding the disposition of excess fissile material from weapons, and the demand by end-users for weapons material. The United States should not exaggerate its ability to influence the course of these developments. It can, however, make a difference and should endeavor to do so. As part of its long-term strategy to contain fissile material proliferation, the United States should seek to create a safeguards regime that extends to all nuclear weapons-usable material in the weapons states.[48] In 1994 the United States took a step in this direction when it voluntarily took one ton of plutonium and 10 tons of HEU out of its active weapons inventory and agreed to place the material under IAEA safeguards. In March 1995 President Clinton announced that the United States had "permanently withdrawn" another 200 tons of fissile material from its nuclear stockpile.[49]

It will not be easy to persuade Russia to participate in such a comprehensive multilateral regime, given Minatom's current opposition to an IAEA presence at its military facilities. One also can anticipate resistance on the part of some U.S. governmental actors. For that reason, it may be preferable, at least initially, to pursue the idea of an expanded safeguards regime with Russia on a bilateral R & D basis. As Tom Cochran at the NRDC has argued persuasively, the primary focus of the initiative should not be to compel the parties to make a political commitment to adopt comprehensive bilateral or multilateral safeguards, but rather to engage them in a fully reciprocal research, development, and demonstration program. This approach not only embraces the principle of truly joint U.S.-Russian cooperation for nonproliferation, but has the virtue of redirecting U.S. and Russian nuclear weapons scientists and laboratories to work in non-weapons areas.

Appendix A

Chronology of Proliferation-Significant Cases of Diversion of Probable FSU-Origin HEU and Plutonium

Date of Diversion:	May-September 1992
Date of Seizure:	October 9, 1992
Amount:	1.538 Kg of HEU in the form of UO2
Description of Material:	HEU (90% enrichment level)
Point of Origin:	Luch Scientific Production Association, Podolsk
Point of Seizure:	Podolsk, Russia

Date of Diversion:	July 29, 1993
Date of Seizure:	August 1993
Amount:	1.8 Kg of enriched uranium
Description of Material:	HEU (approximately 36% enrichment level)
Point of Origin:	Andreeva Guba Fuel Storage Area, Russia
Point of Seizure:	Andreeva Guba

Date of Diversion:	November 27, 1993
Date of Seizure:	June 1994
Amount:	4.5 Kg enriched uranium
Description of Material:	HEU (approximately 20% enrichment level)
Point of Origin:	Fuel Storage Area 3-30, Sevmorput Shipyard near Murmansk
Point of Seizure:	Polyarny (near Murmansk, Russia)

Date of Diversion:	?
Date of Seizure:	May 10, 1994
Amount:	5.6 grams Pu-239
Description of Material:	99.78 pure Pu-239
Point of Origin:	?
Point of Seizure:	Baden-Wuertemberg (Tengen), Germany

Date of Diversion:	?
Date of Seizure:	June 13, 1994
Amount:	800 milligrams

Description of Material: HEU (enriched to 87.7 %)
Point of Origin: ?
Point of Seizure: Landshut, Germany

Date of Diversion: ?
Date of Seizure: August 10, 1994
Amount: 560 grams of mixed-oxide of pluto-
                                 nium and uranium (363 grams of Pu-
                                 239)
Description of Material: Mixed-Oxide (MOX) fuel
Point of Origin: ?
Point of Seizure: Munich, Germany

Date of Diversion: ?
Date of Seizure: December 14, 1994
Amount: 2.72 Kg of HEU in the form of UO2
Description of Material: HEU enriched to 87.7% U-235
Point of Origin: ?
Point of Seizure: Prague, Czech Republic

Notes

1. The author wishes to thank Clay Moltz, Sarah Jacobson, and Oleg Bukharin for their comments on an earlier version of this study, which appeared as "Before the Deluge? Assessing the Threat of Nuclear Leakage from the Post-Soviet States," *Arms Control Today* (October 1995): 9-16.

2. The most systematic effort probably is that conducted by the Department of Energy, which maintains a database on illicit trafficking of nuclear materials. An open-source database on illicit nuclear transactions also is maintained by the Center for Nonproliferation Studies at the Monterey Institute of International Studies.

3. A study by Phil Williams and Paul Woessner makes a laudable effort to relate the subject of nuclear smuggling to the broader literature on organized, international criminal activity, but is flawed by methodological problems that result in errors of omission and inclusion. See "Nuclear Material Trafficking: An Interim Assessment," *Ridgeway Viewpoints*, Working Paper No. 95-3 (1995).

4. See Craig R. Whitney, "Smuggling of Radioactive Material Said to Double in a Year," *The New York Times*, February 18, 1995.

5. Russia's eight nuclear-powered icebreakers, for example, use uranium-enriched to 90 percent as do some other naval reactors. For more details, see Oleg Bukharin and William Potter, "Potatoes were guarded better," *The Bulletin of the Atomic Scientists* (May/June 1995): 46-50.

6. Interview with Mikhail Kulik, *Yadernyi kontrol* (January 1995): 12-13.

7. Most prior instances involved attempts to market plutonium ionization sources used in minute quantities in smoke detectors in the former Soviet Union and Eastern Europe. These cases appear to have been linked to the theft of several crates of plutonium ionization sources from a warehouse in Bulgaria in late 1991.

8. See Mark Hibbs, "Russian Data Suggests PU Was Enriched By Arzamas-16 Calutron," *Nuclear Fuel*, August 14, 1994, pp. 9-10; Mark Hibbs, "Which Fissile Fingerprint?" *The Bulletin of the Atomic Scientists* (May/June 1995): 10; and Steve Coll, "Stolen Plutonium Tied to Arms Labs," *The Washington Post*, August 17, 1994.

9. This view is propounded by Williams and Woessner, p. 12.

10. See Mark Hibbs, "Plutonium, Politics, and Panic," *The Bulletin of the Atomic Scientists* (November/December 1994): 26.

11. Mark Hibbs, "U.S. Agencies Lacking Data on Source of Seized Plutonium," *Nucleonics Week*, May 25, 1995, p. 17.

12. This allegation was made by a BND official at the trial of the three defendants in the Lufthansa case. See Mark Hibbs, "BND Offered Cash Bonus to Agent for Plutonium, Official Asserts," *Nucleonics Week*, July 6, 1995, pp. 2-3.

13. Jane Perlez, "Tracing a Nuclear Risk: Stolen Enriched Uranium," *The New York Times*, February 15, 1995.

14. See Hibbs, "Which Fissile Fingerprint?," p. 11.

15. See William C. Potter, "Nuclear Exports from the Former Soviet Union: What's New, What's True," *Arms Control Today* (January-February 1993): 3.

16. Thomas Cochran identifies fifty-eight sites in Russia alone that are likely to have weapons-usable fissile material. See his "Safety and Control of Nuclear Materials and Nuclear Weapons." Paper presented at the Round-Table on Economic and Social Developments in the Former Soviet Union and the Problem of Nuclear Disarmament, Como, Italy, July 3-4, 1995.

17. In 1994 several deaths were attributed to black market trade in cesium 137 and cobalt 60.

18. Iranian interest in Ulba prompted Kazakhstan and the United States to cooperate in the airlift of 600 kilograms from the Ulba plant to the United States in November 1994.

19. See, for example, the intriguing but largely unconfirmed case for a Bulgarian-Iraqi supply chain made by Williams and Woessner, p. 12.

20. See Thomas B. Cochran, Robert S. Norris, and Oleg A. Bukharin, *Making the Russian Bomb: From Stalin to Yeltsin* (Boulder, CO: The Westview Press, 1995), p. 51.

21. The U.S. government's explanation that the reactor in question, an IR-100, is a naval training reactor not subject to IAEA reporting requirements is disputed by the IAEA. The reactor should have been declared previously unless it was still under Russian custody.

22. U.S. Office of Technology Assessment, *Nuclear Proliferation and Safeguards*, Vol. 1 (New York: Praeger, 1977), p. 194.

23. Interview with Project Sapphire member, June 1995. Allison et al., p. 23, report that the United States recovered 104% of the declared inventory.

24. An excellent summary of the MPC & A problem and U.S. efforts to address it is provided by Frank von Hippel, "Fissile Material Security in the Post-Cold War World," *Physics Today* (June 1995): 26-31.

25. See Oleg Bukharin, "Western Assistance to Upgrade Security at High-Risk Fissile Material Processing Facilities in Russia, January 27, 1995, Table 1. Tomsk-7, Krasnoyarsk-26, and Sverdlovsk-44 were recently renamed Seversk, Zelenogorsk, and Novouralsk, respectively.

26. Thomas B. Cochran, "Testimony before the Military Application of Nuclear Energy Panel of the House Armed Services Committee," April 19, 1994, p. 2.

27. Alexei Lebedev, as cited in "Russian Weapons Plutonium Storage Termed Unsafe by Minatom Official," *Nucleonics Week*, April 28, 1994, p. 1.

28. Reported in Graham T. Allison, Owen R. Cote, Jr., Richard A. Falkenrath, and Steven E. Miller, "Avoiding Nuclear Anarchy: Containing the Threat of Loose Russian Nuclear Weapons and Fissile Material," CSIA Discussion Paper 95-08. Kennedy School of Government, Harvard University, July 1995, p. 6.

29. For a more detailed discussion of this issue, see Oleg Bukharin, "The Threat of Nuclear Terrorism and the Physical Security of Nuclear Installations and Materials in the Former Soviet Union," Occasional Paper No. 2, CRES, Monterey

Institute of International Studies, August 1992. See also Karl-Heinz Kamp, "Nuklearterrorismus: Fakten und Fiktionen," Konrad Adenauer Stiftung Interne Studien No. 96, 1994.

30. See "Threat Seen to Russian Nuke Plant," *The Washington Times*, July 2, 1995.

31. See *Nucleonics Week*, April 16, 1992, p. 8. It is unclear if the instigator sought to damage the plant or simply to cause problems that he could subsequently fix in order to receive a financial bonus.

32. According to former CIA Director James Woolsey, in 1994 there were 5,700 criminal gangs in Russia, about 200 of which were large, sophisticated groups involved in criminal activity throughout the former Soviet Union and in twenty-nine other countries. See Draft of Proposed Remarks by R. James Woolsey before the House Foreign Relations Committee, International Organizations, International Security and Human Rights Subcommittee, June 27, 1994.

33. Discussions with U.S. government officials suggest that much more work also could be done at the classified level. No one, for example, appears to have sought interviews with many of the parties arrested and/or sentenced for their involvement in illicit nuclear trafficking.

34. On this point, see Stephen Handelman, *Comrade Criminal: The Theft of the Second Russian Revolution* (New Haven: Yale University Press, 1995), especially pp. 227-228.

35. According to VATESI, the Lithuanian Nuclear Power Safety Inspectorate, the cache consisted of 3,860 kg of pure beryllium and 140 kg of a beryllium-uranium alloy containing 150 grams of uranium enriched to approximately 50 percent. These figures have been corroborated by other sources and appear to be more reliable than the two kilogram quantity of U-235 cited by U.S. officials in a letter to Tom Cochran of November 23, 1994.

36. Personal communication with reporters, August 17, 1995.

37. Rensselaer W. Lee, III, "The Organized Crime Morass in the Former Soviet Union," *Demokratizatsiya* (Summer 1994): 400.

38. See Louise Shelley, "Post-Soviet Organized Crime," *Demokratizatsiya* (Summer 1994): 343. I am grateful to Jessica Stern for calling this citation to my attention.

39. These changes are discussed in detail in Elina Kirichenko and William Potter, "Nuclear Export Controls in Russia: The Players and the Process," forthcoming, 1996.

40. One of the new political constraints is the emergence of Russian parliamentarians as vocal champions of exports with little regard for their proliferation implications.

41. For a discussion of this problem in Ukraine, see "Trip Report of Dan Hoydysh, January 18-February 5, 1995, Kiev, Ukraine," Lawyers Alliance for World Security, 1995.

42. The lab-to-lab program has had more flexibility in these respects. The

1994-1995 authorization for the CTR Program also relaxes the "buy America" requirement.

43. See Allison et al., pp. 87 and 96.

44. Minatom, to be sure, is not a homogenous entity and its different directorates may differ on what constitutes useful assistance. For a discussion of this point with reference to the CTR Program, see Oleg Bukharin, "Minatom and Nuclear Threat Reduction Activities," paper prepared for the Conference on the Nunn-Lugar Cooperative Threat Reduction Program: Donor and Recipient Country Perspectives, Monterey, CA, August 20-22, 1995.

45. On this point, see Jessica Stern, pp. 16-18, who creatively applies economic theory to explain the divergence of interests between the Russian president and Minatom.

46. See "U.S.-German Cooperation in the Elimination of Excess Weapons Plutonium," Report of the German-American Aacdemic Council and the National Academy of Sciences, 1995.

47. The fledgling Russian nuclear regulatory body, Gosatomnadzor (GAN), recently suffered a major defeat when on July 25, 1995, President Yeltsin declined to sign a new Atomic Energy Act that had been passed by the Duma. The legislation would have codified GAN's MPC & A oversight responsibilities in both the military and civilian sectors. On June 26, Yeltsin signed a new decree stripping GAN of at least some of its regulatory authority in the military domain. See *Rossiiskaya gazeta*, August 2, 1995, p. 4.

48. This proposal is developed at greater length by Thomas Cochran and Christopher Paine, "U.S. Assistance to Improve Physical Security and Accounting of Fissile Materials in Russia." Paper presented to the Panel on U.S.-Russian Cooperation to Control and Account for Fissile Material, President's Commission for Advisors on Science and Technology, Washington, D.C., January 27, 1995.

49. For a breakdown of this material, see Thomas Cochran, "Dismantlement of Nuclear Weapons and Disposal of Fissile Material from Weapons." Paper presented at the Round Table on Economic and Social Developments in the Former Soviet Union and the Problem of Nuclear Disarmament, Como, Italy, July 3-4, 1995, Table 3.

Index

Air travel, safety of, 7

Aitmitov, D., 107

Allison, Graham, 156

Alperovitz, Gar, 15n

Andreeva Guba (Russia), 141, 146

Andropov, Yuri, 21

Antwerp, 147

Arendt, Hannah, 104

Armenia, Armenians, 2, 22, 38, 50, 72, 111, 150, 153
  1988 earthquake in, 50, 79n
  civilian nuclear safety in, 85
  energy shortages in, 50, 78n
  war with Azerbaijan, 50

Arratibel, J.B., 144, 145

Arzamas-16 nuclear weapons laboratory (renamed Kremlev) (Russia), 142, 143, 152

Athens, 143

Atlanta, 79n

Atomic Energy Act (Russia), 165n

Austria, Austrians, 13n, 46

Automobile safety, 47-48

Azerbaijan, Azeris, 50, 78n

Baker, James, 124

Balakovo nuclear power plant (Russia), 22, 23, 33, 68

Baranov, Oleg, 141-142

Belarus, Belarusians, 8, 24, 30, 35, 39, 40, 50, 110, 122, 124, 136n, 146, 149, 150, 155, 156
  declaration of independence in, 26
  energy, energy industry, 33-35
  radiation fallout from Chornobyl in, 27
  thyroid gland cancer in, 31-32

Bellefonte nuclear power plant (United States), 3

Beloyarsk nuclear power plant (Kazakhstan), 21

Benitez, J.T., 144, 145

beryllium, 146, 147, 153, 154

Bilibino nuclear power plant (Russia), 80n

Black Sea Fleet, 123, 129, 132, 134

Blix, Hans, 37

Bochvar Institute of Non-Organic Substances (Moscow), 151

Brest Oblast (Belarus), 27
  thyroid gland cancer incidence in, 31

Brezhnev, L.I., 19

Britain, British, 36

Bronnikov, Vladimir, 68, 80n

Brussels, 84

Bryansk Region (Russia), 27

Bulgaria, Bulgarians, 23, 38, 143, 162n
  civilian nuclear safety in, 85

Bush, George, 124, 127
  "Chicken Kyiv" speech, 128
Bushehr nuclear power plant (Iran),
  155

Canada, Canadians, 4, 41n, 130
CANDU nuclear reactor, 23
Carnegie, Dale, 56
Center for Radiation Measurement
  (Kyiv), 118n
Cernavoda nuclear power plant
  (Romania), 23
cesium-137, 24, 26, 27, 28, 163n
Challenger disaster (1986), 78n
Chechenya, Chechens, 152
Chelyabinsk-65 nuclear fuel cycle
  facility (Russia), 157
Chernihiv Oblast, 28, 29, 36
Chernomyrdin, V., 85, 87
China, Chinese, 2, 41n, 83, 93
  nuclear power industry, 2, 155
Chkalovsk (Tajikistan), 143
Chornobyl disaster, 1, 3, 4, 5, 8, 10,
  11, 12, 23, 25-26, 33, 40, 45, 51, 55,
  63, 72-73, 76n, 77n, 80n, 83, 85,
  98, 107-109, 112
  deaths from, 29
  effect on U.S. nuclear power
    industry, 3, 10, 48
  projected casualties of, 24
  evacuations of population as a
    result of, 25, 26, 28-29
  medical impact of, 29-33
  psychological problems caused by,
    30
  radiation fallout from, 24-25, 26-29
  radiation toleration levels for those
    suffering from, 24, 28
  "radiophobia" as a result of, 50-51
  response to in Soviet Union, 108-
    110
  Tenth Anniversary of, 1

Chornobyl nuclear power plant, 2,
  25, 35, 45, 57, 65, 72
  efforts to shut down, 13n, 32, 35-
    38, 40, 66-67, 80n, 85, 95, 97, 114
  safety problems of, 25, 38, 98
Chretien, Jean, 41n
Churchill, Winston, 102
  Fulton Speech of, 102
Civil War (USSR), 103
Clinton, Bill, 72, 131, 159
coal, 20, 34, 50, 92, 105, 114
cobalt-60, 163n
Cochran, Tom, 159
Cold War, 51, 64, 102, 124, 136n, 156
  nuclear "arms race" and, 102
Comanche Peak nuclear power plant
  (United States), 14n
COMECON, 105
Committee for Hydrometeorology
  (Russia), 118n
Committee for the State Supervision
  of Safety in Industry and Nuclear
  Power (USSR), 118n
Committee on the Questions of the
  Chornobyl Catastrophe
  (Ukrainian Parliament), 32
Commonwealth of Independent
  States (CIS), 33, 38, 39, 70, 110,
  122, 123, 125, 126, 131, 132, 135n,
  156
Communist Party of the Soviet
  Union (CPSU), 64, 80n, 103, 106,
  108, 109
  19th Party Congress (1988), 108
Congdon, Michael, 12
Council for Mutual Economic
  Assistance, 20
Crimea, 4, 74n, 105, 133
  as a Ukrainian-Russian issue, 129,
    131-132
Cyprus, 147

Czech Republic, Czechs, 46, 53, 76n, 144, 146-147

Czechoslovakia, 23, 110

DeBardeleben, Joan, 106

Demidchik, Evgeny, 31

Dewing, Martin, 130

Diablo Canyon nuclear power plant (United States), 14n, 74n

Dniprodzerzhinsk (Ukraine), 147

Donbas coalfield, 20

Donetsk Basin, 20

Duke Power Company (United States), 72

Dukovany nuclear power plant (Czech Republic), 146

East Germany, East Germans, 23

Eisenhower, Dwight D., 2, 6, 15n, 16n
"Atoms for Peace" plan, 6, 10

Electrostal nuclear fuel cycle facility (Russia), 147, 151

Eleventh Five-Year Plan (1981-1985), 23

Energy Reorganization Act (United States), 15n

Energy Research Institute (ERI) (Russia), 97

Energy Strategy for Russia, 90

Energy Technology and Design Institute (Moscow), 73

Enerhodar (Ukraine), 34, 37

Estonia, Estonians, 150

European Bank for Reconstruction and Development (EBRD), 84, 85
Nuclear Safety Account at, 84

European Investment Bank, 85

European Union, 37, 84, 129, 132
Corfu meeting (July 1994), 97

Export Control Commission (Russia), 155

Federal Weapons of War Control Act (Germany), 145

Financial Times, 128

Finland, Finns, 23, 53

Foreign Intelligence Agency (BND) (Germany), 145, 162n

France, French, 2, 66, 80n
nuclear power industry, 2, 34

Freeh, Louis, 147

Gagarin, Yuri, 11

Gale, Robert, 64, 79n

Geneva, 30

Germany, Germans, 80n, 102, 116n, 142-145, 148

Glasnost, 108

Glennan, T. Keith, 6

GOELRO Plan (USSR), 103

Gofman, John, 24

Gorbachev, M.S., 25, 50, 51, 62, 79n, 107, 108, 110, 122, 129

Gore, A., 85

Gore-Chernomyrdin Commission (GCC), 55, 85, 87, 88
agreements arising from, 55, 85, 87

Gosatomnadzor (Russian nuclear regulatory commission), 68, 70, 165n

Goskomatom (Ukrainian agency for nuclear power production facilities), 67, 68

Group of Seven Countries (G-7), 37, 55, 67, 84, 98, 127
Action Plan for assisting Ukraine's energy sector, 97
Halifax Summit (1995), 85, 97
Naples Summit (1994), 84-85, 97

Group of Twenty-Four Countries (G-24), 84

Gutsalov, Aleksandr, 68, 69

hafnium, 147

Hammer, Armand, 64

Hanau (Germany), 157

Hanford nuclear power plant (United States), 54

Harrisburg (United States), 16n, 45

Heisenberg uncertainty principle, 77n

Hibbs, Mark, 145, 146

Highly-enriched Uranium (HEU), 139, 146, 149, 150, 151, 154, 159
  purchase of by United States, 157
  smuggled from the former Soviet Union, 140-144,145-147, 148

Hiroshima, 6, 8, 15n, 46, 101
  fiftieth anniversary of nuclear attack on, 46

Homel' Oblast (Belarus), 27
  thyroid gland cancer incidence in, 31

Hryshchenko, V., 81n

Hungary, Hungarians, 23, 38, 110

Ignalina nuclear power plant (Lithuania), 22, 25, 35, 39, 50, 65, 80n, 153

India, Indians, 2
  nuclear power industry, 2, 155

Institute for Nuclear Power Operations (United States), 72, 79n

Institute for Nuclear Research (Kyiv), 147

Institute for the Problems of Safe Development of Atomic Energy (Russia), 118n

Institute of Nuclear Power Operators, 3

Institute of Physics and Power Engineering (Obninsk), 151, 154, 158

Institute of Radiation (Minsk), 118n

Institute of Radiation Safety (Belarusian Ministry of Health), 32

International Atomic Energy Agency (IAEA), 16n, 29, 30, 37, 38, 39, 76n, 149, 150, 159, 163n

International Chornobyl Report (ICR) (1991), 29-30

International Ecological Academy (Belarus), 35

International Red Cross, 79n

International Users Group of Soviet Designed Reactors (IUG), 96

iodine-131, 28, 31
  deficiency of in soil, 31

Iran, Iranians, 2, 155, 163n
  nuclear power industry, 2
  Savak (secret police), 56

Iraq, Iraqis, 143

Italy, Italians, 97

Jaekle, Adolf, 142-143, 149

Japan, Japanese, 34, 51, 83, 86, 102
  nuclear power industry, 34-35

Johnson, L.B., 81n

Joint Parallel Nuclear Alternatives Study (JPNAS), 87, 96

Kalinin nuclear power plant (Russia), 22, 23, 33

Kazakhstan, Kazakhs, 2, 61, 65, 109, 110, 122, 124, 135n, 136n, 145, 147, 149, 150, 155, 156, 163n
  nuclear power industry, 2

Kewanee nuclear power plant (United States), 14n

Khabarovsk nuclear power plant, 33

Kharkiv (Ukraine), 69, 75n

Khmelnytsky nuclear power plant (Ukraine), 23, 34, 66

Khrushchev, N.S., 103

Kirovohrad (Ukraine), 28
Kola Peninsula (Russia), 22, 33, 70, 78n
Komsomolskaya pravda, 140
Koodangulan nuclear power plant (India), 155
Kopchinsky, Georgy, 69
Kostroma nuclear power plant (Russia), 22, 33
Kozloduy nuclear power plant (Bulgaria), 23
safety of, 82n
Kozyrev, A., 132
Krasnoyarsk-26 nuclear fuel cycle facility (Russia), 151, 157
Kravchuk, Leonid, 36, 37, 121, 122, 123, 126, 134
Kronstadt uprising (1921), 104
Krzhizhanovsky, G. 103
Kuchma, Leonid, 37, 69, 80n, 85, 95, 97, 125
Kurchatov Institute of Atomic Energy (Moscow), 22, 151, 158
Kursk nuclear power plant (Russia), 22, 25, 33, 80n
Kyiv Oblast, 28
Kyiv, 25, 26, 34, 45, 66, 72, 80n, 109, 114, 121, 123, 125, 126, 127, 129, 131, 147
Kyshtym (Russia), 10
1957 disaster at, 10, 40

Landeskriminalant (LKA) (Bavaria), 144, 145
Landshut (Germany), 144, 145, 146, 147
Lapshin, Vladimir, 79n
Latvia, Latvians, 150
Launer, Michael, 40
Lee, Bill, 72, 73

Lee, Rensselaer, 154
Legasov, Valery, 29
Lenin, V.I., 103, 104
Leukemia, 30
Ligachev, Egor, 26
Lisbon initiative for nuclear safety, 77n, 84
Lithuania, Lithuanians, 22, 25, 35, 37, 38, 50, 65, 72, 111, 112, 146, 150, 153, 154
civilian nuclear safety in, 85
Nuclear Power Safety Inspectorate (VATESI), 164n
organized crime in, 153-154
Sajudis, 39
Lobov, Vladimir, 123
Lockerbie (Scotland), 7
PanAm flight 103 and, 7
Lovisa nuclear power plant (Finland), 53
Luch Scientific Production Association (Podolsk), 140-141, 146, 151

Mahileu Region (Belarus), 27
Malibu, California, 4
Marples, David, 11
Massandra (Crimea), 126
Massandra Protocol (1993), 136n
Mayak Chemical Combine (Russia), 151
McNamara, Robert S., 130
Metzamor nuclear power plant (Armenia), 2, 22, 38, 50, 153
Minsk, 32, 35, 109
MIR (peace) electrical power grid, 23
Mohovce nuclear power plant (Slovakia), 13n, 46
Mongolia, Mongolians, 23
Morozov, Kostiantyn, 123

Moscow, 40, 65, 68, 69, 72, 114, 118n,
    123, 124, 125, 127, 128, 129, 131,
    134, 135, 140, 144, 145, 147

Munich, 84, 144, 146

Murmansk, 141

Mykolaiv nuclear power plant
    (Ukraine), 22, 23, 43n

Nader, Ralph, 47
    Unsafe At Any Speed

Nagasaki, 6, 8, 15n, 46
    fiftieth anniversary of nuclear
    attack on, 46

Nagorno-Karabakh, 50

Narodychi Raion (Ukraine), 26

National Aeronautics and Space
    Administration (NASA), 78n

National Resources Defense Council
    (NRDC) (United States), 159

natural gas, 35, 50, 63, 78n, 90, 92,
    105, 113-114, 133

Nesterenko, V.B., 32

Nevada, nuclear testing in, 8

North Atlantic Treaty Organization
    (NATO), 129, 132, 136n

North Caucasus (Russia), 93

North Korea, 143

North Slope (Alaska), 5

Norway, Norwegians, 141

Novosibirsk Chemical Concentrate
    Plant (Russia), 151

Novovoronezh nuclear power plant
    (Russia), 22, 33
    implementation of emergency
    operating procedures at, 55-56,
    70-71

"Nuclear Legitimation Gap", 102

Nuclear Non-proliferation Treaty
    (NPT), 98, 123, 124, 126, 127, 150

Nuclear power industry
    equipment supply for, 59

safety culture and, 60
    safety of, 46, 48, 83, 86
    spent fuel storage and, 65, 79n

Nuclear power, 2
    history of, 2, 6-7

Nuclear Research Institute (Rez,
    Czech Republic), 146

Nuclear Suppliers Group (NSG), 147

Nuclear weapons
    history of, 101-102
    nuclear terrorism and, 152-153
    Ukraine as a nuclear weapons
    state, 121-128, 130-134

Nunn-Lugar appropriations for
    disarmament, dismantlement, and
    nuclear materials accountancy
    (United States), 64

Obninsk nuclear power plant
    (Russia), 19, 21

Odesa, 105

oil, 34, 35, 50, 63, 65, 78n, 90, 113-114,
    133
    West Siberian, 105

Oklahoma City bombing, 1

Oroz, Julio, 144, 145

Paks nuclear power plant (Hungary),
    23

Parashyn, Sergey, 38

Parsons, R.M., 6

Pasedag, Walter, 8, 14n

perestroika, 62, 100, 107-110

Perrow, Charles, 5, 47, 73

Physical-Technical Institute
    (Kharkiv), 149

plutonium, 24, 146, 150, 159
    smuggled from the former Soviet
    Union, 139, 140, 142-145, 148

Point Beach nuclear power plant
    (United States), 14n, 49

Poland, Poles, 20, 23, 62, 78n, 110, 132
  Communist Party of Poland (CPP), 78n

Poliske Raion (Ukraine), 28

Polyarny (Russia), 146

Portner, Stuart, 121

Potter, William C., 12

Powers, Francis Gary, 16n

Prague, 144, 145-146, 147

Prairie Island nuclear power plant (United States), 14n

Pridneprovsky Chemical Factory (Dniprodzerzhinsk), 147

Pripyat (Ukraine), 10, 29, 44n
  evacuation of, 25

Pripyat Industrial and Research Association, 29

Project Sapphire, 151, 163n

Pschennikov, Bronislav, 36

Rancho Seco nuclear power plant (United States), 3

Rasputin, V., 107

Reagan, Ronald, 11

Rivne nuclear power plant (Ukraine), 22, 23, 34, 66

Rivne Oblast (Ukraine), 28

Romanenko, Anatoly, 30

Romania, Romanians, 23, 132

Rosenergoatom (Russian nuclear power operating agency), 33, 70, 71,

Rostov nuclear power plant (Russia), 22, 23

Rotterdam, 147

Russia, Russians, 4, 11, 36, 37, 38, 39, 45, 50, 51, 52, 53, 54, 55, 56, 57, 61, 63, 65, 67, 69, 75n, 76n, 83, 84, 87, 88, 90, 108, 110, 111, 122, 123, 147, 148

civilian nuclear safety in, 72-74, 84, 85, 90
  Duma (Parliament) of, 65, 112, 128, 165n
  economic reform in, 62, 133
  economic system of, 62-63, 90, 100
  energy, energy industry, 33, 40, 63, 90, 91, 92-96, 114
  nuclear power industry, 33, 40, 45, 50, 59, 63, 90, 100, 110-111, 112, 113-115
  nuclear regulatory procedures, 69-71, 86, 101
  nuclear warhead disassembly factories in, 152
  radiation fallout from Chornobyl in, 27
  smuggling of weapons-grade nuclear materials from, 139-148
  safeguards of nuclear materials in, 150-152, 155-158
  Ukrainian nuclear weapons and, 128-130

Russian Academy of Sciences, 118n
  Commission for Atomic Energy, 118n

Russian Ministry of Atomic Energy (Minatom), 87, 88, 140, 144, 151, 155, 157, 159, 165n

Russian Ministry of Ecology, 118n

Russian Ministry of Foreign Affairs, 155

Russian Ministry of Foreign Economic Relations, 155

Russian Revolution (1917), 101, 103

Russian-Ukrainian Treaty of Friendship and Cooperation, 128

Ryazan Oblast (Russia), 27

Ryzhkov, Nikolay, 26

St. Petersburg (Leningrad), 22, 70, 114, 118n, 141, 146, 147

Salin, Ivan, 44n

San Andreas fault, 74n

Sarkofag, 109

Savitsky, B.P., 35

Scientific Research and Construction
  Institute of Electro-Technology
  (USSR), 22

Scientific Research Institute for
  Atomic Reactors (Dmitrovgrod),
  151

Seabrook nuclear power plant
  (United States), 49

Selin, Ivan, 86, 88

"Semipalatinsk Polygon", 109

Sequoyah nuclear power plant
  (United States), 3

Sevastopol, 132, 149

Sevmorput Shipyard (Murmansk),
  141-142

Shcherbak, Yuri, 12, 13n

Shcherbyna, Borys, 29

Shekhovstov, V.S., 128

Shevchenko, Volodymyr, 29

Shippingport nuclear power plant
  (United States), 16n

Shoreham nuclear power plant
  (United States), 3

Shteinberg, Nikolay, 43n, 68-69

Shushkevich, Stanislau, 122

Shute, Neville, 8
  On The Beach, 8

Siberia, 20, 40
  hydroelectric capacity of, 93

Slavutych (Ukraine), 29, 36, 43n

Slovakia, Slovaks, 46, 132, 144

Smirnov, Leonid, 140-141

Smolensk nuclear power plant
  (Russia), 22, 25, 35, 80n

Sosnovy Bor nuclear power plant
  (Russia), 22, 25, 33, 70, 80n

South Korea, South Koreans, 35
  nuclear power industry, 35

Soviet Union (USSR), 6, 8, 10, 11, 25,
  39, 51, 52, 57, 61, 63, 64, 65, 73,
  84, 100, 102, 116n, 122, 134, 139
  Chornobyl accident and, 8, 11, 12,
    25-26, 108-110
  collapse of, 109, 111
  economic system of, 62, 78n, 104
  energy, energy industry, 19-21, 105
  industrial design and construction
    philosophy in, 52-53
  management philosophy and
    practice in, 56-57, 95
  nuclear power industry, 21-24, 40,
    52, 83, 103-110
  nuclear power procedures in, 55-
    56, 57, 76n, 81n, 84
  nuclear regulatory procedures, 84
  opposition to nuclear power in, 50,
    109-110
  reactor design safety of, 53, 54,
    79n, 84, 86, 96, 109
  reactor types of, 21-23, 25, 53, 65,
    82n
  technology in, 100, 104

Spain, Spaniards, 37, 144

Spizhenko, Yury, 30

Sputnik I, 11

State Atomic Safety Committee
  (Russia), 118n

State Chernobyl Committee (Russia),
  118n

State Committee for Extraordinary
  Situations (Russia), 118n

Strategic Arms Reduction Treaty
  (START-1), 123, 126, 127, 151

strontium-90, 24, 27, 28

Supreme Council of Ukraine, 122

Sverdlovsk (Yekaterinburg) (Russia),
  154

Sverdlovsk-44 nuclear fuel cycle
  facility (Russia), 151

Sweden, Swedes, 37

Switzerland, Swiss, 143

Tajikistan, Tajiks, 143

Tambov Oblast (Russia), 27

Technical Assistance to the Commonwealth of Independent States program (TACIS), 84, 85

Temelin nuclear power plant (Czech Republic), 53, 146

Tengen (Baden-Wuertemberg) (Germany), 142, 145, 146

Tennessee Valley Authority (TVA), 3

Three Mile Island (TMI) nuclear power plant, 3, 8, 45
1979 accident at, 3, 4, 5, 14n, 45, 46-47, 76n, 77n, 79n, 83

Thyroid gland
cancer of esp. among children, 30-32, 43n

Thyroid Tumor Clinic (Minsk), 31

Tikhomirov, Alexei, 141-142

Tomsk-7 nuclear fuel cycle facility (Russia), 151, 157

Total Quality Management, 56

TransBaikalia (Russia), 93

Trilateral Agreements (1994), 127

U.S.-Russian Joint Electric Power Alternatives Study (JEPAS), 85, 86, 87-89, 96
methodology of, 89-90
priorities of, 91
recommendations of, 92-96

Ukraine, Ukrainians, 2, 4, 8, 11, 22, 23, 24, 25, 29, 30, 37, 38, 39, 40, 45, 50, 51, 52, 54, 55, 56, 57, 59, 61, 63, 65, 66, 67, 69, 75n, 83, 84, 94, 105, 108, 110, 111, 122, 123, 145, 146, 147, 150, 155
as a nuclear weapons state, 121-128, 130-134
civilian nuclear safety in, 72-74, 84, 85

declaration of independence in, 26, 122, 129, 135n
economic crisis in, 57, 133-134
energy, energy industry, 33-35, 51, 57, 63, 97-98, 118n, 132-133
nuclear power industry, 45, 50, 51, 59, 63, 67-68, 112, 113-115
nuclear regulatory procedures, 67-69, 71, 86
parliament of, 112
Popular Movement for Perestroika (Rukh), 125-126
radiation fallout from Chornobyl in, 27
Republican Party of Ukraine, 125-126
Social-National Party of Ukraine, 126
Supreme Soviet of, 34

Ukrainian Ministry for the Protection of the Environment and Nuclear Safety, 43n

Ukrainian Ministry of Defense, 122, 150

Ukrainian Ministry of Health, 30, 69

Ukrainian National Committee for the Radiation Protection of the Population, 29

Ukrainian State Committee for Nuclear and Radiation Safety, 118n

Ukrainian Supreme Soviet, 121

Ulba Metallurgy Plant (Ust-Kamenogorsk, Kazakhstan), 149, 151, 163n

Umanets, M.P., 80n

United Nations, 2, 102

United States, Americans, 1, 37, 47, 48, 51, 53, 55, 56, 61, 65, 72, 76n, 80n, 83, 88, 102, 123, 124, 125, 154
denuclearization assistance programs of, 156-158, 159
energy conservation in, 49
fossil fuel imports, 5

nuclear power emergency
operating procedures in, 55
nuclear power industry, 2-4, 49, 52,
58, 71
nuclear power regular operating
procedures in, 58-59, 77n, 78n,
81n
nuclear safety assistance programs
of, 55, 84-86
oil industry, 5
recognition of Ukrainian
independence by, 124
Ukrainian nuclear weapons and,
124-128, 130, 134

United States Atomic Energy
Commission, 6, 15n

United States Department of
Defense, 64

United States Department of Energy,
66, 69, 71, 77n, 142, 147, 162n
nuclear smuggling from the former
Soviet Union and, 157-158

United States Department of State,
64, 66

United States Nuclear Regulatory
Commission, 3, 13n, 15n, 37, 49,
71, 78n, 81n, 84, 86, 87, 88, 89
nuclear safety assistance programs
of, 84

Ural Mountains (Russia), 93, 105,
109, 110

U.S.-Russia Joint Electric Power
Alternatives Study (1995), 12

USSR Academy of Medical Sciences,
24

USSR Academy of Sciences, 106

USSR Central Committee of the
CPSU (CC CPSU), 106

USSR Committee for State Security
(KGB), 56, 139, 143

USSR Council of Ministers, 106

USSR Ministry of Defense, 106, 152

USSR Ministry of Energy, 78n

USSR Ministry of Health, 26
Third Department of, 26

USSR Ministry of Medium Machine
Building, 21

USSR Ministry of Nuclear Energy
and Industry, 118n

USSR Ministry of Nuclear Power and
Engineering, 33, 78n, 79n, 80n

USSR Ministry of Power and
Electrification, 21

USSR Nuclear Society, 75n

USSR State Committee for Science
and Technology, 106

USSR Supreme Soviet, 106

Uzbekistan, Uzbeks, 150

V.I. Lenin nuclear power plant, see
Chornobyl nuclear power plant

Vagner, Jaroslav, 145-146

Vancouver, 131

Varna (Bulgaria), 143

Vienna, 147

Vietnam, Vietnamese, 23

Vilnius, 146, 147, 153, 154

Vitebsk region (Belarus), 31

Volgodonsk nuclear reactor
construction plant (Russia), 22,
105

Volhynia (Ukraine), 25

Volyn Oblast (Ukraine), 28

Washington International Energy
Group, 2

Washington, D.C., 123, 125

Watts Bar nuclear power plant
(United States), 2-3

Weart, Spencer, 9-10

Wegmarshaus, Gert-Ruediger, 12,
15n

Wisconsin Public Utility
Commission, 49

Woolsey, R. James, 164n
World Association of Nuclear Operators, 72, 79n, 96
World Bank, 88
World Health Organization (WHO), 30, 31
World War II, 6, 51, 103, 125

Yankee Rowe nuclear power plant (United States), 3
Yatsenko, Volodymyr, 32
Yeltsin, B.N., 62, 70, 122, 123, 129, 131, 132, 165n
Young, Marilyn, 11
Yugoslavia, 23
Yukhnovsky, Ihor, 126
Yuriev, A.I., 81n

Zaporizhzhya nuclear power plant (Ukraine), 22, 23, 34, 37, 59, 66, 68, 69, 74n, 79n, 80n, 81n
  safety problems of, 38
  spent fuel storage at, 65-66, 68
  staffing problems at, 57-58
Zelenyi Svit (Green Movement of Ukraine), 24, 110
Zhirinovsky, Vladimir, 133, 137n
Zhytomyr Oblast (Ukraine), 26, 28
zirconium, 147
Zurich, 143
Zyla, Roman, 12

About the Book

Only several years after the collapse of the Soviet Union, nuclear security issues are again at the forefront of international concern. This timely collection addresses issues of cleanup at Chernobyl and other sites of nuclear disasters, nuclear smuggling, safety concerns in the Ukrainian and Russian nuclear industries, and Ukraine's negotiations with Russia and the West regarding the transference of its nuclear weapons to Russia. Preeminent scholars in their fields, the contributors provide up-to-the-minute information and fresh insights into questions critical to the future of the former Soviet Union and to Russian and Ukrainian relations with the West.

About the Editors and Contributors

Michael B. Congdon is manager of the Washington, D.C., offices of Pacific Northwest National Laboratory's nuclear safety programs in Ukraine. Formerly he specialized in nuclear safety assistance and cooperation with the former Soviet Union, first with the State Department and later (1988–1995) with the U.S. Nuclear Regulatory Commission as deputy to the director of International Programs.

Michael K. Launer is professor of Russian at Florida State University. He is the author of *Elementary Russian Syntax* (1974) and coauthor of *Flights of Fancy, Flight of Doom: KAL 007 and Soviet-American Rhetoric* (1988).

David R. Marples is professor of history at the University of Alberta and director of the Stasiuk Program on Contemporary Ukraine, Canadian Institute of Ukrainian Studies.

William C. Potter is a professor and director of the Center for Nonproliferation Studies at the Monterey Institute of International Studies. His most recent book is *Nuclear Profiles of the Soviet Successor States* (1993).

Gert-Rüdiger Wegmarshaus teaches political science at the Europe-University Viadrina Frankfurt (Oder) School for Cultural Studies.

Marilyn J. Young is professor of communications at Florida State University. She is a specialist in rhetoric, political communication, public argument, and evidence and the author of *Coaching Debate* (1976).

Roman P. Zyla is a Ph.D. candidate at the School of Slavonic and East European Studies, University of London, England.